This study reconstructs the apocalyptic eschatology in Matthew's gospel so that we may understand Matthew's time and his concerns. Apocalyptic eschatology can be broadly defined as a comprehensive world view which emphasises the final judgement and its aftermath within a dualistic and deterministic framework. This distinctive and often vengeful vision of reality was vigorously adopted by Matthew and dominates his gospel. Sociological analysis of apocalypticism in Judaism and early Christianity has shown that such a world view was adopted by minority or sectarian groups which were undergoing great crises, and Dr Sim looks at the social setting of the Matthean community, which reveals that after the first Jewish war against Rome, it came into conflict with the Jewish and gentile worlds and the larger Christian church.

The gospel of Matthew was held in high regard in the early church but may repel the modern reader with its division of humanity into righteous and wicked, and its emphasis on the fires of hell. But by understanding the social circumstances of the evangelist and his community, we can see that Matthew wrote not simply to condemn but out of an acute need to protect and enhance his community's sense of distinctiveness, and from pastoral concern for his troubled church. Dr Sim offers for the first time in English an extended and comprehensive analysis of Matthew's eschatological outlook which interprets his gospel in the light of contemporary literature which shares the same view.

SOCIETY FOR NEW TESTAMENT STUDIES

MONOGRAPH SERIES

General editor: Margaret E. Thrall

88

APOCALYPTIC ESCHATOLOGY IN THE

GOSPEL OF MATTHEW

Apocalyptic eschatology in the gospel of Matthew

DAVID C. SIM

Lecturer in New Testament,
Australian Catholic University, Brisbane

CAMBRIDGE
UNIVERSITY PRESS

Published by the Press Syndicate of the University of Cambridge
The Pitt Building, Trumpington Street, Cambridge CB2 1RP
40 West 20th Street, New York, NY 10011–4211, USA
10 Stamford Road, Oakleigh, Melbourne 3166, Australia

First published 1996

Printed in Great Britain at the University Press, Cambridge

A catalogue record for this book is available from the British Library

Library of Congress cataloguing in publication data

Sim, David C.
    Apocalyptic eschatology in the Gospel of Matthew / David C. Sim.
        p.   cm. – (Society for New Testament Studies monograph series : 88)
    Revision of the author's thesis (doctoral) – King's College, London,
    1992.
    Includes bibliographical references
    ISBN 0 521 55365 2 (hardback)
    1. Bible. N.T. Matthew – Criticism, interpretation, etc. 2. Eschatology –
biblical teaching. 3. Eschatology – History of doctrines – Early church, ca.
30–600. 4. Eschatology, Jewish. I. Title. II. Series: Monograph series
(Society for New Testament Studies) : 88.
BS2575.2.S49 1996
226.2'06–dc20 95–17551 CIP

ISBN 0 521 55365 2 hardback

To Robyn

CONTENTS

ix

PREFACE

This study marks a significant stage in a long-held interest in the eschatology of the synoptic gospels and their sources. My interest in Matthew's eschatology was sparked by a Master's thesis on the eschatology of Q when, in the course of reconstructing the text of this hypothetical source, I was struck by Matthew's constant insertion of apocalyptic-eschatological themes. I was then of the opinion that this phenomenon had never been adequately explored or explained, and I decided that my doctoral research would be devoted to this important and neglected subject. The present study is a revised version of my doctoral thesis which was undertaken at King's College London and submitted in October 1992. There are many people who have contributed to the production of this book in its various stages and to whom I wish to give due acknowledgement.

My first debt of thanks is to my supervisor, Professor Graham Stanton of King's College London, who nurtured the thesis in its early stages and saw it through to its completion. While I was in London, Graham was unstinting in his support and always made himself available, even at very short notice, to discuss ideas and drafts. His support continued after I returned to Melbourne in February 1990 to take up a position at La Trobe University. Whether he was responding to queries by letter or on the telephone, Graham's enthusiasm and encouragement provided the guidance and inspiration which enabled me to complete the thesis 'long-distance' while coping with a full-time teaching load. At all times Graham willingly shared his immense knowledge of the gospel of Matthew and encouraged me to develop my own ideas. I can truthfully say that I have learnt much from him.

Sincere thanks must also be given to the British Council for awarding me a Commonwealth Scholarship which enabled me to realise a dream and undertake doctoral study in London. Further funding from this institution also made it possible for me to have two extended trips to the Middle East in 1988 and 1989. I must single out two administrators, Kathy Roberts of the Association of Commonwealth Universities and Alison Edwards of the British Council, who were always very helpful during my association with them.

A special vote of thanks is due to Dr Margaret Thrall for accepting this study into the SNTS monograph series, and for her helpful comments and suggestions for revision. Other readers of the original thesis who have provided perceptive criticisms include Professor Christopher Rowland, Dr Judith Lieu and the reader for the SNTS monograph series, and I also express my gratitude to them. The final revision of this study was completed at the Australian Catholic University campus in Brisbane, and I must thank the departmental secretary, Ms Fran Wilkinson, for providing much needed assistance in the production of the final draft.

I would be remiss if I did not acknowledge the debt which I owe to certain members of my family. My parents, Gordon and Norma Sim, helped me in many ways in the initial stages of my career and provided the opportunity for my doctoral work. Special thanks are due as well to my brother, Mr Bruce Sim, who agreed to proof-read the whole manuscript at the thesis stage and I thank him for taking on such an unenviable task. Finally and most importantly, I must express my enormous thanks to Robyn, who has lived with this study from beginning to end and consequently has shared the 'highs' and the 'lows'. Whether we were in the heart of London, the middle of the Syrian desert, or the suburbia of Melbourne or Brisbane, her love, support and understanding have been unyielding. Though she has contributed little in terms of the content of this book, I feel that her contribution to it is no less than mine. It is therefore with much love and gratitude that I dedicate this book to her.

While I acknowledge the assistance of all those mentioned above, and emphasise that this study is considerably better for their assistance, I alone remain responsible for any of its errors and deficiencies.

ABBREVIATIONS

AB	Anchor Bible
AnBib	Analecta Biblica
ANRW	*Aufstieg und Niedergang der römischen Welt*
ASNU	Acta Seminarii Neotestamentica Upsaliensis
BETL	Bibliotheca Ephemeridum Theologicarum Lovaniensium
BEvT	Beiträge zur Evangelischen Theologie
BJRL	*Bulletin of the John Rylands Library*
BSR	Biblioteca di Scienze Religiose
BuL	*Bibel und Leben*
BZ	*Biblische Zeitschrift*
BZNW	Beiheft zur *ZNW*
CBNTS	Coniectanea Biblica New Testament Series
CBQ	*Catholic Biblical Quarterly*
CBQMS	*CBQ* Monograph Series
CMT	*Currents in Mission and Theology*
CRINT	Compendia Rerum Iudaicarum ad Novum Testamentum
CTM	Calwer Theologische Monographien
EKKNT	Evangelisch-Katholischer Kommentar zum Neuen Testament
ETS	Erfurter Theologische Studien
FB	Forschung zur Bibel
FRLANT	Forschungen zur Religion und Literatur des Alten und Neuen Testaments
HBT	*Horizons in Biblical Theology*
HeyJ	*Heythrop Journal*
HSM	Harvard Semitic Monographs
HTKNT	Herders Theologischer Kommentar zum Neuen Testament
HTR	*Harvard Theological Review*

HTS	Harvard Theological Studies
ICC	International Critical Commentary
IDBSupp	*Interpreter's Dictionary of the Bible Supplement*
JBL	*Journal of Biblical Literature*
JSNT	*Journal for the Study of the New Testament*
JSNTSS	*JSNT* Supplement Series
JSOT	*Journal for the Study of the Old Testament*
JSOTSS	*JSOT* Supplement Series
JSP	*Journal for the Study of the Pseudepigrapha*
JSPSS	*JSP* Supplement Series
JTS	*Journal of Theological Studies*
LD	Lectio Divina
LTPM	Louvain Theological and Pastoral Monographs
MeyerK	H. A. W. Meyer, Kritisch-exegetischer Kommentar über das Neue Testament
NCB	New Century Bible
NIGTC	New International Greek Testament Commentary
NovT	*Novum Testamentum*
NovTSup	*NovT* Supplements
NTAbh	Neutestamentliche Abhandlungen
NTD	Das Neue Testament Deutsch
NTS	*New Testament Studies*
OBO	Orbis Biblicus et Orientalis
PNTC	Pelican New Testament Commentary
RSB	*Religious Studies Bulletin*
SBEC	Studies in the Bible and Early Christianity
SBLDS	Society of Biblical Literature Dissertation Series
SBLMS	Society of Biblical Literature Monograph Series
SBLSBS	Society of Biblical Literature Sources for Biblical Study
SBLSCS	Society of Biblical Literature Septuagint and Cognate Studies
SBS	Stuttgarter Bibelstudien
SBT	Studies in Biblical Theology
SJT	*Scottish Journal of Theology*
SNTSMS	Society for New Testament Studies Monograph Series
SUNT	Studien zur Umwelt des Neuen Testaments
SVTP	Studia in Veteris Testamenti Pseudepigrapha
TDNT	*Theological Dictionary of the New Testament*
TPINTC	Trinity Press International New Testament Commentary

TS	Theological Studies
TZ	*Theologische Zeitschrift*
WBC	Word Biblical Commentary
WMANT	Wissenschaftliche Monographien zum Alten und Neuen Testament
ZNW	*Zeitschrift für die Neutestamentliche Wissenschaft*
ZTK	*Zeitschrift für Theologie und Kirche*

INTRODUCTION

1. The aims of this study

The apocalyptic-eschatological sections of the gospel of Matthew continue to fascinate the specialist New Testament scholar and general reader alike. Throughout the gospel the Matthean Jesus prophesies the arrival of the Son of Man who would sit on his throne of glory and preside over the final judgement. The fate of the wicked in particular is recounted in the most graphic terms. They will weep and gnash their teeth as they burn forever in the unceasing fires of Gehenna. While this sort of 'hell-fire and brimstone' material appeals to some Christians, for others it is a source of acute embarrassment which should be either ignored or downplayed considerably. Yet this sort of approach is clearly unsatisfactory since it avoids rather than confronts the problem. A better policy is to acknowledge that this apocalyptic-eschatological material is an important component of Matthew's gospel, and then try to understand why this is the case.

Before specifying the primary aims of this study, a few brief comments on the term 'apocalyptic eschatology' are in order. Since many scholars equate 'apocalyptic' or apocalyptic eschatology merely with speculation about the final judgement, it might be thought that such a study need involve little more than an assessment of the gospel's judgemental material. This view would be very much mistaken, however, for an identification of apocalyptic eschatology merely with the notion of judgement is simplistic at best and inaccurate at worst. A detailed analysis of the concept of apocalyptic eschatology will be provided in Part I, but it can be said at this point that it is an all-embracing religious perspective which considers the past, present and future within a dualistic and deterministic framework. Apocalyptic eschatology is thus far broader in scope than mere speculation about the judgement and its aftermath. It follows from this that the notion of the future judgement is merely one component of apocalyptic eschatology, albeit an extremely important one, which must be approached in conjunction with the other components of this religious perspective and not in isolation from them. A further point to note at the outset is that the latest studies of apocalyptic eschatology accept that this perspective does not arise in a vacuum. Its comprehensive and distinctive world view has an identifiable social setting, and its acceptance and promotion by authors or groups serve a number of specific functions in response to that social setting. Consequently, the study of apocalyptic eschatology in any given document necessarily involves three related areas – the content of the apocalyptic-eschatological scheme in question, the social setting which gives rise to it, and the particular functions it serves for the author or group which adopts it.

This observation brings us to the three specific aims of the present study. The first of these is basically descriptive and is concerned with identifying precisely the nature and extent of apocalyptic eschatology in the gospel of Matthew. To what extent does Matthew embrace this schematic world view and how is it presented in his gospel? How does the gospel's scheme compare with contemporary apocalyptic-eschatological schemes and are there any direct points of contact between them? The second aim is primarily explanatory and attempts to account for the evangelist's adoption of this particular perspective. What were the historical and/or social conditions which prompted Matthew and his community to adopt their particular apocalyptic-eschatological vision of reality? The third aim follows on from the first two and is concerned with identifying the practical purposes of this religious perspective. What are the precise functions of apocalyptic eschatology in the gospel of Matthew?

2. Survey of earlier studies

That such a study of Matthew's gospel has its place in the mass of Matthean literature published each year is best justified by documenting the history of research appropriate to this particular subject. It will be shown that, despite past scholarly recognition of the importance of apocalyptic eschatology in this gospel,[1] and

---

[1]   In 1957 F. C. Grant commented that Matthew is '... the most thoroughly

despite growing interest in this aspect of Matthew's theology in the past decade or so, no *full-scale* treatment has yet been undertaken. The present work is thus an attempt to fill this gap.

A number of works written in the early decades of this century devoted a good deal of attention to Matthew's apocalyptic eschatology. That this was the case should occasion no surprise. The works of Johannes Weiss and Albert Schweitzer had put (apocalyptic) eschatology at the forefront of New Testament scholarship. Moreover, these years witnessed an increasing interest in the non-canonical apocalyptic literature through the agencies of R. H. Charles and others. Given this environment, it is only to be expected that many works of this period (though by no means all) emphasised this particular aspect of Matthew's gospel. We need mention only one such study, that of B. H. Streeter.

It is appropriate that Streeter's classic work on the four gospels should commence our survey, since he was the first scholar both to emphasise Matthew's apocalyptic eschatology and to offer an explanation of its prominence in the gospel. This book, though sadly neglected over the past few decades, is still a challenging and valuable work of scholarship. His study of the Matthean gospel in particular is worthy of far closer attention than it presently receives. According to Streeter, 'No Gospel makes so much as does Matthew of the expectation that the visible Return of Christ will be within the lifetime of those who saw and heard Him' (*Four Gospels*, p. 520). In support of this claim, Streeter appealed to a number of texts which imply an imminent end expectation in Matthew (pp. 520–1). He then followed this with a discussion of another group of texts in which the evangelist betrays his interest in apocalyptic concepts (pp. 521–2). All this led Streeter to the conclusion that the gospel 'must have been written during a period of intense Apocalyptic expectation' (p. 523). He dated Matthew to c.85 CE, a period when the Jewish war and the destruction of Jerusalem had led to a resurgence of apocalyptic thinking (pp. 517, 523–4). In addition Streeter placed the composition of the gospel in Antioch on the Orontes (pp. 500–23), and this factor too played a crucial part in shaping the evangelist's apocalyptic-eschatological perspective. As the eastern gate of the Roman empire, Antioch was particularly susceptible to the *Nero redivivus* myth which served to fuel even further the flame of apocalyptic

"apocalyptic-eschatological" of the gospels in its general outlook', *The Gospels*, p. 137.

speculation which the Jewish war had ignited. This was especially the case in the Antiochene Christian community where the myth of the return of Nero at the head of the Parthian armies was fused with the expectation of the antichrist (p. 523). Thus for Streeter, Matthew's intense concern with apocalyptic-eschatological themes is to be explained by both the time and the place of the gospel's composition.[2]

Even before Streeter had published his work, the new method of form criticism had been brought to scholarly attention by Martin Dibelius and Rudolf Bultmann. This method was to dominate synoptic studies up to the outbreak of the second world war. As a consequence, the emphasis shifted from the gospels as whole works to the analysis of their individual pericopae, and the study of Matthean eschatology was neglected in the process. The next major contribution to this subject came in the wake of the heir to form criticism, redaction criticism, when the focus of attention shifted back to the editorial and theological interests of the evangelists. In 1956 G. Bornkamm published what was to prove to be a very influential essay, 'End-Expectation and Church in Matthew'.

In this study Bornkamm focused primarily on the role of the judgemental material in Matthew's gospel. He argued that the gospel as a whole was written from the perspective of the coming judgement. The evangelist's view of the church was interwoven with and definitively shaped by this particular theme. Bornkamm began his essay with an analysis of the Matthean discourses and observed that all of them combined teaching for the church with the notion of the future judgement (pp. 15–24). According to Matthew everyone is to be judged, the church included, and the standard by which each is to be judged is the attainment (or not) of the higher righteousness (p. 24). The higher righteousness consists in adherence to the Torah but governed by the twofold love command (pp. 24–32). Matthew comes to this radical understanding of the law on the basis of his view of the universal judgement (p. 32). This understanding of the law shapes Matthew's christology; the future judge Jesus is also the weak and humble servant who shows mercy to the meek in strict accordance with the principles of the higher righteousness (pp. 32–8). The church is urged to follow Jesus' example. Its members will be judged by

---

[2]   Streeter's historical type of explanation seems to be accepted by Grant, *The Gospels*, p. 137, who states that Matthew's apocalyptic eschatology '... suggests a milieu and a time when apocalyptic messianism was in the ascendant'.

the success or otherwise of their imitation of the example set by Jesus – love of God and neighbour, suffering and obedience. Matthew stresses that the church is a *corpus mixtum* whose constituent elements will be separated only at the judgement (pp. 38–49).

The obvious merit of Bornkamm's study is that it attempts to define the purpose of Matthew's eschatological material. The evangelist's emphasis on the coming judgement serves to exhort his readers to strive for the higher righteousness as defined by the life and teaching of Jesus. The gospel's judgemental material therefore has primarily a paraenetic function. In this respect Bornkamm's work marks a step forward from the earlier study of Streeter. But in other respects Bornkamm's redaction-critical analysis of the judgement in Matthew is less satisfying than Streeter's work. Since Bornkamm confines his study only to the gospel material, there is no attempt to understand Matthew's emphasis on the judgement in a broader context. Bornkamm merely takes for granted the presence of these eschatological traditions in the gospel and, unlike Streeter, does not try to explain why Matthew adopted them in the first place. It might be true that the theme of judgement serves the evangelist's paraenesis, but why did he choose this particular vehicle of expression and not another? Moreover, by examining the judgement as a general concept, Bornkamm tends to neglect the specific details of this theme in the gospel. Matthew's view of the fate of the wicked, for example, is painted in the harshest of terms; this group will be tortured eternally in the fires of Gehenna (see further chapter 6 below). Why does the evangelist promote such a terrible picture of the fate of the wicked? How are this theme and Matthew's apocalyptic eschatology as a whole related to contemporary eschatological schemes? Bornkamm's study overlooks these important questions. In view of this, it does not take us very far in explaining why Matthew places such emphasis on the judgement in the first place and why he portrays it in the terms he does. Despite these failings, Bornkamm's study of Matthew's eschatology became the standard work for the next generation and its legacy is well attested in later studies.

After the appearance of Bornkamm's essay, and in no small part because of it, the study of Matthew's eschatology moved to the periphery of Matthean scholarship. The redaction-critical studies which followed focused attention on other aspects of the evangelist's thought, notably his ecclesiology and his christology;

eschatology was moved well and truly from the centre stage.[3] That this proved to be the case can be seen from a brief review of two of the most important redaction-critical studies of Matthew's gospel, those of W. Trilling and G. Strecker.

Trilling's study, which concentrates on the rejection of Israel and the status of the church as 'the true Israel', has very little to say on the subject of Matthew's apocalyptic eschatology. In a small section devoted to the general area of eschatology, he argues that the evangelist is far more interested in the present than in speculating on the time of the end events. For Matthew the end of the existing world order is neither particularly near nor particularly distant (*Wahre Israel*, p. 30). What Matthew does wish to express, according to Trilling, is the present experience of the Lord in the church, no matter how long or short the interim period might prove to be. Thus the evangelist is more concerned with the strong faith of the church in the present than with apocalyptic speculation (p. 29). These statements are echoed in later sections. The uncertainty over the date of the end (cf. 24:36) leads Matthew in 24:37–25:13 to exhort his readers to extreme vigilance (p. 125). In order to serve this exhortation, the evangelist dispenses with the notion of the judgement's imminence and focuses instead on its severity (p. 126). It is the threat of judgement which shapes Matthew's paraenesis and not the imminence of the event (p. 126 n. 24).

Matthew's apocalyptic eschatology is likewise of little concern in the work of Strecker, which openly focuses on the gospel's christology and ecclesiology. At the beginning of his study, Strecker disputes the view of Streeter (and others) that Matthew is dominated by an imminent end expectation (*Weg*, pp. 41–5). Rather, the evangelist emphasises the suddenness of the event which excludes any calculation of its date (p. 242). But Matthew does not entirely abandon this notion, since he wishes his community to reckon continually with the possibility of the end. In a statement echoing the position of Trilling, Strecker maintains that both the near end expectation and the notion of its further delay have their part to play in Matthew's thought (p. 242). That Matthew has little interest

[3]   It is worth noting that a recent survey of Matthean scholarship between 1945–80 had in its treatment of 'Matthew as Theologian' no section devoted to Matthew's eschatology. See Stanton, 'Origin and Purpose', pp. 1889–951. That such a comprehensive survey as this has no individual treatment of Matthew's eschatology is proof enough that this particular theme had been all but omitted from the agenda during the period in question.

in the end events themselves is evident from the fact that he makes no attempt to systematise the diverse accounts of the judgement which he found in his sources (pp. 236–7). For Strecker, Matthew's real purpose for this judgemental material is entirely paraenetic. In his presentation of these traditions, Matthew directs the readers away from the future and back to the present ethical demands which are the central elements in the ongoing process of salvation history (p. 242).

The influence of Bornkamm's study is well illustrated in the works of Trilling and Strecker. The eschatology of Matthew's gospel was no longer to be taken on its own terms; rather, it must be viewed only in conjunction with or as a component of Matthew's ecclesiology. Matthew uses his eschatological material only for the purpose of exhortation and paraenesis in the present. Contrary to the view of Streeter, the evangelist, far from upholding the imminence of the judgement, hardly gives its time of arrival a second thought. So complete had been the change of opinion with regard to Matthew's eschatological expectations, that in 1980 H. C. Kee could write, 'The church of Matthew, with the apostolic foundation going back to Peter as sovereign and arbiter ... is an established institution, not an apocalyptic sect.'[4]

The very next year saw the appearance of the first major contribution to Matthew's eschatology since the essay of Bornkamm, D. Marguerat's massive revised doctoral dissertation devoted to the theme of judgement in Matthew's gospel. There are five distinct parts to his book. The first of these, which deals with the theme of judgement in the gospel, is basically introductory and raises many of the issues with which the present study is concerned. The more salient points can be summarised as follows. According to Marguerat the theme of judgement is the fundamental theme of the Matthean gospel. Of the 148 pericopae which comprise this gospel, no less than 60 are concerned with this feature (*Le Jugement*, p. 13). Matthew adopts from his sources, notably Q and his special traditions, the metaphorical language of judgement and accentuates it (pp. 17–22). Much of this language is found in the contemporary apocalyptic literature (pp. 22–3). Taking up Strecker's observation, Marguerat notes that Matthew makes no attempt to synthesise the disparate material which he inherited from his sources; the evangelist has little interest in presenting a

---

[4] Kee, *Christian Origins*, p. 143.

coherent picture of the actual event of judgement (pp. 23–5). The same is true of the material pertaining to the (consummated) kingdom where the righteous will reside (pp. 41–4). What does hold Matthew's interest is not so much the concrete events associated with the judgement, but the criteria by which people are to be judged (pp. 25–6). This observation leads Marguerat to the rhetorical function of the announcement of judgement in Matthew's gospel. He maintains with Bornkamm that this type of material concludes all the major discourses of Jesus in Matthew. The purpose of this method of composition is clear. The words of Jesus are given the utmost authority; fidelity to his teaching becomes the yardstick by which all will be judged (pp. 32–7). In addition, the announcement of the coming judgement puts the hearers in a position of radical responsibility whereby they are ultimately responsible for their fate (pp. 37–41). The threat of judgement in Matthew is addressed to two groups – the disciples (the church) and the people of Israel represented by their leaders (pp. 45–8).

The remainder of Marguerat's work follows on from these preliminary findings and examines the judgement from a number of perspectives. The second part of his dissertation, Christ is the Law (pp. 67–235), establishes that Jesus of Nazareth is the judge of the world and that the major criterion for judgement is Jesus' interpretation of the law. In the third section, the church and the failure of Israel (pp. 239–407), Marguerat argues that on account of her disobedience Israel is now rejected by God, this being illustrated by the destruction of Jerusalem. The Christian church effectively replaces Israel, but in doing so the threat of judgement now rebounds on its members who should learn from Israel's fate and take care not to repeat her mistakes (pp. 398–405). This point is elaborated in part 4, the church faces the judgement (pp. 411–75), where Marguerat examines Matthew's notion of the church as a *corpus mixtum* which will inevitably be exposed to the judgement. In the fifth and final section of his book, on vigilance (pp. 479–561), Marguerat analyses the responsibility of the church in the interim. Her members must be watchful and remain faithful to the standards of conduct enjoined by Jesus if they are to escape eschatological punishment.

It can be seen from the above summary that Marguerat's position is closely related to that of Bornkamm. Although his monograph is clearly broader in scope and far more detailed than the essay of Bornkamm, it still argues that Matthew's intense focus on the judgement primarily serves a paraenetic function. The church is warned both by direct threat and by the example of Israel that it too faces the judgement. In view of this, Matthew exhorts his readers not to be complacent about their salvation but to ensure that they live according to the precepts set down by Jesus himself. While Marguerat's discussion of all these issues contains much that is valuable, it suffers from many of the same limitations as those of his predecessors. Like Bornkamm's essay, Marguerat's work is basically descriptive and not explanatory. There is, for example, no sustained attempt to explain why Matthew used such extreme measures, the threat of eternal punishment, in the service of his paraenesis. Moreover, Marguerat pays little attention to the content of Matthew's judgemental expectations, though he notes that much of it is found in the contemporary apocalyptic tradition. He follows Strecker's argument that since Matthew made no attempt to systematise his disparate traditions regarding the judgement, it is legitimate to conclude that he was more interested in the criteria of judgement than the actual event itself.

But this supposition needs to be questioned. It presumes that Matthew was a systematic theologian of sorts who aimed for consistency on important matters and was happy to be inconsistent on unimportant matters. As G. N. Stanton has recently warned, however, the view of Matthew as a (systematic) theologian requires serious modification.[5] Matthew wrote primarily as an evangelist with many purposes in mind and not as a theologian who was concerned with presenting a coherent and consistent theology. We should not expect absolute consistency from such an author, nor should we judge as unimportant those themes which he had not assimilated into a coherent whole. In fact, a critical examination of the gospel reveals that there is very little on which the evangelist is absolutely consistent. Even the criteria by which individuals will be judged are not constant throughout the gospel. We need only compare the criteria in 12:31–2 with those in 25:31–46 to illustrate this point. In view of this, the particulars of Matthew's eschatological scheme cannot so easily be set aside. Nor should we, as does Marguerat, bypass the relationship between the apocalyptic-eschatological tradition and Matthew's judgemental material. Like the redaction-critical studies before him, Marguerat

---

[5] Stanton, *Gospel for a New People*, pp. 41–5.

investigates the judgement theme in Matthew within the limited context of the gospel alone, and outside influences and historical factors are given very little consideration.

It is perhaps fitting that the work of Marguerat, which has so many affiliations with the earlier study of Bornkamm and which stands as the most comprehensive defence of Bornkamm's position, might well prove to be its final representative. The last decade or so has seen a significant shift in scholarly attitudes toward Matthew's apocalyptic eschatology. The reason for this shift is not difficult to discern. In the last fifteen years or so there has been a dramatic renewal of interest in the apocalyptic writings and related literature. Not since the days of Charles have these documents been translated and interpreted with such vigour. This activity has rekindled interest in this theme in the field of New Testament studies and the gospel of Matthew has not been immune to it. Thus Matthean scholarship is in the process of turning the full circle. Just as Streeter and others were deeply influenced by the contemporary study of the apocalyptic literature, so too today are Matthean scholars heavily influenced by modern apocalyptic scholarship.

In 1984 G. N. Stanton made the first attempt since Streeter to offer an explanation for the apocalyptic-eschatological content of the first gospel.[6] Although Stanton was primarily concerned with Matthew's severe anti-Jewish polemic, he argued in the course of his discussion that there is a direct link between the gospel's anti-Jewish attitude and the prominence of its apocalyptic features. Stanton claims that the evangelist and his church had recently parted company with Judaism and were trying to come to grips with the trauma occasioned by that separation (pp. 273–4). In support of his claim Stanton produces four arguments. He first builds a case from a number of Matthean texts that the evangelist's community perceived itself to be threatened by Jewish opposition (pp. 274–7). The sectarian nature of Matthew's group is further evidenced, argues Stanton, by the fact that it was very much at odds as well with the gentile world (pp. 277–8). Stanton's third argument is the most important for our purposes and concerns the prominence of apocalyptic-eschatological motifs in Matthew. Not content merely with noting and describing this phenomenon, Stanton asks, 'Why is there increased prominence given to apocalyptic themes in this gospel? What is the *function* of these

---

6   Stanton, 'Matthew and Judaism'. This study also appears in his *Gospel for a New People*, pp. 146–68. The page references apply to the original article.

traditions?' (p. 278, original emphasis). In answering this question Stanton turns to a sociological explanation. Apocalyptic language and motifs are evoked by historical crises and/or an intense feeling of alienation from the outside world. They serve to comfort and console those who feel alienated and in doing so reinforce group solidarity (p. 279). Stanton goes on to argue that this is precisely the function of the apocalyptic features of Matthew (pp. 279–80). He concludes with the claim that Matthew's heightened apocalyptic interest can be seen as a response to a number of crises which the Matthean community faced, including the painful separation from Judaism (p. 281). Stanton then turns to his final argument which demonstrates that other early Christian texts also bear the twin characteristics of opposition to Judaism and increased emphasis on apocalyptic themes (pp. 281–3).

Stanton's essay is an important contribution to the study of Matthew's apocalyptic eschatology. Not only did it raise anew the question why Matthew is so oriented toward this perspective, but it opened up new possibilities for the solution of this puzzle. By stressing the social setting of the evangelist and his readers, Stanton's explanation took the enquiry a significant step further on from the historical and geographical explanation of Streeter. After the publication of Stanton's essay, it became clear that this aspect of the gospel could not be interpreted without reference to the historical and social forces which affected the evangelist and the community for whom he wrote.

Another important contribution to our subject came the following year in an article by D. A. Hagner which seems to have been written without knowledge of Stanton's essay. Beginning with an overview of the apocalyptic viewpoint ('Apocalyptic Motifs', pp. 54–7), Hagner devotes the remainder of his study to the author of Matthew, his gospel and his church. With regard to the members of Matthew's church, Hagner maintains that they were Jewish Christians who were experiencing hostility from both non-Christian Jews and gentiles. He affirms, 'Just this simple a realization will prepare us to expect apocalyptic in the Gospel of Mt ... alienation and the experience of hostility and persecution have been shown to be the key sociological factors that stimulate apocalyptic thought and form apocalyptic movements' (pp. 57–8). Having produced a sociological explanation for Matthew's apocalyptic orientation, Hagner then proceeds to detail more fully the evangelist's point of view. He notes that the gospel's presentation of the story of Jesus, from his birth to the great commission, is replete with 'apocalyptic-like' motifs (pp. 60–2). Hagner then turns to the gospel's 'apocalyptic viewpoint proper', which means the apocalyptic-eschatological material that, from the standpoint of the evangelist, refers to the future. According to Hagner, this is the more prominent apocalyptic feature in Matthew and is found in the preaching of the Baptist as well as the five major discourses of Jesus (pp. 63–8). He argues that Matthew's double-edged apocalyptic stance, the use of apocalyptic language and motifs to present the past story of the messiah and his future-oriented apocalyptic viewpoint proper, is a conscious alteration by the evangelist of the traditional apocalyptic view which was always directed toward the future (pp. 68–73). The final pages of Hagner's study are devoted to the role of apocalyptic-eschatological features in the gospel which he categorises under four headings (pp. 74–6). 1 Instruction: Matthew instructs his community in the glories of two apocalyptic realities, the one having already occurred in the life and mission of Jesus and the other which will come at the consummation of the age. 2 Encouragement: the evangelist, like other apocalyptic authors, encourages his community to persevere in the face of present persecution and suffering. 3 Paraenesis: Matthew uses the apocalyptic viewpoint as a motivation to moral and righteous conduct. 4 Readiness: this is related to the third category. The end of the age is imminent, so wakefulness and watchfulness are demanded. Hagner's study, though brief and quite general, is none the less an important one. Not only does it make a conscious effort to understand the apocalyptic stance(s) of Matthew, but it lends support to the position of Stanton that the explanation of this viewpoint lies in the gospel's historical and social setting.

The next important contribution to this subject was an article by O. L. Cope published in 1989. Cope admits that he is building upon the earlier work of Bornkamm, but he attempts to fill in the gaps in Bornkamm's essay. For example, he claims that Bornkamm actually understated the pervasiveness of the apocalyptic element in the first gospel and so supplements his predecessor's arguments ('Role of Apocalyptic', pp. 115–17). Moreover, Cope asks the very question which Bornkamm did not ask; just why is this apocalyptic theme so strong in Matthew's gospel? In similar vein to Stanton and Hagner, Cope adopts a sociological approach and examines the many functions of apocalyptic language and imagery; these functions include providing hope in difficult times, assuring the readers that their enemies will be punished and warning them that they too must walk the straight and narrow lest they be punished as well (pp. 117–18). While acknowledging that Matthew's gospel uses apocalyptic material to provide hope and to satisfy the need for vengeance, Cope argues that its primary purpose is to direct the behaviour of the gospel's readers. Matthew uses apocalyptic categories to promise rewards for good deeds and punishment for evil deeds. Cope writes, 'The continued repetition of this punishment/ judgement theme as a warning to the disciples throughout the Gospel is so powerful as to represent one of *the* major stresses of the book ... The vision of the future in this Gospel is a two-edged motivator to obedient discipleship' (p. 119, original emphasis). On the question why Matthew uses apocalyptic themes in this way, Cope maintains that the cause lies in the recent history of the Matthean church. By contrast with Stanton, he does not see the cause as a painful separation from Judaism; according to Cope the Matthean community is still a part of Judaism. Rather, there is a whole set of alternative circumstances – the Jewish war, the experience of persecution and inter-church division over allegiance to Christ (p. 120). Cope concludes that after the Jewish revolt the Matthean community had turned to the apocalyptic hope of the return of the Son of Man; in the meantime its members should devote themselves to strict obedience to both the Torah and the teachings of Jesus (p. 120). It is to this end that the first evangelist makes use of apocalyptic concepts.

The work of Cope, though offering an alternative explanation to those provided by Stanton and Hagner, is very much at one with them in terms of the method of approach. All three agree that, in order to understand and explain Matthew's interest in apocalyptic eschatology, we need to make use of appropriate sociological analyses. The gospel of Matthew must be examined in the same way that other apocalyptic-eschatological writings are investigated. While these three scholars agree with their predecessors that Matthew's judgemental material plays an important role in paraenesis and exhortation, they each identify further functions it plays in the gospel.

This brief survey of the relevant scholarly literature has shown that the study of Matthew's (apocalyptic) eschatology has turned the full circle. The early work of Streeter, though less concerned with the function of this material in the gospel, at least understood that its presence there needed to be explained. He argued that historical and geographical factors contributed to the prominence of this theme in Matthew. By contrast, the redaction-critical studies from Bornkamm's programmatic essay to Marguerat's full-scale discussion tended to ignore the broader context of the evangelist's judgemental material and focused solely upon its paraenetic function. They claimed that the evangelist was less interested in the events of the future and more concerned with the present life of the church. Since the judgement in Matthew was analysed only within the context of the gospel itself, the parallels in content between this theme and the wider apocalyptic-eschatological tradition and the question of external influences on the evangelist were either downplayed or ignored. The more recent studies of Stanton, Hagner and Cope witnessed a return to the tradition of Streeter. They highlighted the parallels between the gospel's eschatology and the apocalyptic tradition and explained these as a result of similar social settings.

By way of concluding this survey, I wish to return to a point made at its beginning, the justification of the present work. The studies of Stanton, Hagner and Cope, though all important in their own particular way, were only on a small scale. Because these three authors composed articles and not monographs, none of them attempted to amass and comprehensively assess all the relevant evidence. There is then a need for a larger and more complete treatment of all aspects of this subject.[7] It is this task which the present study sets itself. Before attempting to do so, it is necessary first to state precisely the presuppositions on which this study proceeds and the methods it will employ.

3. Presuppositions concerning the gospel of Matthew

The presuppositions concerning Matthew's gospel upon which the present study proceeds stand in agreement with the consensus of critical scholarly opinion. The author of the first gospel is not known. I follow the common view in rejecting the traditional identification of Matthew as the disciple of Jesus. However, for the sake of convenience and in deference to convention, this study will refer to both the writer of the gospel and the gospel itself as

---

[7]   Recently D. Orton has noted the desirability of further investigations of the relationship between Matthew and the apocalyptic literature. See his *Understanding Scribe*, p. 175.

Matthew. On the more debated question whether Matthew was a Jew or a gentile, it is accepted here that he belonged to the former group. This contention will be confirmed in Part II as we establish that Matthew is quite at home in the world of Jewish apocalyptic eschatology, and in Part III where it will be argued that the evangelist harboured anti-gentile sentiments which are incompatible with gentile authorship. Both the internal and external evidence strongly suggest that Matthew was written at some point in the final quarter of the first century, perhaps earlier rather than later within this period. A date of around 80 CE is most consistent with the evidence, though it is possible that it could have been written some five to ten years later than this.[8] The general area of composition was probably Syria, and the most likely location is the provincial capital, Antioch on the Orontes.[9] It is also assumed that Matthew composed his gospel using Mark and Q as his major sources. This acceptance of the two source (or two document) hypothesis does not presume that the theory itself has been proven beyond all shadow of doubt. Rather, it means that this hypothesis, whatever its limitations, offers a better explanation of the complex interrelationships between the synoptic gospels than any of its competitors.

4. The methods employed in this study

The methods adopted in this study are those most appropriate to the tasks at hand. The major tool for the descriptive section of this study, the reconstruction of Matthew's apocalyptic-eschatological scheme in Part II, will be redaction criticism. This method has been chosen because I accept the proposition that we can learn much about editors and authors by the manner in which they treat their sources. It is important to emphasise that in the present work redaction criticism is meant in its broadest sense. This means that it covers *all* facets of Matthew's treatment of his sources. These can be roughly classified into four major categories.

The first of these involves Matthew's alteration of his source material. This phenomenon has attracted the keenest interest and has provided the basic starting point for many redaction-critical studies. Its importance lies in the fact that redaction of this nature

---

[8] On the dating of the gospel, see Davies and Allison, *Matthew*, I, pp. 127–38.

[9] See the comprehensive discussion of Matthew's provenance by Meier, 'Antioch', pp. 18–26.

presumes a conscious decision on the part of the evangelist which in turn indicates the subjects of importance to him. This principle, though perhaps exaggerated at the expense of others in past studies (see below), still remains a crucial tool of the Matthean redaction critic. Closely related to the first category is the second which takes into account Matthew's creation of material to supplement or complement his sources. This type of redaction is also a significant indicator of authorial interests since it too results from a deliberate decision of the evangelist and obviously betrays his particular concerns. The third category of editorial activity, Matthew's omissions from his sources, works in the opposite way by identifying his dislikes. Of course, any one of a number of reasons might lie behind his omission of a particular passage – it was theologically or christologically offensive or inappropriate, it was superfluous, it did not fit well into his own narrative structure and so on. Each instance of this type of redaction needs to be assessed on its own merits. The fourth type of redactional practice is Matthew's retention of his source material either unchanged or almost unchanged. Unlike the three other types, all of which reveal the evangelist's dissatisfaction with his sources, this editorial procedure indicates where the evangelist agreed with the sources at his disposal. This is a point which has been too little appreciated in redaction-critical studies on Matthew, and it requires further comment.

The early redaction critics assumed that Matthew's characteristic interests could be detected only in his alterations of his sources and in his free compositions (categories 1 and 2 above), and that nothing of importance could be learnt from those sections of the gospel where the evangelist's editorial hand played only a minor role. The unstated principle behind this view is that editors betray their interests only when they consciously alter the works they are using. The retention of sources, on the other hand, should be seen as a passive act which is silent concerning authorial intent or interest. This approach, however, is based upon a false view of editorial practice. It hardly needs saying that at every point in the composition of his gospel Matthew had the freedom to choose how he would treat his sources. To put the matter in bald terms, he could choose either to revise (or omit) any part of the material he had before him or to accept it as it stood. When he chose the former option, it must be inferred that at that point he disagreed with his source and so altered it to a more agreeable form. Conversely, when he opted to follow a certain section closely, it must be concluded that at this particular point his own view coincided with that of his source. Thus both phenomena, revision and retention, clearly involve the concept of choice and each is an important indicator of Matthew's point of view. The active/passive principle on which so much earlier redaction-critical work was based is thus a false one. No editorial activity, not even straight copying, can be deemed passive in any meaningful sense of the term. This point is well made by C. M. Tuckett in regard to the gospel of Luke. Tuckett writes,

> if we are interested in discovering Luke's overall theology, we must be prepared to consider not only the changes Luke has made to his tradition, but also the places where Luke has preserved his tradition unaltered ... For Luke's decision to adopt, and *not* adapt, a tradition may be just as revealing of his overall concerns as the changes he makes to his sources elsewhere.[10]

What Tuckett says of Luke holds just as true in the case of Matthew.[11] Finally, it needs to be said that noting those sections where Matthew closely follows his sources might not reveal what was *distinctive* in his thought, as might categories 1 and 2 above, but it is no less important for that. In order to study the evangelist fully, we need a complete picture of him and not just a glimpse of his distinctive features.

It is clear from this that the redaction-critical approach to Matthew's gospel in the present study is a comprehensive one. We are interested in the gospel as a whole and not just those sections where the evangelist altered his source material. While the question of the evangelist's modifications of his sources is still of paramount importance, it is not the only significant indicator of his intentions. The totality of his composition, which incorporates both creative redaction and retentive redaction, is the true object of study.

In the light of this a few comments are in order with regard to the application of redaction criticism in the present study. In the case of Matthew's treatment of Mark, there is no problem since both texts are available and can be readily compared. It is clear when

---

[10] Tuckett, *Reading the New Testament*, p. 122 (original emphasis).
[11] So too Stanton, *Gospel for a New People*, pp. 41–2, 52. The same point is made in the recent study of Charette, *Theme of Recompense*, pp. 16–18, who prefers to call this approach composition criticism.

Matthew chose to follow his Marcan source and when he chose not to do so. The same does not apply, of course, to Matthew's Q material. Here we have only the parallel Lucan text for comparison, and it is not always easy to discern where Matthew has followed the wording of Q and where he has edited it. There is a similar problem with regard to the passages which appear only in Matthew. With nothing available for comparison, any one of three possibilities can account for each of these gospel pericopae. It might have been taken from a source with little change or it might have been traditional material which Matthew subjected to heavy redaction. On the other hand, it could be the case that Matthew created the passage outright. Many redaction-critical studies subject these Q and special source passages to painstaking analysis in an attempt to sort out these problems, but I do not propose to do so in the following chapters. My reasons are twofold. The first is that such minute redactional work, which would take up valuable space, is not necessary. There has been much excellent work done in this area, particularly in the larger Matthean commentaries of recent years, and nothing is to be gained by repeating their discussion. When the issue of Matthew's redaction in these Q and unique pericopae arises, I will direct the reader in the notes to those studies whose analysis of the problem I accept and where all the relevant evidence and arguments can be found. This dependence on earlier studies is all the more permissible since in almost all cases my own view coincides with the consensus position. Secondly, in the final analysis the extent of Matthew's modifications to these sources does not affect our understanding of Matthew to any significant degree. As noted above, all Matthean passages inform us about the evangelist, and this applies no matter whether he has created them or copied them. So even if we took the extreme (and rather improbable) position that in every case Matthew copied slavishly from Q and his special traditions, then we would come to the conclusion that Matthew stood very close to these sources. This might mean that the evangelist was not such a distinctive thinker, but it does not mean that he is unworthy of study.

While redaction criticism is entirely appropriate for reconstructing Matthew's apocalyptic-eschatological perspective, it cannot take us very far in terms of the explanatory aims of this study in Part III. Other methods are required at this point as a supplement to redaction criticism. The essays of Stanton, Hagner and Cope have demonstrated the necessity of applying sociological analysis to the study of the gospel of Matthew.[12] This is an important step forward, since the evangelist has too often been depicted as 'an armchair theologian' quietly musing over abstract theological issues in a historical vacuum. The application of social-scientific methods completely overturns this particular view by acknowledging that both Matthew and his gospel were influenced by their historical, geographical, cultural and social contexts. Thus insights will be gleaned from the social sciences and applied where appropriate to the gospel of Matthew in an attempt to understand the evangelist's apocalyptic-eschatological perspective. It should be noted, however, that the methods of the social sciences must be used with due caution. They should never be employed as primary methods at the expense of the historical data. On the contrary, they must be used where applicable only when the historical evidence has been accumulated by other means.[13] For this reason, the reconstruction of Matthew's social setting in chapter 8 will focus mainly on the historical evidence with the social sciences providing subsequent illumination at certain points. The dangers of using social-scientific criticism as a substitute for historical reconstruction will be highlighted in chapter 2 when we examine the social setting of apocalypticism.

[12] In his groundbreaking study of Luke–Acts, P. F. Esler suggests that such a marriage of redaction criticism and the social sciences should be called 'socio-redaction' criticism. See *Community and Gospel*, pp. 2–6.

[13] For similar comments, see Esler, *Community and Gospel*, pp. 12–13 and Watson, *Paul, Judaism and the Gentiles*, p. x.

PART I

Apocalyptic eschatology and apocalypticism

This first part is concerned with the related notions of apocalyptic eschatology and apocalypticism. The first chapter begins with a discussion of the current terminology and identifies in broad terms what is meant by apocalyptic eschatology and apocalypticism in the present study. The remainder of the chapter will then present a survey of the major characteristics of apocalyptic eschatology. Such a survey will provide a firm basis from which we may approach the apocalyptic-eschatological content of Matthew in the second part of the study (chapters 3–7). The second chapter moves from the realm of description to that of explanation. Here the focus of attention will be on the phenomenon of apocalypticism. What factors contribute to the rise of apocalypticism? What is it which causes certain individuals or groups to resort to apocalyptic eschatology? Does this phenomenon have an identifiable social setting? Finally, we shall look at the related issue of the function of apocalyptic eschatology in the works (or groups) where it is prominent. The investigation of these questions will put us in a position to examine in chapters 8 and 9 the social setting of Matthew's apocalyptic eschatology as well as the function it plays within that gospel.

1

THE MAJOR CHARACTERISTICS OF APOCALYPTIC ESCHATOLOGY

1. The problem of terminology

It is well recognised in the field of apocalyptic studies that this area of study is plagued by considerable and continuing difficulties. First and foremost of these is the problem of confusing and ambiguous terminology which has its origin in the past. For many decades scholars conducted research into what was then called apocalyptic. This term came into English as an adaptation of the German 'Apokalyptik', which itself derives from the Greek word for revelation (ἀποκάλυψις), specifically from its presence in the first verse of the book of Revelation where it denotes the contents of that document. The word was eventually used to express two quite distinct ideas. On the one hand, it denoted a specific literary genre of ancient Jewish and Christian texts which focused on the revelation of heavenly secrets. This identification of an apocalyptic genre traces back to early Christian practice where a number of documents, similar in form to Revelation, were grouped together and referred to as apocalypses. On the other hand, the word 'apocalyptic' was also employed to describe a particular eschatologically oriented world view which was thought to dominate the apocalyptic literature. Almost inevitably this dual sense of the same term led to semantic confusion. Because the same word covered quite different concepts, a literary genre and a world view, it was often difficult to decide which of the two senses was intended in any given reference to apocalyptic.[1] For this reason a number of scholars abandoned the then current terminology and attempted to lessen the confusion by arriving at a new set of descriptive terms.

The first attempt at a revision was that of K. Koch who distinguished between the literary genre apocalypse and the historical

---

[1] For discussion of this point, see Knibb, 'Prophecy and the emergence of the Jewish apocalypses', pp. 157–8.

movement underlying it which he called apocalyptic.[2] This process
of revision was taken a significant stage further by P. D. Hanson
who argued that the whole subject would be better served by a
threefold classification of the phenomena. According to Hanson,
we must speak of the literary form as apocalypse, the dominating
(eschatological) religious perspective as apocalyptic eschatology
and the socio-religious movement as apocalypticism.[3] The last two
categories are not to be confused with one another. Apocalypticism
is born at that point when a group tries to codify its identity and
particular interpretation of reality by recourse to apocalyptic
eschatology. Hanson's scheme, which draws a useful distinction
between the religious perspective (or world view) and the underlying socio-religious movement, has been adopted by many scholars
in preference to the ambiguous dual use of the word 'apocalyptic'.[4]
It is questionable, however, whether these developments have really
assisted our understanding of this very complex subject.

The problem resides in the fact that the two sets of terms listed
above operate on the assumption that the phenomena they
describe are all necessarily related to one another.[5] This is quite
clear from the chosen terminology. In the original nomenclature,
the same word was employed to describe two distinct concepts,
and this in turn was intended to convey the impression that they
were inextricably connected. Thus almost by definition the world
of ideas denoted as apocalyptic was necessarily related to the
apocalyptic genre. The revised terminology of Hanson, though a
semantic improvement on its predecessor, made precisely the same
assumption in exactly the same way. Since the names given to
apocalyptic eschatology and apocalypticism were derivatives of
the word 'apocalypse', the assumption was plain that the three
phenomena enjoyed a necessary relationship. With some qualifica-
tions this relationship was thought to operate both ways. First,
apocalypticism always involved the adoption of apocalyptic eschatology and its expression via the apocalyptic genre. Secondly, the
apocalyptic genre always involved apocalyptic eschatology and

---

[2]   Koch, *Rediscovery*, pp. 23–33.
[3]   Hanson, 'Apocalypticism', pp. 28–34 and *Dawn of Apocalyptic*, pp. 429–44.
[4]   Those who follow Hanson's scheme include Collins, *Apocalyptic Imagination*,
       pp. 2–11 and Aune, *Prophecy*, p. 107. There are, of course, exceptions to this
       revision of the terminology. Both Rowland, *Open Heaven*, p. 2 and Sturm,
       'Defining the Word "Apocalyptic"', p. 17 are happy to retain the twofold
       nominal use of the word 'apocalyptic'.
[5]   The same point is made by Davies, 'Social World', p. 252.

was always the result of apocalypticism. In more recent studies, this assumption of a necessary relationship has been raised almost to the status of an accepted fact. This can be evidenced by citing the words of one of the acknowledged authorities in this field, J. J. Collins, who writes, 'Since the adjective apocalyptic and the noun apocalypticism are derived from "apocalypse", it is reasonable to expect that they indicate some analogy with the apocalypses.'[6] What Collins says here must be clearly understood. He does *not* argue that scholars have correctly identified a number of related phenomena – a genre, a world view and a social movement – which they named accordingly using similar terms. Rather, he assumes that the phenomena in question are related because they have been given the names they have. In other words Collins allows modern scholarly language to determine the relationship between certain historical realities. The terminology and all it implies has now become the tool which enables historical reconstruction. In terms of the study of apocalypticism and apocalyptic eschatology, this means that these subjects can be approached only through the apocalyptic literature. As we shall see below, this is precisely how Collins approaches them. All this is patently questionable, however, and we ought to ask whether the current terminology does in fact reflect the historical situation.

An examination of the evidence reveals that on the threefold classification of the phenomena the only necessary relationship seems to exist between the socio-religious movement apocalypticism and the world view denoted as apocalyptic eschatology. While I will say more about this shortly, it can be noted at this point that since we identify an apocalyptic group only where there is an apocalyptic-eschatological perspective, it stands to reason that the former, almost by definition, must involve the latter. But as a number of scholars have pointed out, there appears to be no necessary connection between the genre apocalypse and the other two phenomena. On the one hand, some books from the Jewish apocalyptic corpus contain hardly any eschatological material, but focus on completely different themes such as the heavenly world, cosmology and astronomy. Obvious examples of this type of apocalypse are 2 Enoch and 3 Baruch.[7] On the other hand, some of the clearest expressions of apocalyptic eschatology (and therefore apocalypticism) are found in texts which do not belong to the

---

6   Collins, *Apocalyptic Imagination*, p. 10.
7   See Stone, 'Lists of Revealed Things', p. 440 and Rowland, *Open Heaven*, p. 28.

apocalyptic genre.[8] The prime example here is the corpus of texts composed by the Qumran community. These documents are replete with apocalyptic-eschatological material, and provide a wealth of information regarding Jewish end-time notions at the time of the birth of Christianity. Even Collins admits that the eschatological orientation of this group marks it as a representative of ancient Jewish apocalypticism.[9] Yet there is no evidence at all that this sectarian group ever produced an apocalypse of its own. While it collected and clearly cherished works of this type – Daniel and parts of 1 Enoch were found amongst its library – it clearly favoured other literary forms for expressing its own eschatological convictions.

The examples of 3 Baruch, 2 Enoch and the Qumran community demonstrate that the current terminology does not accurately reflect the historical situation. There is no necessary connection between the genre apocalypse and the religious perspective apocalyptic eschatology and its accompanying social movement. This in turn raises serious doubts about the continued use of the present terms. If we persist with the current system by which all three phenomena bear similar names, then we must be prepared for a semantic nightmare. We must accept that there is apocalyptic eschatology and apocalypticism outside the apocalyptic genre, apocalypses which have little or no apocalyptic eschatology, and apocalyptic groups which did not produce apocalypses. For obvious reasons, such a situation would be both impractical and unworkable. Consequently, there is a definite need to revise radically the revised terminology and arrive at a more appropriate set of terms. This new terminology must do justice to the disparate phenomena under discussion and not imply necessary relationships where they do not exist. In other words, we must not repeat the mistakes of the past by continuing to describe all three historical realities using cognates of the same word.

One possible way to avoid the current impasse would be to retain apocalypse for the literary genre and rename the distinctive eschatological perspective and its accompanying social movement. A suggestion along these lines has already been proposed by C. C. Rowland who has criticised the prevailing scholarly view for exaggerating the importance of eschatology in the apocalyptic

---

[8]   Stone, 'Lists of Revealed Things', pp. 440, 443, 451–2 n. 78.
[9]   Collins, 'Was the Dead Sea Sect an Apocalyptic Movement?', pp. 25–51.

literature.[10] Rowland argues that the very term 'apocalyptic eschatology' is a misnomer on the grounds that there is no unity of thought in the eschatological schemes of the apocalypses and that their end-time themes are found both within and without the apocalyptic genre. Since there is no necessary connection between the genre apocalypse and what is normally defined as apocalyptic eschatology, Rowland contends that the former should remain and that the latter should be dropped. The word 'apocalyptic' should be reserved to denote the distinctive outlook of the apocalypses, while the broad range of eschatological ideas might be referred to as transcendent eschatology.[11] Although Rowland does not discuss the social movement, it is clear that such a change of name for apocalyptic eschatology would necessitate an alteration of the word 'apocalypticism'. One possible alternative is millennialism (or millenarianism),[12] but the application of this word to early Jewish and Christian movements would be both anachronistic and misleading. Another possibility might be the adoption of the term 'messianic movements', yet this too is unsatisfactory since not all ancient apocalyptic groups emphasised the idea of a messiah.

The other and more drastic alternative is to retain apocalyptic eschatology and apocalypticism and find another name for the literary genre. This would doubtless meet with staunch resistance, since the very words 'apocalyptic' and 'apocalypse' as descriptive terms for the literary form have become so entrenched in current scholarship that nothing short of a miracle would see their demise. Moreover, such a change of name would be disputed on the grounds that it was coined in ancient times and therefore has a firm historical precedent. But there are practical reasons for at least giving serious thought to the abolition of the idea of *an* apocalyptic genre. To begin with, we should not be bound automatically by ancient practices. We must face the possibility that the early Christians were simply wrong in their identification of this genre. Further, it is no secret that there are serious problems associated with defining this particular literary type. The reason for this

---

[10] Rowland, *Open Heaven*, pp. 23–48. While Rowland's point is well taken, his attempt to emphasise the other important features of the apocalypses leads him to downplay the importance of the crucial role which eschatology plays in many of them. For a similar criticism, see Collins, *Apocalyptic Imagination*, p. 8 and Vanderkam, 'Prophetic-Sapiential Origins', p. 165.

[11] Rowland, *Christian Origins*, p. 57.

[12] So Isenberg, 'Millenarianism', pp. 26–46, who is followed by Davies, 'Social World', p. 253.

resides in the disparate nature of the texts under discussion. Even J. J. Collins, who has done most to set a standard definition, acknowledges that there are two different types of apocalypses and even sub-categories within these different types.[13] Of the two major types, one incorporates visions and an interest in the development of history up to its eschatological conclusion, while the other involves otherworldly journeys with an emphasis on cosmology rather than eschatology. Rather than imposing an artificial uniformity on these diverse writings, might it not be a better policy to dispense altogether with the notion of one apocalyptic genre with sub-types, and accept that there are a number of different genres with different concerns which should bear different labels?[14] We already differentiate between the genre apocalypse and related kinds of revelatory literature, Oracles and Testaments for example, so there is a precedent for this course of action.

I do not wish to settle this question here; that would take us too far afield. The point I wish to make is that the current terminology is no longer serviceable and is in dire need of revision. We must arrive at terms which do not imply that apocalyptic eschatology is the dominant religious perspective of the apocalyptic genre or that apocalypticism is simply the social movement which produced the apocalypses. The historical reality is that apocalypticism is the social phenomenon underlying an apocalyptic-eschatological perspective which can be given expression in the genre apocalypse as well as other literary types. Needless to say, some scholars stand in principle against any changes of this sort. J. J. Collins, who is well aware of the problems associated with the current terminology, argues none the less that they are serviceable, provided they are adequately qualified and the proper distinctions made.[15] In response to the criticisms of Rowland (and others), Collins adopted broader definitions of apocalyptic eschatology and apocalypticism than those which then prevailed in order to do justice to the diversity within the apocalyptic literature.

Collins defines apocalyptic eschatology as an end-time scheme which looks to retribution or judgement beyond the realm of history. This appears on the surface to be a reasonable definition,

---

[13] Collins, 'Morphology of a Genre', pp. 1–21 and his later statement in *Apocalyptic Imagination*, pp. 2–8.

[14] The same question is posed by Himmelfarb, *Tours of Hell*, p. 60.

[15] Collins, *Apocalyptic Imagination*, p. 10. See also his later affirmation in 'Genre, Ideology and Social Movements', p. 24.

since this sort of eschatology is clearly different from earlier (i.e. prophetic) eschatological convictions in Judaism. But just as Collins is impelled by the diversity of the apocalyptic texts to define two distinct sub-types within the genre, so too is he forced to identify two types of apocalyptic eschatology.[16] The more common type is reflected in the historical apocalypses and involves the notion of the two ages, including concrete descriptions of the end-times woes, the process of a universal judgement and the bestowal of eternal rewards or punishments. The second type is more characteristic of those apocalypses which focus on other-worldly journeys and cosmological matters. These apocalypses contain no reference to the end of history, but advance an alternative concept of individual judgement after death. Collins' assessment of apocalypticism follows the same pattern. He defines apocalypticism as '...the ideology of a movement that shares the conceptual structure of the apocalypses', and is again led by the diversity of the apocalyptic texts to posit (at least) two types of apocalypticism. One is concerned with the end of history and all that entails, while the other betrays a less eschatological and a more mystical orientation.[17]

It is not certain, however, whether this development is helpful. By clinging to the current terms and accepting the necessary relationship between them, Collins has merely complicated matters. The diversity within the apocalyptic genre which led Collins to postulate two sub-types is now carried over to the eschatological world view and the social movement. Apocalyptic eschatology thus comprises two very different end-time schemes, while apocalypticism consists of an eschatological and a mystical manifestation. While I readily accept in general terms the distinction which Collins draws between the genres, the eschatological schemes and social movements, I have concerns over the appropriateness of relating them so closely to one another and labelling them in the same way. The two eschatological schemes seem so far removed from one another in real terms that it is difficult to see any significant points of contact. Precisely the same can be said of the eschatological and mystical movements which Collins identifies. The concerns of each group appear so different that we need to question whether they

---

[16] Collins, *Apocalyptic Imagination*, p. 9. For an earlier statement of his views, see 'Apocalyptic Eschatology', pp. 21–43.
[17] Collins, *Apocalyptic Imagination*, pp. 10–11 and 'Genre, Ideology and Social Movements', p. 16.

belong together at all. By grouping together such different ideas and movements, Collins defines apocalyptic eschatology and apocalypticism in such broad terms that each definition becomes impractical, if not meaningless. The solution to the problem is to accept Collins' identification of different eschatological schemes and socio-religious movements, but to reject his presupposition that they are necessarily connected because they appear in a very broadly defined apocalyptic genre.

It seems clear to me that what Collins has actually identified are two distinct streams within early Judaism, an eschatologically oriented movement which focused on the end of the age and the universal judgement, and a mystically based movement which was concerned with other matters. The fact that each of them sometimes uses a revelatory genre to express its particular convictions is not in itself significant. Since these movements had little of substance in common, they should not be grouped together under the one label. They should be differentiated from one another and given different names as a result. Precisely the same applies to the different types of eschatology which we find in these movements. The eschatological scheme which is characterised by a continuation of history and individual judgement after death might be better described as post-mortem eschatology, while a more appropriate name for the mystical movement should be coined. On the other hand, the religious perspective and its accompanying socio-religious movement which emphasise the end of history and the universal judgement require a different set of terms.

Although most scholars would describe these phenomena as apocalyptic eschatology and apocalypticism, these terms are not really apt because of the confusion they engender; they seem to imply a necessary relationship between these phenomena and the genre apocalypse where none exists. I would therefore agree with Rowland that they should be dropped in preference to other terms which are more appropriate. But the temptation to propose new terms here will be resisted, and with some misgivings the current terminology will be retained in this study. The reason for its retention is that ever since the term was coined, apocalyptic eschatology has generally been understood in the sense of the eschatology of the historical apocalypses (and other texts). The debate over the terms and the phenomena they describe, which is an important debate, has had little impact on New Testament scholarship, and most scholars continue to define the religious perspective and the social movement in terms of the end of history and the universal judgement. In view of this, there seems little point in adding to the confusion here by proposing another set of terms. Therefore, the term apocalyptic eschatology, which will be defined more precisely shortly, will be used here in a sense which approximates the normal understanding of this term. Conceptually the term corresponds to what Rowland would call transcendent eschatology and to the more common of the two forms of apocalyptic eschatology on the understanding of Collins. Similarly, apocalypticism refers to the social movement which produced and transmitted this distinctive eschatological outlook. But it is essential to note that neither the religious perspective nor the social movement is confined to the apocalyptic genre. What is accepted here as apocalyptic eschatology (and apocalypticism) can be found in texts of other genres as the evidence of Qumran demonstrates.

The importance of this point in the context of the present study should be apparent. If apocalyptic eschatology and apocalypticism are viewed as enjoying a necessary relationship with the apocalyptic literature, then it becomes difficult to relate them to the *gospel* of Matthew which obviously belongs to a completely different genre. On the other hand, if it is accepted that these phenomena can be found both within and without the apocalyptic genre, then there is no impediment to examining the gospel of Matthew in terms of this eschatological scheme and its associated social movement.

2. The major characteristics of apocalyptic eschatology

The discussion thus far has spoken of apocalyptic eschatology only in very broad terms. There is a need at this point to narrow the discussion and specify in more detail what is meant by apocalyptic eschatology. This is necessary because many scholars have a limited understanding of this religious perspective and appreciate merely its eschatological motifs. But as stated in the Introduction, apocalyptic eschatology is broader in scope than just speculation about the final judgement. It contains non-eschatological themes which provide the framework for the eschatological material, and these should not be overlooked. The best way to define apocalyptic eschatology is to isolate and expound the major characteristics of this religious perspective as they appear in the relevant documents. But prior to doing so, a number of preliminary questions need to be settled.

2.1 Preliminary questions

The first question for discussion concerns the texts to be reviewed. Which documents are relevant for reconstructing the apocalyptic-eschatological perspective in the time of Matthew? Documents must meet two criteria for inclusion in the following survey. The first is that the dominating concern of the text must be the eschatological scheme of the end of history and its aftermath. The second criterion is that they must fall within a certain time-frame. The gospel of Matthew, written c.80 CE, belongs to the latter part of the age of 'classical apocalyptic(ism)' which is normally set between 250 BCE and 100 CE. Consequently, it stands to reason that our documents should belong to this period. The number of documents for consideration is quite large and they belong to many genres.

Of the Jewish apocalyptic corpus, the relevant texts include Daniel, 1 Enoch, 2 Baruch, 4 Ezra and the Apocalypse of Abraham. In terms of the Christian apocalyptic literature, the only document which falls within the time-frame is the book of Revelation. This is an important text in so far as it provides evidence of (Jewish) Christian apocalyptic eschatology at roughly the same time as the gospel of Matthew. We shall see that the evangelist and the seer have much in common in terms of this perspective. In addition to these documents are a number of writings from the related revelatory genres, Testaments and Oracles. The Testament is a last speech delivered by a revered figure, normally a patriarch, either to his sons or to his successor prior to his death. The single text belonging to this genre which meets our criteria is the Testament of Moses. The Oracle is a prophecy or other form of inspired utterance delivered on behalf of God. The works of this genre which fall within the relevant period and emphasise the end of history and its aftermath are books 3–5 of the (Jewish) Sibylline Oracles.[18] Also of paramount importance are the documents produced by the Qumran community which are a mine of information regarding the apocalyptic-eschatological notions of this period. The writings of this group thus provide a concrete example of apocalypticism in (or near) the time of Matthew, though it should not be assumed that all apocalyptic groups functioned in precisely the same way, nor held the same set of beliefs. When

---

[18] See Collins, *Apocalyptic Imagination*, p. 93.

speaking of the eschatology of the Qumran community, it is perhaps more advisable to speak of its eschatologies, since the scrolls evidence a number of end-time expectations, some of which are not entirely compatible with one another. Such a variety of notions is only to be expected. The Qumran sect existed for more than two centuries and we must reckon with some development of eschatological ideas over such a long period of time.[19] Whether the later Qumran community was aware of such inconsistencies, or even cared about them, is impossible to say.[20] In any event, it will become clear in ensuing chapters that the Matthean community has many affinities with this Jewish sectarian group.

All the above-mentioned texts provide the best witnesses to the apocalyptic-eschatological notions in existence at the time of Matthew. This is not to say that such ideas are not found in other works of this period. Apocalyptic-eschatological motifs do feature in many other texts, but they are less prominent and so of less importance to the overall concerns of the authors in question. Even the Psalms of Solomon, which is an important guide to the messianic beliefs of the time, contains little in the way of apocalyptic eschatology proper. The following survey will thus be based primarily upon the more important texts identified above, though reference to other Jewish documents of the specified period will sometimes be made. These texts include Jubilees, 2 Enoch, 3 Baruch, the Testaments of the Twelve Patriarchs and the Testament of Abraham. With the exception of Revelation, no Christian documents will appear in the following review. A comparison of Matthew's apocalyptic eschatology with other early Christian schemes will be undertaken in Part II.

A further preliminary point concerns the intention and scope of the following survey of the major characteristics of apocalyptic eschatology. This survey does *not* propose to offer a systematic 'apocalyptic theology'. The religious perspective or world view which we call apocalyptic eschatology is an extremely diverse and unsystematic phenomenon, and any discussion of it must take this diversity into account. While there is general agreement that history

---

[19] So too Davies, 'Eschatology at Qumran', p. 54; Pryke, 'Eschatology in the Dead Sea Scrolls', p. 57 and Davidson, *Angels at Qumran*, pp. 138–9.

[20] M. Smith has argued that the inconsistency in eschatological beliefs in the Qumran writings points to the reduced importance of eschatology for this community. See his 'What is Implied by the Variety of Messianic Figures?', pp. 66–72. Smith's remarks have been convincingly refuted by Collins, *Apocalyptic Imagination*, pp. 138–40.

is drawing to a close and that the eschatological judgement will ensue, there can be enormous diversity between schemes, either in emphasis or in detail. Therefore, rather than offering an artificial 'theology' of apocalyptic eschatology which applies to every document, we shall attempt here to isolate the major characteristics or motifs of this religious perspective. This is a permissible alternative, for it is clear that in the midst of this extremely diverse phenomenon a number of basic elements recur with great frequency. While few of these perhaps can be said to be *essential* aspects of apocalyptic eschatology, since one can always point to a document in which particular motifs do not appear or are given minimal treatment, these features represent the more common characteristics. An apocalyptic-eschatological perspective, therefore, consists of a substantial cluster of these elements and need not necessarily contain them all. Moreover, the following survey will not cite every instance of a given characteristic from the available documents; limitations of space do not make this feasible and the availability of more comprehensive surveys makes it unnecessary.[21] Rather, it will attempt to give an overview of these basic elements, providing examples from the documents and noting where applicable any important exceptions to the rule. Such an overview is all that is necessary to help identify and assess the apocalyptic-eschatological material of Matthew's gospel.

In the following survey eight characteristics of apocalyptic eschatology have been isolated. These include two concepts which provide the context in which the eschatological themes function, dualism and determinism, and six motifs which are purely eschatological in nature – eschatological woes, the appearance of a saviour figure, the judgement, the fate of the wicked, the fate of the righteous, an imminent end expectation. These eight characteristics can be readily compared with the eightfold scheme proposed by K. Koch for the apocalyptic movement (apocalypticism) from his reading of the apocalyptic literature.[22] Using slightly different terminology, Koch also isolated a near end expectation (number i), eschatological woes (number ii), determinism (number iii), dualism (number iv), the fate of the righteous (number v), the judgement

---

21 More detailed recent surveys are to be found in Russell, *Method and Message*, pp. 205–390 and Schürer et al., *History*, II, pp. 514–47. The revised Schürer gives a survey of apocalyptic-eschatological notions within the general context of messianism.

22 Koch, *Rediscovery*, pp. 28–33. A similar but less complete list is to be found in Vielhauer, 'Apocalypses and Related Subjects', pp. 587–94.

(number vi) and the appearance of a saviour figure (number viii). Koch's eighth category, which has no equivalent in the scheme proposed here, is the catchword 'glory' to describe the conditions of the new age in which the righteous participate. This theme properly belongs to the category of the fate of the righteous and does not require classification on its own. The characteristic included in the present work which has no parallel in the scheme of Koch, the fate of the wicked, is a very important component of apocalyptic eschatology. As the antithesis of the fate of the righteous, this theme is inextricably tied up with the dualistic context in which this religious perspective is set. No system of categorisation is complete without this particular motif.

2.2 The survey of the literature

Dualism

As stated above, the end-time speculations of apocalyptic eschatology function within the context of dualism. This dualism can be manifested in a variety of ways and each needs to be specified. One important dualistic motif which is integral to all apocalyptic-eschatological schemes is the notion that history is divided into two ages, the present age which began with creation and a fundamentally new age which will be realised at some point in the future. The beliefs about this new age will be delineated more fully in the following sections. A further important dualistic component of many apocalyptic schemes is that the cosmos or supernatural realm is divided into two opposing forces. On one side stands God and the holy angels and on the other stands a host of evil angels who have fallen from grace. It is well known that in the centuries prior to the turn of the eras, the angelology and demonology of Judaism underwent considerable development and we find in the contemporary texts a rather complex set of ideas relating to these opposing angelic groups.

The order of holy angels is arranged according to a strict hierarchy and each class of angel has its set function. To choose only a few examples, there are angels responsible for the natural elements and astral phenomena (cf. 1 En. 60:11–23; 2 En. 4:1–6:1; 19:2–6; Jub. 2:2), angels who pray on behalf of humans (1 En. 39:5; 47:2; Rev. 8:3–4), recording angels who keep a record of sins (1 En. 89:61–4; T.Ab. 12:12), angels who administer eschatological punishment (1 En. 53:4–5; 55:3; 56:1–4; 62:11; 63:1; 2 En. 10:3; T.Levi 3:2; T.Ab. 12:1–2), personal guardian angels (Jub. 35:17; Dan. 3:6; 3 Bar. 12–13) and guardian angels of the nations (Dan. 10:13, 21; 12:1; 1 En. 89:59–62; Jub. 15:31–2). At the very top of this hierarchy and closest to God are the archangels, four in number according to some traditions (1 En. 40:2–9; 54:6; 71:8) or seven in number according to others (1 En. 20:1–7; 81:5; 90:21–2). This class of angel has a variety of functions, including the imprisonment of the fallen angels (1 En. 10:4–5) and the consignment of them into the fiery furnace on the day of judgement (1 En. 54:6). In those apocalypses which describe an otherworldly journey, it is normally one of these archangels who transports and guides the purported author of the apocalypse through the heavenly regions and explains the heavenly secrets.

These holy angels have their evil counterparts.[23] One very influential tradition in relation to this theme is that of the Watchers which is found in its most complete form in the Book of the Watchers (1 En. 1–36). Developing the story of Genesis 6:1–4, the early section of this document explains how a group of evil angels, known as Watchers, descends from heaven, marries human women and reveals a whole host of heavenly secrets (1 En. 6–8). Their sins are reported to God who directs the archangels to bind and imprison them until the judgement (chs. 9–11). This story is recounted in abbreviated form in the Animal Apocalypse (1 En. 85–90) where the fallen angels are represented as stars (86:1–88:3; 90:24). Another less detailed account of these fallen angels is found in Jubilees 5:1–11; 10:1–12, where the leader of the wicked angels is Mastema and only nine-tenths of his company is bound and imprisoned; one tenth is permitted to remain free and is subject to Satan. The mention of Satan here introduces the point that the mythical story of the Watchers, though exercising widespread influence, did not form the backdrop to all demonological traditions of the period. An entirely different set of beliefs in which Satan assumes a major role also explains the origin and activities of evil angels who oppose God.

Satan is something of a minor figure in the Old Testament period (cf. Job chs. 1–2; Zech. 3:1–2; 1 Chron. 21:1) but had become very important by the time of the New Testament. He is very prominent in the Parables of Enoch (1 En. 37–71), 2 Enoch and Revelation.

---

[23]   More detailed accounts of this subject can be found in Russell, *Method and Message*, pp. 249–57 and Langton, *Essentials of Demonology*, pp. 107–44.

The first of these speaks of many Satans led by a chief Satan (1 En. 53:3; 54:6). These angels had presumably rebelled against God prior to the fall of the Watchers, since two of them were responsible for counselling the Watchers to sin (69:4–5; cf. 54:6) and one was guilty of tempting Eve (69:6). They are unlike the Watchers in so far as they were able to traverse between heaven and earth in order to accuse humans before God (40:7). Curiously enough, these Satans seem to be the ones responsible for punishing the human sinners at the time of the eschatological judgement (53:3–5; 62:9–11; 63:1). The Satan tradition in 2 Enoch is both similar to and different from the account in the Parables of Enoch. Here the patriarch visits the second heaven where he sees a group of condemned angels who had rebelled against God (7:1–3). In the fifth heaven he sees the Watchers and the prince of all the fallen angels, Satanail (18:1–3), who had earlier tried to make himself equal to God (29:4) and who was responsible for the sin of Eve (31:3–6). An important development of the Satan tradition is reflected in the book of Revelation. In this work he is the eschatological adversary *par excellence* and is prominent in certain parts of the book. Satan appears in chapter 12 as the dragon who deceives the whole world and persecutes the mother and her offspring, the righteous community and the messiah (verses 1–6, 13–17). He and his evil company are expelled from heaven by Michael and the other holy angels (verses 7–12). Satan exercises dominion over the earth until his imprisonment for one thousand years in the bottomless pit (20:1–3), and then for a short time until he receives his final and decisive defeat and ensuing punishment (20:7–10). Here we find not just a division in the cosmic order, but an implacable battle between the opposing forces of good and evil.

This representation of Satan as the wicked opponent of the heavenly realm is found in other traditions but he is given different names. In the Qumran texts he is known at times as Melkiresha (4Q280–2; 4QAmram), but most often he is called Belial. Like Satan in Revelation, this figure is the leader of the forces of darkness, both human and divine, who are opposed to the human and divine forces of light which are led by the archangel Michael (1QS 3:20–1; CD 5:18). He and his evil agents are responsible for the sins of the Qumran sectarians, the sons of light (1QS 3:22–3), and for directing the human forces which oppose them (see further below). Though it is admitted that Belial currently has the upper hand in this conflict (e.g. 1QS 1:17–18; 2:19), which brings suffering to the elect (1QpHab 5:7–8; 1QSa 1:3), the Qumran scrolls affirm strongly in a number of places that he will be eventually defeated and punished (4Q286–7; 11QMelch; 1QM). Belial, though known as Beliar, is also prominent in the Testaments of the Twelve Patriarchs. In these writings he is the cause of human sin (T.Reub. 4:7; T.Dan 1:7; T.Ash. 1:8–9; T.Ben. 6:1) but, as at Qumran, he will ultimately be defeated (T.Levi 18:12; T.Jud. 25:3; T.Dan 6:10–11). It should be noted that in the Testaments Beliar is also known as Satan (T.Dan 3:6; T.Gad 4:7).

It is clear from this brief summary that the Satan tradition as we find it in Revelation and at Qumran, and to a lesser extent in the Testaments of the Twelve Patriarchs, reflects a developed cosmic dualism. The cosmic order is not merely divided into those angels who rebelled against God and those who have not, but these angelic forces are currently engaged in a fierce struggle for supremacy, a conflict which will only be resolved at the eschaton (see further below).[24]

The distinction between good and evil in the cosmic order is likewise reflected in the human realm. This introduces the third significant element of apocalyptic-eschatological dualism, that of human dualism. In those texts which most emphasise the present struggle in the supernatural arena, human dualism is inextricably linked with its angelic or cosmic counterpart. Of utmost importance in this respect is the doctrine of the two spirits which we find in the Testaments of the Twelve Patriarchs and at Qumran. In the first of these, the Testament of Judah specifies that there are two spirits at work within each individual, the spirit of truth and the spirit of error (20:1–3). Further detail is supplied in the Testament of Asher. God has given people two ways to act, the way of good and the way of evil (1:3–5). The way of good is overseen by the angels of the Lord, while the way of evil is ruled by Beliar and his angels (1:8–9; 6:4; cf. also T.Levi 19:1). Here the point is made that the dualism on the angelic level and the battle for supremacy it reflects are likewise reflected on the individual human level. This doctrine is also found at Qumran, notably in 1QS 3:13–4:26.[25] In this text it is maintained that God has created humans with a mixture of two

---

[24] Davidson, *Angels at Qumran*, p. 321 correctly makes the point that the Qumran Belial material reflects a more marked dualism than the Enochic Watchers tradition, though he fails to mention the scheme in Revelation or the Testaments of the Twelve Patriarchs.

[25] For recent discussion of this subject, see Davidson, *Angels at Qumran*, pp. 144–62.

spirits, the spirit of truth and the spirit of falsehood (3:18–19). These spirits struggle for supremacy (4:18, 24–5) and are governed respectively by Michael the Prince of Light and Belial the Prince of Darkness (3:20–1). Thus, as in the Testaments of the Twelve Patriarchs, the struggle between good and evil on the cosmic level is manifested on the individual human level.

The notion of the two spirits reflected in the Qumran scrolls and the Testaments of the Twelve Patriarchs is a development from the earlier Jewish doctrine of the two ways. The antithesis between the way of the righteous and the way of the wicked is found throughout the Old Testament, particularly in the Psalms and Proverbs,[26] but these earlier texts refer merely to two courses of human action, the way which accords with the will of God and the way which does not. In the apocalyptic-eschatological material mentioned above, by contrast, this theme is merged with the developed demonology which enjoyed widespread currency at that time. Choosing to follow one way or the other now entails taking sides in a cosmic conflict and pledging allegiance either to the side of God or to his cosmic adversary. The upshot of this, at least in the scheme at Qumran, is that the human world necessarily divides itself into two opposing camps. As the ones who choose to walk in the ways of light, the Qumran sectarians consider themselves to be the sons of light. Conversely, the ones who walk in the ways of darkness, the opponents of the sect, are seen as the sons of darkness. This dualistic terminology or similar nomenclature is found throughout the scrolls and testifies plainly to the entrenched Qumran belief that the human realm, like its supernatural counterpart, is divided into two distinct groups. As the War scroll makes clear, the final eschatological war will witness the complete drawing of the battle lines; on one side will stand the human and angelic forces of good and on the other will stand their wicked counterparts.

The book of Revelation also advances a strict dualism on the group human level and associates it with the cosmic conflict. In this document the Johannine communities comprise the group of right-eous humans, while the Roman empire represents the evil mani-fested on the group human level. The two beasts of chapter 13, the antichrist and the false prophet, represent different aspects of the imperial cult and exercise authority on behalf of the dragon (verses 2–4, 12) who is none other than Satan (20:2). The whole earth

---

[26] See Michaelis, 'ὁδός', pp. 54–5.

(excluding the saints) follows and worships these three figures (13:3–4, 8, 11) and each person is given a special mark as a sign of this (verses 16–18). Moreover, Pergamum, an important centre for the worship of the emperor, is called the throne of Satan (2:13), and the seer also perceives Satan standing behind the sins of the synagogues of Smyrna (2:9–10) and Philadelphia (3:9). For this author, then, human wickedness is inextricably linked to angelic wickedness. Evil human individuals and institutions work in the service of Satan and his wicked forces.[27]

It would be wrong to suggest, however, that this explicit linking of cosmic and human dualism is representative of all apocalyptic-eschatological schemes. Many documents say little or nothing at all of the struggle in the angelic orders. While it might be the case that some schemes presume it, this cannot be taken for granted. Yet these texts still accept the basic division of good and evil on the group human level and draw a sharp distinction between those who perform the will of God and those who do not. This is reflected in the antithetical terminology which these documents adopt – right-eous/sinners (1 En. 5:6; 38:1; 81:7–8; 97:1; 100:7; 103:4–5; 2 Bar. 24:1–2; 30:2–4; 48:48), righteous/ungodly (4 Ezra 7:17), elect/ungodly (1 En. 1:2), elect/wicked (1 En. 5:7–8), wise/wicked (Dan. 12:10), pious/impious (Sib. Or. 4:40). These groups are not always juxtaposed, of course, and one is often referred to without reference to the other. Despite the variation of descriptive terms both between texts and sometimes within texts, there is no doubt that a unity of perspective lies behind this classificatory system. Almost without exception, the documents which emphasise the end of history and the universal judgement take great pains to classify humanity into two diametrically opposed groups. On one side stand the author and his readers, and on the other stand those who are opposed to them. Thus the notion of human dualism is a constant element in apocalyptic eschatology. As we might expect, the identities of the two opposing human groups differ from author to author and depend upon the perspective from which he writes or the circumstances which prompted him to write. A consistent factor, however, is that in distinction to the texts of the Old Testament the division is not drawn along racial lines, Jews and non-Jews. It is not so much the Jews as a race who are the elect and earmarked for salvation, but a remnant within the chosen people.

---

[27] See further Thompson, *Book of Revelation*, pp. 80–1.

The wicked therefore encompass the remaining Jews as well as the 'heathen' nations. The book of Revelation is an obvious exception to this rule and defines the wicked and the righteous according to their allegiance or otherwise to Jesus.

Determinism

The second conceptual element providing the framework of apocalyptic eschatology is that of determinism. Many texts specify time and again that from the creation history is determined by God who remains ultimately in control of everything (e.g. Dan. 11:36; Jub. 1:29; 4 Ezra 4:36–7; T.Mos. 12:4–5; 1QS 3:15). The course of history has been schematised into distinct divisions. In the Apocalypse of Weeks (1 En. 93:1–10; 91:11–17), the present age is perceived as consisting of ten 'weeks' (cf. Sib. Or. 4:47), while in 4 Ezra (14:11) and the Apocalypse of Abraham (29:2) it comprises twelve parts. The method of pseudonymity combined with a historical review, which was favoured by many of those who composed apocalypses, is also an obvious attempt to lend support to this conviction. By writing in the name of a great figure of the past, who seemingly predicted in accurate fashion the course of history from his own time up to and beyond the time of the readers, the apocalyptists intended to portray history as totally foreordained. The future will therefore unfold in the manner predicted just as the past had done so. The Qumran community, which did not compose any apocalypses, expressed this conviction using a different scheme of prophecy and fulfilment, the *pesher* method of interpretation. In the commentaries on the Old Testament prophetic books, the predictions of the prophets were interpreted as meeting their fulfilment in the life of the Qumran community. It hardly needs saying that such a scheme of prophecy and fulfilment also presupposes the determined nature of history. Like the historical review of the apocalyptic literature, it involves the belief that God has fixed the course of history and has revealed aspects of it to certain individuals.

On the individual level, a softer and perhaps less consistent form of determinism was in operation. While most writers maintained that an individual's life and thus his or her lot in the afterlife was determined in advance, they still accepted the concept of human free will.[28] Even at Qumran, where much is made of the elect status

---

[28] For full discussion of this theme, see Russell, *Method and Message*, pp. 232–4.

of each member (1QS 3:15–16), this still holds true. The doctrine of the two ways discussed above emphasises that the choice for good or for evil remains in the hands of the individual. This point of view is best summed up in a statement attributed to Rabbi Akiba in the rabbinic literature; 'All is foreseen, but freedom of choice is given' (Pirke 'Aboth 3:19).[29] In this way apocalyptic eschatology was able to combine two fundamentally important notions: divine control over and foreknowledge of all aspects of human activity and human responsibility for individual actions. As we shall see in the following chapter, each form of determinism, the hard determinism concerning the whole sweep of history and the softer form on the individual level, has an important function.

Eschatological woes

Having discussed the two primary elements which comprise the conceptual framework of apocalyptic eschatology, we may now turn to the eschatological events proper. One of the more constant features of apocalyptic eschatology is that before the end of history a number of signs will herald its arrival. These signs are more often than not of a terrible nature and are better called eschatological woes than the less accurate messianic woes. There is no consistent notion of these terrible signs of the end.[30] They can take the form of a progressive breakdown of human society whereby the wicked prosper and intensify the suffering of the righteous (1 En. 93:9–10 and 91:11–12; 99:4–5; 100:1–4; Dan. 8:13–14; 9:26–7; 12:1; T.Jud. 23:3–4). Alternatively, they can involve in addition to the above the onset of plagues, earthquakes, wars and other afflictions which wreak havoc upon the earth (1 En. 91:5–7; Jub. 23:13–23; Apoc. of Ab. 29:15; 30:2–8; 4 Ezra 9:1–3; 2 Bar. 25:1–27:15; 48:31–9; 70:2–10; 1QH 3:13–16; Rev. 8:1–9:21; 16:1–21; Sib. Or. 3:635–51; 4:130–51; 5:361–80) or the appearance of human prodigies or abominations (4 Ezra 5:8; Jub. 23:25; 6:21–4). In many cases the signs can be of a purely cosmic nature involving the complete breakdown of the cosmic order (1 En. 80:2–8; T.Mos. 10:4–6; T.Levi 4:1; Sib. Or. 3:796–807; 5:155–61, 512–31). Sometimes there is a combination of more than one of these types of phenomena in

---

[29] Russell, *Method and Message*, p. 232.
[30] For some of the major variations of this theme, see Allison, *End of the Ages*, pp. 5–25.

these descriptions of the eschatological upheavals (4 Ezra 5:1–12; Sib. Or. 5:447–83).

A number of texts speak of a major war as the final event in history, though it is depicted in different ways. Daniel 11:40–5 refers to a great conflict between major world powers at the time of the end, and in later times this appears in the form of the *Nero redivivus* myth. As the concluding event of history and as the culmination of the period of distress, Nero will return from the east leading the Parthian armies against the Romans. This myth is especially prominent in the Sibylline literature (Sib. Or. 3:63–74; 4:137–52; 5:93–109, 214–27, 361–74). A different form of this tradition represents the final conflict in terms of a specific battle between the righteous and their evil enemies (1 En. 56:5–6; 90:10–19; 91:11). In those schemes which reflect a developed cosmic dualism, we have yet a further variation. The struggle between the righteous and their wicked opponents is not confined to the human sphere; it includes their supernatural counterparts as well, and the final battle between good and evil is of cosmic proportions. The full complement of demonic powers is unleashed against the righteous, and this leads to an all-out eschatological conflict. According to Revelation, the evil forces rise from the bottomless pit for this purpose (6:8; 9:1–11; 11:7; 17:8; 20:7–8), while the War scroll from Qumran predicts the final conflict between the righteous and the wicked army of Belial and his company of demons. The myth of the returning Nero figures in Revelation as well (13:3; 17:11), but here he is depicted almost as a supernatural being working in the service of Satan (13:2, 4) who declares war on the saints (13:7).

The arrival of the saviour figure

According to many apocalyptic-eschatological schemes, the end-time woes come to their conclusion with the appearance of a saviour figure whose arrival relieves the plight of the embattled righteous and signals the turning of the eras. There is no consistency at all on the identity of this individual.[31] In a few cases it is the arrival of God himself which brings history to its close (1 En. 1:3–9; 90:15–19; T.Mos 10:3–7), but more often than not it is his agent who acts in this capacity. Sometimes

[31] So correctly, Koch, *Rediscovery*, pp. 31–2.

this figure is identified as the messiah whose nature might be either human or supernatural. The Psalms of Solomon provide the clearest example of the human messiah, especially in chapter 17, while 2 Baruch and 4 Ezra illustrate the expectation of a supernatural messiah. The first of these states that at the end of the period of tribulation the pre-existent messiah will arrive (29:3; 30:1; 70:9) and punish the wicked nations who oppressed Israel (39:7–40:3; 72:2–6). The pre-existent messiah of 4 Ezra (12:32) was also expected to defeat the Roman empire and punish it for its sins against Israel (12:31–4), while 13:32–8 relates his assembling and punishing of the ungodly nations. A slightly different perspective on this figure is given in chapter 7. Here the text speaks of the messiah establishing a four hundred year messianic kingdom (verse 28) at the end of which he dies. His death is followed by the earth returning to its primeval form and the occurrence of the resurrection and the judgement (verses 29–44).[32]

At Qumran we find two and possibly three messianic figures. The two certain messianic figures are the priestly messiah of Aaron and the kingly messiah of Israel who were to play important roles in the end-time, including the eschatological war against Belial and the sons of darkness (cf. CD 7:19–20; 12:23–13:1; 14:19; 1QM 15:4; 16:13; 18:5; 1QSa 2:11–22; 1QSb 5:20–8). In 1QS 9:11, these two messianic agents are associated with a third figure, 'the prophet', whose messianic status is less easy to determine.[33] Despite their great importance, these messiahs do not perform as saviour figures in the manner of the respective messianic agents in 2 Baruch and 4 Ezra. According to 1QM, relief will be brought to the army of the human righteous (which includes the messiahs) first in the form of Michael leading the angelic armies of heaven (13:9–13; 17:5–8; cf. 1QH 3:35) and then by the decisive appearance of God himself (1:14; 14:15). The tradition of the archangel Michael acting as a saviour figure is likewise reflected in Daniel 12:1. Here Michael the

---

[32] M. E. Stone has published a number of studies treating the figure of the messiah in 4 Ezra. For his most recent statement, see 'The Question of the Messiah in 4 Ezra', pp. 209–24.

[33] A similar expectation of multiple messianic figures is attested as well in the original Jewish core of the Testaments of the Twelve Patriarchs. In this corpus of texts, the messiahs of Levi and Judah are prominent throughout (cf. T.Reub. 6:10–11; T.Sim. 7:2; T.Levi 18:1–12; T.Jud. 1:6; 24:1–6), the first being a priestly figure and the second a secular and kingly agent. As at Qumran, the Testaments have a sole reference to an eschatological prophet who might or might not have messianic status (T.Ben. 9:2).

guardian angel of Israel will deliver his people at the time of their greatest distress.[34]

A similar scenario is envisaged in the book of Revelation, though in this case it is presented in strictly Christian terms. Although this text knows of a battle between Michael and his angelic army and Satan and his company of fallen angels (12:7–8), the end of the period of tribulation is signalled by the arrival from heaven of Jesus, the word of God. In the eschatological scenario of 19:11–19, the return of Jesus is described in military terms. He sits upon a white horse accompanied by the armies of heaven and faces the beast and his army of wicked followers (cf. 17:14). Though lacking the detail of the final battle which is found in the Qumran War scroll, and having a different set of participants in the ensuing conflict, this picture of the last and decisive battle between good and evil shares much in common with the Qumran document.[35] The final events of history witness an all-out attack on the human righteous by the forces of evil, both angelic and human, which can only be repulsed by a supernatural army. At Qumran it is Michael who commands the angelic forces, while in Revelation it is Jesus.

The judgement

The arrival of the saviour figure prepares the way for the important event of the final judgement. Many texts contain some reference to the resurrection of the dead as the necessary prelude to this event, but there are a number of exceptions. Most notable of these are the Apocalypse of Abraham and perhaps the Qumran texts.[36] These

---

[34] See further Davidson, *Angels at Qumran*, p. 226.

[35] For full discussion of this point, see Bauckham, 'Revelation as a Christian War Scroll', pp. 17–40.

[36] It is now generally agreed that the notion of bodily resurrection played no real role in the eschatology at Qumran. Texts such as 1QH 6:34–5, which could be interpreted in terms of this belief, were more likely than not intended to be taken metaphorically. This resurrection language alludes to the raising of the members of the Qumran sect to the same status as the angels of God which, in turn, ensured their salvation and eternal life (1QS 11:5–9; 1QH 3:19–22; 11:10–14). For recent discussion of the fellowship between the Qumran community and the holy angels, see Davidson, *Angels at Qumran*, pp. 317–19. This association between the sectarians and the angels presumably continued after death, in which case the primary afterlife doctrine was that of the immortality of the soul and not that of bodily resurrection. This conclusion coheres with Josephus' statements concerning this aspect of the Essenes' religious beliefs. See Collins, *Apocalyptic Imagination*, pp. 133–4; Pryke, 'Eschatology in the Dead Sea Scrolls', pp. 55–6 and Schürer et al, *History*, II, pp. 582–3.

exceptions notwithstanding, the general view was that the dead, both wicked and righteous, would be raised to face the final judgement (Dan. 12:2; T.Ben. 10:6–8; 1 En. 51:1 62:15; 67:8–9; Sib. Or. 4:181–2; 4 Ezra 7:32, 37; 2 Bar. 30:1–2; 42:8; 50:1–3; 51:1–6). In Revelation there are no less than two resurrections from the dead. The first involves only the martyrs who died for Christ and who reign with him for the thousand years after Satan is imprisoned (20:4–5), while the second sees the resurrection of everybody else after the final defeat of Satan (20:11–13).

The resurrection leads immediately to the universal and decisive judgement, a very important component of apocalyptic eschatology. The majority of texts specify that God himself will preside over the judgement and mete out punishments and rewards (e.g. 1 En. 1:7–9; 90:24–7; 91:7; 100:4; 2 En. 66:6; 2 Bar. 5:2; 13:8; Apoc. of Ab. 31:1–8; T.Levi 4:1; T.Ben. 10:9; Jub. 23:31; Rev. 20:11–15; Sib. Or. 3:741–3; 4:42; 5:110), but there are an important number of variations from this theme. In the Psalms of Solomon it is the messiah alone who presides over the final judgement of Israel and the nations (17:26–46). 4 Ezra also accepts that the messiah oversees the judgement (13:33–4), but since 7:33 specifically states that God performs this task, the document is not consistent on this point. There is likewise no consistency in the Qumran texts on this issue. According to 11QMelch it is Melchizedek, a pseudonym for the archangel Michael,[37] who presides over the final judgement of Belial and his company of evil angels and delivers them to eternal punishment. On the other hand, the commentary on Isaiah 11 (4Q161) affirms that all the people shall be judged by the Davidic messiah. It is possible that two distinct judgements were envisaged at Qumran, the angelic Michael and the human messiah respectively judging their evil counterparts, but this is far from certain. The holy angels alone appear to preside over the judgement in the Apocalypse of Weeks (1 En. 91:15). A few texts also assign a role in the judgement to the human righteous (Dan. 7:22; 1 En. 95:3; 96:1; T.Ab. 13:6; Rev. 20:4), though their precise role is never fully delineated.

Of most importance for our purposes is the situation reflected in the Parables of Enoch where the Son of Man acts in the capacity of end-time judge. This pre-existent, heavenly being (48:6; 62:7) is known also as the Elect One (39:6; 40:5; 45:3 and elsewhere), the

---

[37] See Davidson, *Angels at Qumran*, pp. 263–4.

Righteous One (38:2; 53:6) and the Anointed One (48:10; 52:4). He will sit on God's throne of glory and vindicate the righteous and condemn and punish the wicked, both human and angelic (45:3; 51:3; 55:4; 61:8; 62:2, 5; 69:27, 29). In 71:14 Enoch himself is identified as the Son of Man, but it is generally accepted that this chapter is a later addition.[38] Since the function of the Son of Man in the Parables of Enoch is paralleled in the gospel of Matthew, we shall return to this material in chapter 5.

The fate of the wicked

As noted in our preliminary comments, the terrible fate of the wicked is a crucial theme of apocalyptic eschatology,[39] and almost all the documents specify at some point what this will be. Only a few of the very early texts fail to do so. For example, the Apocalypse of Weeks states that the wicked will receive eternal destruction (91:14) without delineating the precise method. Similarly, Daniel merely affirms that those found wanting after the general resurrection are raised to shame and everlasting contempt (12:2). Most texts, however, are quite specific on this point.

The most common notion of the fate of those condemned at the judgement is that they will be punished by eternal fire. There might be other punishments in conjunction with this, confinement to a bed of worms (1 En. 46:6) or putrefying in the belly of the worm Azazel (Apoc. of Ab. 31:5), but the punishment by everlasting fire runs through the literature like a common thread. In the majority of cases the ones punished in this way are those humans considered wicked by the author (1 En. 54:1; 90:26–7; 91:9; 100:9; 102:1; 103:7; 4 Ezra 7:35–8, 61; 2 Bar. 44:15; 48:39, 43; 59:2; 85:13; 3 Bar. 4:16; 2 En. 10:2; Apoc. of Ab. 31:2–6; T.Levi 3:2; T.Zeb. 10:3; Rev. 20:15). The Qumran texts also express the conviction that the lot of the wicked will be punishment by eternal fire (so 1QS 2:8; 4:12–13; CD 2:5–6; 4QAmram) and the Wicked Priest, the opponent of the

---

[38] So Collins, *Apocalyptic Imagination*, pp. 151–2.

[39] Some texts spell out the state of the righteous and the wicked in the intermediate state between death and the final judgement. According to these texts the usual pattern is that in the interim period the righteous and the wicked are separated, each group receiving a taste of the rewards or punishments which will come after the judgement; the event of judgement thus merely confirms, finalises and perhaps increases one's lot in the intermediate state (cf. 2 Bar 36:11). This theme is most clearly outlined in 4 Ezra 7:75–101. For further discussion see Schürer et al, *History*, II, pp. 540–2 and literature cited there; also Russell, *Method and Message*, pp. 361–3.

Teacher of Righteousness, is singled out for such a fate (1QpHab 10:4–5). The Sibylline corpus testifies to a variation on this theme. Prior to the judgement a great conflagration will envelop the whole earth, burning good and bad alike (Sib. Or. 3:53–4, 84–93, 672–4, 690–2; 4:160–1). According to the fourth book, God will then raise everyone from the dead and pronounce his judgement; the wicked will then be consigned to an eternal fiery fate (Sib. Or. 4:179–86). A similar notion of a universal conflagration immediately prior to the end is found in the Qumran thanksgiving hymns (1QH 3:28–33), though the agent of destruction in this case is Belial. In the Testament of Abraham fire is the means by which one is tested at the judgement (12:10–14; 13:11–14); it is not used as a punishment.

Other texts specify that the supernatural figures who rebelled against God are also consigned to everlasting fire for their sins. This motif is found in the book of the Watchers (1 En. 10:6, 13; 18:10–15; 21:1–10), the Parables of Enoch (1 En. 54:5–6) and the Animal Apocalypse (1 En. 90:24–5). In the Testaments of the Twelve Patriarchs the leader of the demonic powers, Beliar, will be bound at the end-time (T.Levi 18:12) and thrown into eternal fire (T.Jud. 25:3). A similar pattern of punishment by fire for the supernatural enemies of God occurs in Revelation where the beast and the false prophet (19:20), Satan himself (20:10) and even Death and Hades (20:14) are all cast into the lake of fire. In an interesting variation from this theme, the Qumran writings make no mention at all of this particular subject. Though the scrolls testify time and again that the supernatural forces of evil will be utterly defeated, there is no text which specifically refers to their fate in terms of punishment by eternal fire.[40]

The location of the place(s) of punishment is usually specified. While some texts affirm that it is located in one of the lower levels of the heavenly regions (T.Levi 3:1–2; 3 Bar. 3:1–8; 4:3; 2 En. 7:1–4; 10:1–3; 18:1–9), others locate it under the earth (e.g. 1 En. 63:6–10; 103:7; Jub. 7:29; 22:22; Sib. Or. 4:43; Apoc. of Ab. 31:3). The latter location is variously described in general terms as the (fiery) valley (1 En. 27:1–2; 54:1), the fiery abyss (1 En. 90:24–6), the abyss of complete condemnation (1 En. 54:5) or the pit of torment (4 Ezra 7:36). Specific names for this terrible place include Hades, the Greek name for the nether world (Apoc. of Ab. 31:3), Sheol, the Old Testament place of shadows (1 En. 56:8; 63:10; 99:11; 103:7;

---

[40] On the silence in general on the eschatological fate of Belial and his evil angels, see Davidson, *Angels at Qumran*, pp. 298–300.

Jub. 22:22), and Gehenna (4 Ezra 7:36 Latin text; Sib. Or. 4:186; Apoc. of Ab. 15:6).[41] A minor variation on the location of the place of torment appears in Revelation where the wicked are thrown into a fiery lake (19:20; 22:10–15). There is general agreement, however, that the place of punishment, be it in the heavenly realms or the fiery abyss, is characterised not only by fire, but by gloomy darkness as well (e.g. T.Levi 3:2; 3 Bar. 4:3; 2 En. 10:2; 1 En. 63:6; 103:7; Jub. 7:29; Sib. Or. 4:43; 1QS 2:7–8; 4:13).

The fate of the righteous

As we should expect, the fate of the righteous is perceived as the complete contrast of the fate of the wicked. It is a state of pure and eternal bliss. Differences in detail exist between the texts, but the following are some of the more common features. Some texts emphasise that this state is characterised by brilliant light which is in stark contrast to the dark and gloomy residence of the wicked and befits their new existence in the presence of God (Dan. 12:3; 1 En. 1:8; 38:4; 39:7; 50:1; 58:2–6; 96:3; 104:2; 108:12; 2 En. 42:5; Sib. Or. 4:190–1; 1QM 17:7; 4QAmram; 4 Ezra 7:97; Rev. 22:5). Underlying this notion seems to be the view that the righteous will achieve the status of angels, since the angels are also characterised by brilliant light (cf. Dan. 10:6; 1 En. 51:4; 71:1; 2 En. 1:5; 19:1; Rev. 10:1). This idea is also implied in those texts where the righteous will be awarded an eschatological garment which is equivalent to the garb of the holy angels (e.g. 2 En. 22:8–10).[42] In any event, the idea that the righteous will become angels finds explicit expression in 2 Baruch 51:5, 10 and 1 Enoch 104:6. The writings from Qumran emphasise that even now the members of the community have achieved this state (see note 36).

For the righteous, the eschatological era is marked by everlasting peace and great joy (Jub. 23:29–30; 1QS 4:8; 1QM 17:6–8; T.Levi 18:4–5; 2 Bar. 73:1–6; Sib. Or. 3:371–80) as well as eternal abundance

---

[41] Gehenna takes its name from the valley of Hinnom, south of Jerusalem, which had a double association with fire. It was here that children were burnt as an offering to Molech (2 Chron 28:3; 33:6; Jer 7:31; 19:5; 32:35), and in later times it became the place where the refuse of Jerusalem was burnt. Thus in time this location came to symbolise the subterranean place of eternal and fiery torment. See Jeremias, 'γέεννα', pp. 657–8. In the Book of the Watchers, however, there is no symbolism; the wicked will be sent to the actual valley itself to be burnt forever (1 En 26:1–27:4; cf. also 1 En 54:1).

[42] For more detailed discussion of this theme and the relevant texts, see Sim, 'Matthew 22.13a and 1 Enoch 10.4a', pp. 15–17.

and plenty (1 En. 10:18–19; 2 Bar. 29:4–8; 1QS 4:8). A number of texts specify a return to the original Paradise (1 En. 60:8; 2 En. 8:1–9:5; T.Levi 18:10; Rev. 2:7), while others depict this age of plenty in terms of the Old Testament theme of a great banquet (cf. Isa. 25:6; 49:9–10; 65:13; Ezek. 39:17–20), usually in the company of a saviour figure. The Parables of Enoch state that the righteous will eat and rest with the Son of Man forever (1 En. 62:14), whereas in the Qumran scrolls the priestly messiah is expected to take charge of the common meal in the new age (1QSa 2:11–22).[43]

Some texts specify that the new age will be characterised by a renewal of the cosmic order; at the eschaton the old cosmic order will pass away and a new one will replace it. This theme is especially prominent in 4 Ezra which predicts that at the end of the temporary messianic kingdom, the world will return to its primeval state and then be restored (7:30–2; cf. 5:55; 14:10–11). We find precisely the same theme in 2 Baruch where mention is made of the great age of the present creation (85:10), and its future renewal (32:6; 44:12; 57:2; cf. 1QS 4:25). The Astronomical Book (1 En. 72–82), makes reference to the new creation (72:1), while the Apocalypse of Weeks describes the appearance of a new heaven (1 En. 91:16). The explicit mention of the creation of a new heaven and a new earth is found in the Parables of Enoch (1 En. 45:4–5) and in Revelation (21:1). It should come as no surprise that a common theme in many of these Jewish texts is that the new age (or new creation) will see the establishment of either a new Jerusalem (T.Dan 5:12) or a new Temple (T.Ben. 9:2; 1 En. 90:28–9; 91:13; 5Q15), or both (4 Ezra 7:26; 10:25–58; 2 Bar. 4:2–6; 32:4; Sib. Or. 5:420–7). A quite different view is expressed in the Christian Apocalypse in so far as a new Jerusalem is expected (21:10–27), but no new Temple will accompany it (21:22).

The imminence of the end

Apocalyptic eschatology works within the framework of an imminent realisation of the expected end events.[44] As with all aspects of

---

[43] For further discussion of this subject, see Schiffman, *Eschatological Community*, pp. 53–67.

[44] So most scholars; Koch, *Rediscovery*, p. 28; Aune, *Prophecy*, p. 108; Schürer et al, *History*, III.1, p. 243; Hengel, *Judaism and Hellenism*, I, pp. 194–5, and Stone, 'Apocalyptic Literature', p. 383. Even Rowland, who wishes to differentiate between the apocalyptic tradition and the eschatological tradition, appears to presume that the latter normally involved an imminent expectation of the end events. See, for example, *Open Heaven*, pp. 27–8, 32, 35–6.

this religious perspective, there is no one method for expressing this conviction. Some texts prefer to state both regularly and with absolute clarity the imminence of the expected eschatological events. The Epistle of Enoch (1 En. 91–104 minus the Apocalypse of Weeks) is an excellent example, replete as it is with references to the nearness of the final judgement; 'Woe unto those who build oppression and injustice...they shall soon be demolished...(woe unto) those who amass gold and silver; they shall quickly be destroyed...you have become ready for death, and for...the day of great judgement' (1 En. 94:6–8; cf. 95:6; 98:9–10). The book of Revelation provides another good example. This work opens and concludes on a note of the imminence of the end events, 'The revelation of Jesus Christ, which God gave to him to show his servants what must soon take place...for the time is near. (1:1–3)... "God...has sent his angel to show his servants what must soon take place. And behold, I am coming soon" (22:6–7)..."for the time is near" (22:10)..."Behold, I am coming soon" (22:12)..."Surely I am coming soon". Amen. Come, Lord Jesus. (22:20)'[45] Such clear statements are found elsewhere throughout the texts under review (cf. 4 Ezra 4:26; 8:61; 14:10; 2 Bar. 16:1; 20:1; 84:10–12).

Another method is adopted by the author(s) of the book of Daniel. In this work we find precise calculations of the end. There are in fact four such calculations. In 8:14 the period of distress, the persecution by Antiochus Epiphanes, which precedes the arrival of the eschaton, is said to last 1150 days dated from the day of his desecration of the Temple. According to 7:25; 9:27 and 12:7 this period will endure for three and a half years (or 1260 days), while 12:11 and 12:12 offer 1290 days and 1335 days respectively. Most scholars accept that the larger numbers are successive revisions of the original prophecy, either by the author himself or by those of his immediate circle, when the expected events failed to come on time. What is important to note here is that the imminent expectation of the end was in no way rescinded as the revised prophecies were proved wrong. This testifies to the strength of this belief in the circles which produced Daniel.[46] The tradition of the 1260 days is also reflected in Revelation where it is reinterpreted in terms of the length of time the antichrist will rule (13:5; cf. 11:2–3; 12:14).

---

[45] For further discussion of an imminent end expectation in the Apocalypse, see Fiorenza, *Book of Revelation*, pp. 48–50.

[46] So Russell, *Method and Message*, p. 264 and Collins, *The Apocalyptic Vision of the Book of Daniel*, p. 154.

The writings of the Qumran community reflect an imminent end expectation in (at least) two ways. First, it is generally agreed that the *pesher* technique in the biblical commentaries presumes such a belief; the prophets predicted the events leading up to and including the eschaton which the Qumran group interpreted in terms of its own time.[47] The second method is linked to the production of the War scroll (1QM). Although this text contains no definite statements on the nearness of the end, its composition attests that the community was preparing itself for the final eschatological war.[48]

Perhaps the most common method of expressing an imminent end expectation, at least in the apocalyptic and related genres, was to provide a review of history up to a certain identifiable point and then to detail the eschatological events which would follow soon after. The reader would be able to judge from the chronology which events had passed and which were still to come and so make the deduction that the new age was about to replace the old. The Animal Apocalypse may serve as an illustration of the use of this method. This apocalypse uses animal imagery to recount the course of Jewish history from creation to the Maccabean revolt. Our interest lies with chapter 90 which relates the circumstances leading up to the rebellion and concludes its historical survey with the battle at Beth-Zur (verses 6–14). Since this is the last historical reference in the text we may infer that it was composed soon after that event. At this point the narrative leaves the realm of history and moves into the realm of eschatological speculation. God himself will step into the fray, thus ensuring the ultimate victory of the righteous (verses 15–19). This victory sees the commencement of the eschatological events proper. God will execute the final judgement (verses 20–7) and a new Jerusalem will be established for the righteous (verses 28–36). The readers of this document would therefore draw the conclusion that the eschatological events would commence in the imminent future.

Summary

The preceding survey, though necessarily brief and incomplete, is sufficient for our purposes. It has isolated the major motifs which

---

[47] See, for example, Hengel, *Judaism and Hellenism*, I, p. 224; Schiffman, *Eschatological Community*, pp. 6–7 and Nickelsburg, *Jewish Literature*, pp. 126–7.
[48] In agreement with Rowland, *Open Heaven*, p. 31; Schiffman, *Eschatological Community*, p. 6 and Yadin, *Scroll of the War*, p. 15.

appear in the apocalyptic-eschatological schemes of the classical period of apocalypticism. On the basis of the survey, we may offer a general overview of the apocalyptic-eschatological perspective based upon its most prominent recurring elements. As emphasised earlier, the following reconstruction is not intended to be taken as a systematic 'theology' of this perspective, since not every scheme includes all the characteristics.

Apocalyptic eschatology is a comprehensive religious perspective with a distinctive view of reality. It is entirely dualistic. This dualism applies in all cases to the human world where a strict division is made between those few who are righteous and the majority who are wicked and there is no category in between. In some schemes it is explicitly stated that the cosmic realm is similarly divided, and a number of these (the Qumran texts and Revelation) promote the view that this cosmic order is engaged in a bitter battle for supremacy. Here we find the most clear expression that human and cosmic dualism are inextricably linked. The righteous angels and humans who side with God are opposed by their respective counterparts who are led by the fallen angel Satan (or Belial). A distinction is also sharply drawn between this age and the age to come. The course of history is predetermined from the creation to the end of the present age and God remains in control of events. The present era, which is rapidly nearing its conclusion, will witness a number of terrible events as signs that the end is fast approaching. At the very end of the age a saviour figure, either God himself or his agent, will arrive in order to bring the suffering of the righteous to an end. While some schemes reflect the tradition of a final war as the last event in history, those schemes which emphasise the cosmic conflict between God and Satan take this scenario further by promoting the view that the combined forces of evil will unleash a full-scale attack upon the human righteous and that the saviour figure will enter the conflict as a military commander. In all schemes, however, the arrival of the saviour figure introduces the eschatological events proper, beginning with the universal judgement over which God or his representative presides. The righteous will be vindicated and receive salvation. They will reside as angels forever in a blessed and peaceful place, while the wicked will be utterly condemned and burn eternally in a dark and gloomy location.

2

THE SOCIAL SETTING OF APOCALYPTICISM AND THE FUNCTION OF APOCALYPTIC ESCHATOLOGY

1. The social setting of apocalypticism

Having defined in the previous chapter the basic elements of apocalyptic eschatology, we may proceed to the explanatory part of the discussion. As stated earlier, apocalyptic eschatology is the religious perspective of a particular socio-religious phenomenon, apocalypticism. In this section we shall examine the social setting of this phenomenon. Do the various writers (and readers) of the texts which emphasise the end of the age and the universal judgement share a common social setting? If they do, then which social factors contribute to their embracement of this distinctive religious perspective?

In response to these questions, most scholars agree that in general terms there is a common social setting. Apocalypticism, whether it be expressed in an apocalypse or not, arises in minority groups as a direct response to a situation of great crisis or distress.[1] P. D. Hanson has taken this general point an important step further by emphasising the group alienation inherent in ancient apocalyptic groups; the crisis experienced by the group occasions a sense of intense alienation from the wider world.[2] A further point to note in this regard is that the crisis might be either real or perceived to be real. In the latter case, we are dealing with what is known as 'relative deprivation'. Here we must take seriously the

---

[1] So Russell, *Method and Message*, pp. 16–18; Collins, *Apocalyptic Imagination*, pp. 29–30; Nickelsburg, 'Social Aspects', p. 646; Sanders, 'Palestinian Jewish Apocalypses', pp. 456–9; Wilson, 'From Prophecy to Apocalyptic', pp. 84–5; Aune, *Prophecy*, pp. 110–12; Schürer et al, *History*, III.1, p. 243 and Reddish, *Apocalyptic Literature*, p. 24. It should be noted that Rowland accepts that where eschatology does loom large in the apocalyptic literature, it is occasioned by a corresponding situation of crisis (*Open Heaven*, pp. 26–7).

[2] Hanson, *Dawn of Apocalyptic*, pp. 433–4 and 'Apocalyptic Literature', pp. 471–2.

perspective of the author or group involved, no matter what the reality of the situation. What might be viewed by a neutral or objective observer, either ancient or modern, as of trifling importance might have been interpreted by the participants themselves as a situation of great crisis.[3] This means that in those texts which fervently adopt an apocalyptic-eschatological perspective a situation of great moment for the author and his community is evident.[4]

Not all scholars, however, would agree that the social setting of apocalypticism is as neat as this. In a recent study devoted to early Jewish apocalypticism, L. L. Grabbe has challenged the scholarly consensus by using the insights of modern sociological analysis. Grabbe's work stands as the first major attempt to marry the study of ancient apocalypticism and modern social-scientific research, and is for this reason worthy of serious attention. Grabbe sets out the problem of the current study of Jewish apocalypticism in his conclusions,

> Social claims (regarding apocalypticism) have usually been made on the basis of apocalypses, yet these literary works give only a fictitious setting ... Scholars are rightly concerned to begin with the text and work out toward the solution of the broader problems, but in the case of the apocalypses, much work on the sociological level has heretofore been circular: a social situation is first hypothesized from the literature, then this hypothesized situation is used to understand and interpret the literature! ('Social Setting of Early Jewish Apocalypticism', p. 39)

Grabbe then argues that in view of these difficulties an additional insight is required, and this can be supplied by the resources of sociology and anthropology. The information from such sociological

---

[3] See Nickelsburg, 'Social Aspects', p. 646 and Collins, *Apocalyptic Imagination*, p. 30.

[4] Some scholars who define apocalypticism as the movement underlying the apocalyptic genre, state that a situation of crisis occasions all representatives of this literary form. One proponent of this view is D. Hellholm who prefers a definition of the literary genre which makes reference to the social setting which gives rise to it. See his 'The Problem of Apocalyptic Genre', p. 168. But this view serves as a good example of the confusion engendered by the current terms. Some of the apocalypses seem not to reflect any such situation of distress or crisis. One such example might be 2 Enoch (so Collins, *Apocalyptic Imagination*, p. 197) which belongs to a mystical rather than an eschatological stream in Judaism. The situation of crisis is more applicable to those apocalyptic texts (and other texts as well) which emphasise the end of history and its aftermath. So correctly Sanders, 'Palestinian Jewish Apocalypses', p. 456.

and anthropological studies can be used by the historian to construct models which are of benefit in the study of ancient Jewish apocalypticism (p. 39). While I have no problem with this general argument, it is the application of these models in the earlier sections of Grabbe's work which does cause concern.[5]

The way in which Grabbe employs these social-scientific models in his study of ancient Jewish apocalypticism is directly dependent upon a presupposition, and this requires discussion first. At the beginning of his study, Grabbe affirms that early Jewish apocalypticism has much in common with later millenarian movements which have been vigorously studied in the social sciences. This leads him to state his presupposition, 'It seems to me that most communities labelled "apocalyptic" are also millenarian, which would make "apocalyptic community" normally a subdivision of millennial movement' (p. 28). This statement is not self-evident, however, and requires far more discussion than it is given.[6] But even if we concede Grabbe's point that there is a close relationship between these two social phenomena, it is his application of this insight which is questionable. Since apocalypticism is a sub-type of millenarianism, Grabbe concludes that one can make concrete judgements about early Jewish apocalypticism *solely* on the basis of a study of later millenarian groups. Grabbe says as much at the end of his article and his words need to be quoted at length,

> researchers on early Jewish apocalypticism have so far made little use of the many important studies of millenarian groups. Yet *on the basis of such studies*, this first brief sketch has been able to challenge some common sociological assumptions about apocalypticism ... Much more needs to be done in examining actual historical societies and situations to see how apocalyptic attitudes are distributed and function, how apocalyptic movements express themselves, and how apocalyptic literature is produced. *Only then can the Jewish apocalypses and related writings, whose social contexts are largely unknown,*

[5]   See Sim, 'Social Setting of Ancient Apocalypticism', for my full response to Grabbe's article.

[6]   With some justification, J. J. Collins writes, 'We cannot assume a priori that the Enoch literature attests the same phenomenon that anthropologists, on the basis of very different evidence, call a millenarian movement or "an apocalyptic religion"' (*Apocalyptic Imagination*, p. 29). What Collins says of the Enoch literature applies equally to all the texts which reflect apocalypticism.

be socially situated with some methodological rigour. (pp.
39–40, emphasis added)

These words contain in a nutshell Grabbe's particular method for
the study of early Jewish apocalypticism. Because of the difficulty
presented by the ancient texts themselves, we can by and large
dispense with them. In order to understand this particular social
phenomenon in the ancient Graeco-Roman world, we need do no
more than use the models appropriate to later millenarianism
which the social scientists have constructed. All this is questionable,
however. It is clear that Grabbe's argument proceeds not only on
the assumption that apocalypticism and millenarianism enjoy a
close relationship, but also on the premise that each phenomenon
remained substantially the same throughout different historical
periods and is similarly manifested in different cultures. So what
applies to a number of millenarian movements of one or more
cultures can be immediately transferred to ancient apocalyptic
groups of another culture. But this approach is clearly too rigid and
does not adequately consider important variables such as historical
development and cultural diversity. Without ever substantiating his
position, Grabbe simply excludes the possibility that early Jewish
apocalypticism might have functioned in quite different ways from
those millenarian groups which the social scientists have examined.
Despite the problems in this method, Grabbe approaches the social
setting of early Jewish apocalypticism in precisely this way.

In direct contrast to the scholarly consensus, Grabbe contends
that 'Apocalypticism does not necessarily arise in times of crisis, nor
is it always a product of the oppressed, the marginalized and the
powerless' (p. 30). To be fair, it should be stated that Grabbe does
not deny the general validity of the prevailing view on the social
setting of apocalypticism; he wishes merely to show that it is only a
tendency and not a strict rule. In support of his proposed modification to the consensus, Grabbe produces a number of exceptions to
the rule. None of these exceptions, it should be noted, belongs to the
ancient world. On the contrary, all his counter-examples are drawn
from mediaeval and later millenarian movements, and include such
diverse groups as the Russian sect of the Skoptsi and the conservative evangelicals in the modern United States, including the Moral
Majority (pp. 30–1). Since these groups did not arise in response to a
crisis, and since many of their representatives belong to the wealthy
and powerful, Grabbe concludes that not all Jewish apocalyptic

groups were occasioned by a critical situation and not all their members were oppressed and marginalised. But as interesting as these case studies are, it is clear that their applicability to early Jewish apocalypticism involves a rather large leap in the logic of the argument. Grabbe would argue, of course, that these modern examples are relevant in so far as ancient apocalypticism and later millenarianism belong together, and what applies to the latter automatically applies to the former. Yet this asks us to believe that the Moral Majority of modern America, for example, provides a better guide to the social setting of early Jewish apocalypticism than the contemporary texts. This is a rather difficult proposition to accept.

It is clear from this specific example that Grabbe has elevated the sociological data to a position of primacy and neglected the historical data in the process. He makes historical judgements about ancient Jewish apocalyptic groups on the basis of much later Russian and American (and other) millenarian groups which comprise his sociological model. The dangers in this approach are well stated by G. W. E. Nickelsburg, 'These [sociological] theories may serve as useful models that help to understand ancient texts, but primary attention must be given to the documents themselves and their particular contours. The model must not become a die that shapes the ancient materials or a filter that highlights or obliterates textual data in a predetermined way.'[7] These comments of Nickelsburg emphasise the point that our primary evidence for ancient Jewish and Christian apocalypticism must be the texts themselves.[8] The social sciences might be useful in illuminating certain aspects of the subject, but they must not be given primacy over the documents which reflect these early Jewish (and Christian) apocalyptic movements. But this brings us back to Grabbe's objection which was noted above. If we give priority to the texts, do we not then encounter certain hermeneutical problems and circular arguments? I would respond to this objection in two ways. First, it should be clear that whatever problems are associated with reading the ancient texts, these difficulties pose fewer problems for the historian than the alternative approach of Grabbe which pays no attention to the relevant documents. Secondly, the hermeneutical problems which arise from confining the discussion to the relevant texts are not as serious as Grabbe contends. Despite the fictitious

---

[7]   Nickelsburg, 'Social Aspects', p. 648.

[8]   So too Koch, *Rediscovery*, p. 23 and Collins, *Apocalyptic Imagination*, p. 29.

setting of some early Jewish and Christian documents which emphasise apocalyptic eschatology, each of them does refer in concrete ways to an underlying crisis which occasioned the work.

In many cases the crisis is a well known historical event and can thus be pin-pointed with great accuracy, the most obvious examples being the Maccabean crisis and the destruction of Jerusalem and its temple by the Romans in 70 CE. The first of these crises involved the persecution of the Jews by Antiochus Epiphanes who tried to ban the observance of traditional Jewish religion in Palestine as part of his enforced hellenisation policy. This policy met with complicity in some Jewish quarters and fierce resistance in others which remained true to the Torah. The crisis came to a climax in 167 BCE when the temple was defiled by the erection of an idolatrous altar. Certain groups met this crisis with a literary apocalyptic-eschatological response whereby the author and his circle identified themselves as the righteous remnant within Israel. The best known of these texts is the canonical book of Daniel, but the Apocalypse of Weeks and the Animal Apocalypse from 1 Enoch were also composed at this critical time and reflect a similar viewpoint. Another text for consideration in this regard is the Testament of Moses which has two distinct layers.[9] The initial stratum (chapters 1–5, 8–10) reflects the Maccabean crisis and is thus contemporary with Daniel and the two apocalypses from 1 Enoch. On the other hand, chapters 6–7 are later additions which attempt to update the original prophecies. Chapter 6 mentions the Hasmoneans, the life and death of Herod the Great and concludes with the burning of the temple by Varus at the time of Herod's death in 4 BCE. The last events to receive mention provide the clue to the date of this interpolation. The period following the death of Herod was a time of great civil unrest which was met with brutal Roman oppression, and these critical events gave rise to renewed emphasis on apocalyptic eschatology for that group which transmitted the original text of the Testament of Moses.

The second great national disaster for the Jewish people in this period was the unsuccessful revolt against the Romans in 66–70. This conflict led to the deaths of many Jews, both within Palestine and in other parts of the eastern Roman empire, and culminated in the destruction of Jerusalem and its temple. The outcome of the war occasioned a deep sense of alienation in the Jewish people and

---

[9]   For discussion of the dating of the constituent parts of this text, see Collins, *Apocalyptic Imagination*, p. 103 and literature cited there.

clearly raised a number of doubts in the minds of many Jews concerning the justice of God. Why has the just God of the Jews allowed his city, his temple and his people to be destroyed by the godless gentiles? The crisis of the Jewish war evoked no fewer than four apocalypses – the Apocalypse of Abraham, 4 Ezra, 2 Baruch and 3 Baruch – the first three of which attempted to respond to these doubts and questions using the language and themes of apocalyptic eschatology. The destruction of Jerusalem and the Jewish temple also initiated a similar response in the later sections of the third and fourth books of the Sibylline corpus (cf. 4:115–27; 5:396–413).

Not every apocalyptic-eschatological text, of course, was occasioned by a momentous historical catastrophe. At least two documents were written in response to general economic and/or social oppression. The author of the Epistle of Enoch accuses the wicked of a number of religious transgressions (cf. 1 En. 95:4; 96:7; 98:11; 99:2, 7, 14), but he reserves his greatest condemnation for their abuse of wealth and power and for their oppression of the righteous (94:6–9; 96:4–8; 97:8–10; 98:1–3; 99:13–15; 100:7–9; 103:5–15).[10] A similar social setting seems to underlie the Parables of Enoch which criticises unreservedly the rulers and the wealthy who put their trust in riches rather than in God (cf. 46:4–8; 48:7–8; 53:5–7; 54:2–6; 62:1–16; 63:1–12; 67:8–13).[11]

The book of Revelation appears to reflect a rather more complex social setting which can only be outlined in general terms here.[12] There is good evidence that the author and his circle were in direct conflict with local Jewish synagogues (2:9; 3:9) and were being persecuted by the Roman authorities as well. John himself was seemingly banished by the Romans to Patmos (1:9) and the persecution of his churches is also implied in the reference to the

---

[10] For a full analysis of this theme, see Nickelsburg, 'The Apocalyptic Message of 1 Enoch 92–105', pp. 309–28.

[11] According to Suter, *Tradition and Composition*, pp. 29–32, the author had in mind the oppressive Roman occupying forces and their governors and emperors. Nickelsburg, *Jewish Literature*, p. 223 rightly asks whether some Jewish leaders, such as the Hasmoneans and the Herods, might have been included as well in the general category of the wicked who oppress the poor.

[12] For fuller accounts of the social setting(s) of Revelation, see A. Y. Collins, 'Persecution and Vengeance', pp. 732–42; 'The Revelation of John: An Apocalyptic Response to a Social Crisis', pp. 4–8; 'Insiders and Outsiders in the Book of Revelation', pp. 203–18 and Fiorenza, *Book of Revelation*, pp. 192–6. See also the recent review of the scholarly literature by Thompson, *Book of Revelation*, pp. 202–10.

death of Antipas in 2:13. Texts such as 2:2–3, 10, 19; 3:10; 13:10 hint that the seer expected more to come. In the apocalypse proper, constant mention is made of the martyrs who have been killed by the Romans on account of their Christian belief (6:9–10; 16:6; 17:9–17; 18:24; 19:2). It is these righteous dead, probably the victims of Nero's persecution as well as later martyrs, who share in the first resurrection and the thousand year reign of Christ (20:4–6). The seer's attacks on the wealth of Rome (17:4; 18:16) and the merchants who work in her service (18:3, 15, 23) might indicate some economic oppression as well (cf. 2:9). The Apocalypse also attests to divisions within the Christian community. It is generally agreed that John's attacks on the Nicolaitans and the followers of Balaam at Pergamum (2:15–16) and the prophetess Jezebel at Thyatira (2:20) are all directed at the same movement within Christianity. This necessarily brief reconstruction of the social setting(s) of the seer's communities is sufficient for our purposes and reveals that these groups faced a number of critical situations and a resultant sense of alienation from the wider society.

As we might expect, the social setting of the Qumran community is a special case since we are dealing here not with a specific text but with a community which existed over two centuries or so and whose circumstances must have changed over this period. The community originated during the turbulent times of the Maccabean crisis (CD 1:4–7) and went into self-imposed exile at Qumran some twenty years later after a dispute arose between the Teacher of Righteousness and the Wicked Priest. In the early days of the group's existence, it appears to have been persecuted by the Wicked Priest (1QpHab 9:9–10; 11:4–5; 12:6, 10), but such persecution is not clearly in evidence in later periods. Rather, the history of the isolated community at Qumran was marked by an intensifying alienation from both the larger Jewish and gentile worlds.[13] This process of alienation is well attested in the production of the War scroll which contains a more developed dualism than the earlier writings of the group. Here the eschatological battle is fought between the sons of light, the members of the community, and the sons of darkness who are identified with the gentile nations and the remainder of the Jewish world (1QM 1:1). The social setting of the Qumran community, therefore, can be described in general terms as one of increasing alienation from the world at large. This began

[13] So correctly Collins, *Apocalyptic Imagination*, p. 141 and Reddish, *Apocalyptic Literature*, p. 24.

when the Teacher of Righteousness fled from the Wicked Priest to Qumran, and developed throughout its isolated existence until the destruction of the group by the Romans during the Jewish war.

This brief review of the social setting of apocalypticism as provided by the texts themselves confirms the general scholarly view that this phenomenon in the classical period was occasioned by an acute crisis (either actual or perceived) which led to alienation from the wider society. Since human history does not conform to irrevocable laws, it cannot be said with complete certainty that every apocalyptic group in this period embraced apocalyptic eschatology in response to a set of critical circumstances. But the evidence of the texts themselves does suggest that the relationship between the two was more than a mere tendency as Grabbe would have it. On the other hand, it should be noted that not all groups facing conditions of crisis saw the need to embrace apocalypticism. The author of 3 Baruch, for example, dealt with the crisis of the Jewish war but did not respond to it by resorting to apocalyptic eschatology. This means that while apocalypticism (most probably) requires a situation of crisis to occasion it, a set of critical circumstances does not necessarily lead to the formation of an apocalyptic group. The underlying crises which did see the embracement of apocalypticism could take any number of forms. In many cases the crisis was a well known historical catastrophe, though in some cases it was not. Moreover, the resultant alienation could be manifested by actual withdrawal from society, as in the case of the Qumran community, but in the majority of cases it was experienced while the group remained physically within the wider world. The important point to note is that whatever the circumstances the crisis was perceived by the authors (and their readers) as serious enough to warrant a response using apocalyptic eschatology. This brings us to the question of the functions of this religious perspective in the texts under review.

2. The functions of apocalyptic eschatology

As W. A. Meeks has shown in his analysis of the function of apocalyptic-eschatological language in the Pauline letters,[14] the purposes of such language can be many and varied and some of them unique to the author in question. The following discussion

[14] Meeks, 'Social Functions', pp. 687–705. For more detail see his *The First Urban Christians*.

will not be concerned with individual usage; rather, it will attempt to define on a very broad level some of the more common functions of apocalyptic language and themes in the set texts. There is widespread agreement that a direct correlation exists between the desperate situation of the author and his group and the embracement of the apocalyptic-eschatological perspective. Apocalyptic eschatology, which emphasises the imminent reversal of present circumstances, the vindication of the suffering righteous and the punishment of their perceived oppressors, serves to strengthen, comfort and offer hope to the group which is experiencing the crisis.[15] At a more technical level, P. D. Hanson affirms that a group becomes an apocalyptic movement at the point when it adopts apocalyptic eschatology in order to construct a 'symbolic universe' which is at odds with the symbolic universe of the wider and oppressive society but which makes sense of its own situation of distress.[16] The use of apocalyptic eschatology thus exchanges the world view of the opposing group for an entirely new perspective on reality in which the hopes and aspirations of the apocalyptic community are reinforced and validated. As noted in the previous chapter, this symbolic universe can take different forms. These differences in presentation can be seen by comparing the Apocalypse of Weeks with the book of Revelation. Whereas the former makes use of a simple ten period (or week) scheme, the latter presents its vision of reality by employing a complicated and repetitive scheme of bizarre imagery and symbolism.

But despite the differences in detail between these symbolic universes, all the texts which emphasise apocalyptic eschatology attempt to lend weight to their alternative world views by attributing them to a trustworthy and authoritative figure. In the apocalypses and Testaments, which normally employ the device of pseudonymity, it is a great leader or sage of the past (Enoch, Abraham, Moses, Baruch and so on) who presents this interpretation of reality. The same applies to the Sibylline literature where the Sibyl acts as a mouthpiece for God. In those texts which are not pseudonymous the same authoritative tone is given by other means. At Qumran the revered Teacher of Righteousness normally fulfils

---

[15] So Russell, *Method and Message*, p. 18; Collins, *Apocalyptic Imagination*, p. 32; Schürer et al, *History*, III.1, p. 243; Reddish, *Apocalyptic Literature*, pp. 24–7; Hellholm, 'The Problem of Apocalyptic Genre', p. 168 and Fiorenza, 'The Phenomenon of Early Christian Apocalyptic', p. 313.

[16] Hanson, 'Apocalypticism', pp. 30–1 and *Dawn of Apocalyptic*, pp. 432–4.

this function, while in the book of Revelation the risen Lord Jesus speaks to and through the seer. By presenting their alternative world views in this way, the authors of the texts wished to impress upon their readers that the vision of reality they present is believable and trustworthy since it ultimately has divine authority. This brings us to the specific functions of apocalyptic eschatology.

These specific functions can be roughly classified into five categories – 1. identification and legitimation, 2. explanation of current circumstances, 3. encouragement and hope for the future, 4. vengeance and consolation, 5. group solidarity and social control. We will detail each in turn, but it is well to bear in mind at the outset that these categories are not mutually exclusive and some elements of apocalyptic eschatology serve more than one function and belong to more than one category.

2.1 Identification and legitimation

One very important function of apocalyptic eschatology is the setting of boundaries around the apocalyptic community.[17] The strictly dualistic language corresponding to the human sphere is important in this regard. As noted in the previous chapter, apocalyptic eschatology normally speaks of two diametrically opposed groups, 'the righteous', 'the elect' and so on, and their counterparts, 'the wicked' or 'the sinners'. Such language immediately establishes rigid boundaries around the groups in question and identifies, to use the current terminology, the nature of the insider and that of the outsider. Those within the apocalyptic community are the righteous who stand on the side of God, while those outside the community stand in opposition to him. It is clear that the boundaries around some apocalyptic communities were so rigid that the group comprised a well defined sect in opposition to the power structures of the surrounding society.[18] As we might expect, the sectarian nature of the group is most plainly in evidence where the sense of alienation is most clearly felt. Both the collective group addressed by the author of Revelation and the Qumran community have for this reason been described as distinct sects.[19] The degree of

[17] See Meeks, 'Social Functions', p. 692 and Hanson, *Dawn of Apocalyptic*, pp. 435–6.

[18] For discussion of the sectarian nature of second temple Judaism, see Blenkinsopp, 'Interpretation and the Tendency to Sectarianism', pp. 1–26 and Schiffman, 'Jewish Sectarianism', pp. 1–46.

[19] On the sectarian nature of the communities of the Apocalypse, see Stanley, 'The

alienation for each group is indicated by the presence of the very marked dualism which specifically correlates cosmic and human dualism. Each community is depicted as a self-supporting righteous enclave aligned with God in the cosmic struggle for supremacy, while the wider society has thrown in its lot with Satan and is to be avoided. However, even when the evidence does not permit us to speak of a given group as a sect, the dualistic language none the less indicates its perceived minority status within the larger society.[20]

As a result of the drawing of boundaries around the community, groups which adopt apocalyptic eschatology usually designate the requirements for becoming an insider or an outsider. In the Jewish texts the boundary can be marked merely by distinguishing between those who obey the law correctly and those who do not (e.g. 2 Bar. 44:1–15), or it can be marked in a more complicated way as it was at Qumran. In order to become an insider of the Qumran community, one was required to reject the cult of the Jerusalem temple, live a monastic life at Qumran and obey the particular regulations and laws of the group, including its interpretation of the Torah. For all the Jewish texts there was no need to delimit boundaries with regard to the gentiles, who were collectively perceived as wicked, since this was done by virtue of ethnicity; the boundaries needed to be drawn within the Jewish world itself. The same does not hold of course for the Christian book of Revelation. Here Jew or gentile could become an insider and thus a participant in salvation by accepting Jesus as the Christ (in the way desired by the author) and by rejecting the idolatrous cults of the Roman world, if not the Roman empire itself.[21]

This drawing of rigid boundaries around the apocalyptic community and the dualistic language associated with it serve in turn to legitimate both the minority or sectarian status of the group in question and its particular beliefs and practices. The apocalyptic community comprises the righteous and elect who by definition stand with God and obey his will. On the other hand, the wider world is composed of the sinners and the wicked who necessarily stand against God and disobey him. This point is even more marked in those schemes which clearly associate the wicked with

---

Apocalypse and Contemporary Sect Analysis', pp. 412–21. The sectarian status of the Qumran community will be discussed in chapter 8 below.

[20] See the discussion of Overman, *Matthew's Gospel*, pp. 16–19.

[21] On the drawing of boundaries in the Apocalypse, see A. Y. Collins, 'Vilification and Self-Definition', pp. 308–20 and Webber, 'Group Solidarity', pp. 132–40.

the supernatural forces of evil. In all schemes, however, the mere identifying purpose of dualistic language serves to justify both the existence and the peculiar nature of the group.

2.2 Explanation of current circumstances

Another function of apocalyptic eschatology lies in its explanatory power. Its world view, particularly the notion of determinism, offers an explanation for the present circumstances of the group. The suffering of the community has not occurred by chance nor, despite appearances, is it happening contrary to God's will. Rather, the plight of the group is an integral part of the historical and eschatological processes which God determined in advance and which cannot be changed. This in turn serves to console and comfort the members of the community by reinforcing the viewpoint that God has not abandoned them. Their suffering is in fact a sign of their elect status.[22]

2.3 Encouragement and hope for the future

Apocalyptic eschatology offers encouragement and hope for the future by spelling out that the members of the community will ultimately be vindicated and receive magnificent eschatological rewards. They can take heart that the pain they endure now will be more than adequately compensated on the day of judgement. The theme of determinism plays an important role in this regard by adding conviction to the author's eschatological expectations. Just as the past and present were determined and came to pass as predicted by the reputed author of the apocalypse (or another authoritative figure), so too will the future unfold as prophesied. The readers can be assured that according to the predetermined course of history, they will receive magnificent rewards at the conclusion of this age when God or his agent presides over the judgement. The concept of the imminence of the end is an essential aspect of this overall scheme. For reasons which are obvious, it is easier to be hopeful and steadfast in the face of dire circumstances when it is believed that the present situation will be corrected in the immediate future. This is especially true if the reversal of fortunes is deemed eternal and irreversible. A number of texts

---

[22] A similar point is made by Meeks with respect to 1 Thess 3:2–4; 'Social Functions', pp. 691–2.

actively encourage their readers by providing hortatory sections which urge them to retain hope and remain steadfast in the light of the eternal rewards they will receive (e.g. 1 En. 95:3; 96:1–8; 104:1–5; Rev. 2:9–11; 3:9–13).

2.4 Vengeance and consolation

The salvation of the righteous is contrasted with the punishment of the wicked, and this prominent theme also has an important part to play. To put the matter bluntly, the constant claim that those who are responsible for the present suffering will be eternally punished, usually by horrific and torturous means, satisfies the very human desire for vengeance. This theme is especially prominent in the Parables of Enoch which states that the righteous themselves will have a hand in the punishment of the wicked (1 En. 95:3; 96:1; cf. also Dan. 7:22). It is found as well in Revelation where the judgement of the wicked is depicted as divine revenge on the world for the blood of the martyrs.[23] Further examples of this tendency can be seen in 4 Ezra, 2 Baruch and the Apocalypse of Abraham, all of which were written in response to the destruction of Jerusalem by the Romans. While each of these texts states that the people of Israel had sinned and that the events of 66–70 were sanctioned as their punishment (4 Ezra 3:25–7; 2 Bar. 1:2–5; 5:2–4; 77:2–4; 79:1–2; Apoc. of Ab. 27:7–8), they all make the further point that the Romans and the other nations who oppressed Israel will be punished for their crimes (4 Ezra 13:32–8; 2 Bar. 72:2–6; 82:2–9; Apoc. of Ab. 31:1–2). The fifth book of the Sibylline corpus, which was written under similar circumstances, also prophesies the horrific punishment which awaits the Romans (5:162–78, 386–96) and other gentile nations (5:52–93, 111–35, 179–227, 286–327, 333–59, 434–46). Whatever we might think of this particular notion, this important feature of apocalyptic eschatology should not be refined and treated as mere rhetoric or symbolism; it was intended to be taken literally and it is on this level that we should approach it. In its own way, the belief that the wicked will burn forever or receive some other terrible punishment serves to comfort and console the suffering by reinforcing the idea of the justice of God. Just as God's justice is evident in his vindication of the righteous who suffer now,

---

[23] That the theme of vengeance is an important component of the Christian Apocalypse is rightly (and honestly) addressed by A. Y. Collins, 'Persecution and Vengeance', pp. 729–50. Cf. too Fiorenza, *Book of Revelation*, p. 1.

so too is it manifest in his punishment of the wicked who are responsible for their suffering.

2.5 Group solidarity and social control

One further and very important function of apocalyptic eschatology is that of promoting group solidarity by enforcing social control. In minority or sectarian groups which exist in a hostile environment, group solidarity is all-important and dissension cannot be tolerated. Internal disputes can lead to a lessening of resolve and might fragment even further an already fragile community structure. For this reason clear guidelines for becoming an insider need to be established (see 2.1 above) and unity within the community needs to be maintained at all costs. An effective means of ensuring group solidarity is to impose a measure of social control on dissident or potentially dissident members by the use of the threat of judgement.[24] Those within the community who do not conform to the standards of the group will themselves be punished for not being true members of the elect. This threat can be made explicitly as it is in Revelation (2:14–16, 22–3; 3:1–4) and the Community Rule at Qumran (1QS 2:11–17), but it is always implicit in view of the fact that membership in all groups depends upon the observance of certain standards of behaviour. In highly organised sectarian groups like the Qumran community, if the threats did not produce the desired result, then a series of punishments or even the expulsion of the offender could be undertaken (1QS 6:24–7:25). Measures such as these also promote group solidarity by suppressing dissident behaviour or by expelling wholly dissident elements.

The function of social control is also apparent in the material which addresses the eschatological fate of those outside the community. While the constant reminder that outsiders will meet with horrific punishments serves to satisfy the need for vengeance within the group (see 2.4 above), it also functions to deter those waverers in the group who might be tempted to break ranks and leave it. The less than steadfast members would be considerably pressured to remain in the community by the (implicit) threat that leaving the group would see them exchange eternal rewards for

---

[24] This particular function of apocalyptic eschatology is noted by Meeks, 'Social Functions', p. 694 and Fiorenza, 'The Phenomenon of Early Christian Apocalyptic', p. 313.

eternal damnation. Underlying this particular function of apocalyptic eschatology is the concept of human free will and the correlative notion of human responsibility for actions. Rather than promoting a hard determinism at this level, those who embrace apocalyptic eschatology advocate that their readers can choose whether or not to remain within the righteous community. It is therefore in their own hands whether they ultimately receive salvation or punishment at the eschaton.

2.6 Summary

To summarise this section, it was found that the function of apocalyptic eschatology is closely related to the social setting of apocalypticism; apocalyptic eschatology is a response to the situation of crisis and resultant alienation experienced by the author and his circle and encapsulates their efforts to deal with it. It presents a new and authoritative symbolic universe which validates the experience of the group and invalidates the world view of the wider society which is responsible for the desperate situation. By emphasising that the world is composed of only two groups whose boundaries are clearly marked, and that the beliefs and practices of the apocalyptic community alone meet with God's approval, apocalyptic eschatology both identifies and legitimates the community which resorts to it. In spelling out that the righteous will be rewarded and the wicked punished, it serves to offer hope, comfort and consolation, and satisfies the desire for vengeance on the wider oppressive society. Since group solidarity is essential for minority or sectarian groups, apocalyptic eschatology also functions to preserve solidarity and harmony by imposing social control using the threat of judgement.

SUMMARY OF PART I

In this first part of our study, we have attempted to present as full a picture as is necessary for our purposes of both apocalyptic eschatology and apocalypticism in the historical time-frame of the gospel of Matthew. While noting that these terms are confusing and unsatisfactory, it was decided in the interests of avoiding further confusion to retain them. Apocalyptic eschatology is a religious perspective which can be found both within and without the apocalyptic genre. It emphasises dualism on a number of levels and a deterministic view of history, and concentrates on the eschatological reversal of present circumstances in the immediate future. Important eschatological characteristics of this perspective include the lead up to the end of this age, the arrival of a saviour figure, the final and universal judgement and the bestowal of magnificent and eternal rewards or terrible punishments. Apocalypticism is the socio-religious phenomenon which underlies this particular religious perspective. It is embraced by minority groups which are undergoing a situation of crisis, either real or perceived, and experiencing a sense of alienation from the wider, oppressive society. The crisis could take any number of forms and need not necessarily have been a major historical catastrophe. The adoption of apocalyptic eschatology and its alternative symbolic universe is in direct response to the perceived crisis. It legitimates the existence and peculiar nature of the group in question and offers an explanation of the present situation of crisis. Further, apocalyptic eschatology serves to console the group that, despite present appearances, God is on their side and that ultimately they will be rewarded and their enemies punished. Alternatively, it can serve by way of threat to warn wavering members of the consequences of breaking ranks. In this latter usage it serves as a means of social control which is necessary in view of the current critical conditions. Having completed our preliminary and necessary review of the related phenomena apocalyptic eschatology and apocalypticism, we may now turn to the gospel of Matthew and apply the insights of that discussion.

PART II

Apocalyptic eschatology in the gospel of Matthew

This part of the study will attempt to determine the nature and extent of apocalyptic eschatology in the gospel of Matthew. In order to do this, we need to investigate each of the eight major characteristics of this religious perspective which were identified in chapter 1. In all chapters we shall focus upon the evangelist's use of his synoptic sources according to the principles and for the reasons outlined in the Introduction. This will provide a guide as to which elements the evangelist adopted with minimal alteration from these sources and those which he saw fit to alter or to supplement. In those cases where Matthew differs from his synoptic sources, the possibility that he is reflecting source material independent of Mark and Q must be explored. Since apocalyptic eschatology is found to varying degrees in many early Christian documents, most notably in the Apocalypse but by no means confined there, it could be the case that Matthew is reflecting a Christian tradition which is represented in other New Testament texts. On the other hand, in some instances it might be true that the evangelist was dependent upon purely Jewish apocalyptic-eschatological traditions which he knew in either oral or literary form. It is well known that Matthew knew of and utilised the book of Daniel and the claim is sometimes made that he knew other apocalyptic texts. At the conclusion of this part of the study, we will be in a position to offer a complete reconstruction of Matthew's particular scheme of apocalyptic eschatology and to note its similarities to and differences from other schemes. We will be able to identify which elements he accepted from all his Christian sources, both within and without his synoptic sources, and which themes and motifs he adopted from the Jewish apocalyptic-eschatological tradition.

3

DUALISM AND DETERMINISM IN MATTHEW

1. Dualism

The gospel of Matthew accepts the notion of temporal dualism. This doctrine of the two ages is also found in Matthew's major sources, Mark and Q, and is a feature of many early Christian writings. The evangelist's specific notions with respect to this important theme will be fully highlighted in chapters 4 to 7. Matthew also firmly embraces the more developed form of cosmic dualism which is found in the Qumran scrolls and the book of Revelation. In agreement with these texts, he describes the super- natural world in terms of a cosmic struggle between God and his agents on the one hand and Satan and his company of evil angels on the other. Matthew is dependent upon Mark and Q for much of this material, but he edits those sources in an interesting manner and puts his own particular stamp upon them. Let us begin with his depiction of the forces on the side of God in this cosmic conflict.

Like all or most of his contemporaries, Matthew accepts the reality of the holy angels who serve God and mediate between the heavenly and earthly realms. Such angels appear in the birth narratives (1:20–1; 2:13, 19–20; cf. 2:12, 22) and the resurrection episode (28:1–8) and in all cases are the messengers of divine revelation. Matthew also knows of the concept of personal guardian angels. In Matthew 18:10, he writes that 'the little ones' have their own particular angels in heaven who behold the face of God. As with the idea of angels as the instruments of revelation, the notion of personal guardian angels is commonly found in the texts of that time (e.g. Ps. 34:7; 91:11; Tobit 5:2ff; Pseudo-Philo 11:12; 15:5; 59:4; Jub. 35:17; Dan. 3:6; T.Levi 5:3; 3 Bar. 12–13; Acts 12:15).[1]

A more important element of Matthew's angelology concerns the

---

[1] For further discussion of the relationship between Matt. 18:10 and contemporary angelological beliefs, see Davies and Allison, *Matthew*, II, pp. 770–1.

relationship between Jesus and the holy angels. He follows Mark in referring to a group of these angels who serve Jesus after his trials with Satan (4:11//Mark 1:13) and he specifies in a redactional note that at the time of his arrest Jesus could have appealed to twelve legions of angels for help (26:53). The precise relationship between Jesus and these angels, however, is spelt out most clearly in Matthew's eschatological material. When Jesus returns in glory as the judgemental Son of Man, he will be accompanied by an angelic host (16:27//Mark 8:38; 25:31), which will gather the elect (24:31// Mark 13:27) and the wicked (13:41) and separate them prior to the judgement (13:49). It is these angels who have the task of casting the wicked to the eternal fire (13:42, 50; cf. 1 En. 54:6). Of particular interest is that in 13:41, 16:27 and 24:31, Matthew describes the angels who accompany the Son of Man as 'his angels'. While the first of these texts has no synoptic parallel, the evangelist has inserted the genitive pronoun into the Marcan text in the other two (cf. Mark 8:38 and 13:27). In doing so, Matthew testifies that Jesus the Son of Man will return not simply accompanied by angels, but accompanied by his angels; the holy angels therefore belong to Jesus the Son of Man.

This particular theme is peculiar to Matthew in the New Testament. The closest parallels to this Matthean concept appear in 1 Thess. 3:13, 2 Thess. 1:7 and Jude 14–15. The first of these states that at the parousia the Lord Jesus will come with all his holy ones, presumably a reference to his angelic retinue, while the second speaks of his revelation with angels of his power (μετ' ἀγγέλων δυνάμεως αὐτοῦ). In the citation of 1 En. 1:9 in Jude verses 14–15 the coming of the Lord with his holy myriads now refers to Jesus and not to Yahweh. Conceptually these three texts make the same point as the Matthean references – Jesus will return at the end of time accompanied by his holy angels – but only Matthew emphasises that the angels belong to Jesus *the Son of Man*. We may note at this point that Matthew here has brought his angelology into line with his christology; the angels of heaven belong to and serve Jesus the Son of Man. The significance of this point will become clear in later chapters.

Directly opposed to Jesus and his angels are their evil counterparts. While Matthew makes no direct reference at all to the complex mythology of the Watchers,[2] he does know of and utilise

---

[2]   For evidence that Matthew knew the Book of the Watchers, see Sim, 'Matthew 22:13a and 1 Enoch 10:4a'. Apart from this very indirect reference to the Watchers tradition, Matthew seems not to have been greatly influenced by it.

the alternative Satan tradition. Much of this material derives from his Christian sources, though some of it is peculiar to Matthew. The evil angels are headed by the prince of demons (9:35; 12:24) who is known alternatively as Satan (4:10; 12:26; 16:23), Beelzebul (10:25; 12:24, 27), the devil (ὁ διάβολος; 4:1, 5, 8, 11; 13:39; 25:41), the tempter (ὁ πειράζων; 4:3, cf. 1 Thess. 3:5; 1 Cor. 7:5; Rev. 2:10) and the evil one (ὁ πονηρός; 5:37; 6:13; 13:19, 38). The last of these titles requires further discussion, since it is significant in terms of the evangelist's overall dualistic scheme. There is no doubt that ὁ πονηρός, which is found elsewhere in the New Testament as a name for Satan (John 17:15; 2 Thess. 3:3; 1 John 2:13–14; 3:12; 5:18–19; Eph. 6:16), is an important title for Matthew. This is signified by the fact that in 13:19 Matthew omits Mark's 'Satan' (Mark 4:14) and replaces it with 'the evil one' (Matt. 13:19). The evil one also appears in the important apocalyptic-eschatological interpretation of the parable of the tares (13:38) and is there synonymous with the devil (verse 39). He receives further mention right at the end of the saying concerning oaths (5:33–7). While there is no good reason to deny the pre-Matthean character of 5:33–7a, the final clause, τὸ δὲ περισσὸν τούτων ἐκ τοῦ πονηροῦ ἐστιν, looks very much like an addition.[3] The final instance of this particular name for Satan appears at the conclusion of the Lord's Prayer (6:13b) where the petition not to be led into temptation, which concludes the Lucan version, is followed by the request that we be delivered from the evil one. Although it is possible that the addition of this material had occurred prior to the time of Matthew, the fact that he uses the expression editorially elsewhere suggests that the evangelist himself is responsible for it here.[4] This linking of temptation and Satan recalls the temptation narrative; just as Jesus was delivered from temptation at the hands of Satan, so too might be the petitioner.

The Satan tradition plays an important role in the Matthean narrative and sets the story of Jesus in the context of a cosmic conflict between the heavenly forces and the powers of evil. Taking his lead from Mark and Q, Matthew has Jesus tempted

---

[3] So Davies and Allison, *Matthew*, I, p. 538; Gundry, *Matthew*, p. 95; Gnilka, *Matthäusevangelium*, I, p. 173 and tentatively, Luz, *Matthäus*, I, p. 281.

[4] In agreement with Davies and Allison, *Matthew*, I, pp. 614–15; Gnilka, *Matthäusevangelium*, I, p. 215; Gundry, *Matthew*, p. 109; Schweizer, *Matthew*, p. 148 and Schulz, *Q*, p. 86. Both Jeremias, *Prayers*, pp. 89–91 and Luz, *Matthäus*, I, pp. 334–5 view this material as a pre-Matthean expansion.

by Satan right at the outset of his public mission (4:1–13). These temptations take place immediately after the baptism of Jesus when God had confirmed his status as son of God (3:13–17// Mark 1:9–11). Satan is therefore established early on as the adversary of Jesus. As one who is not on the side of God (16:23) but stands opposed to him, he can be described as 'the enemy' (cf. ὁ ἐχθρός in 13:39). After resisting all temptation and then dispensing with Satan, the Matthean Jesus faces and defeats a whole host of lesser demons who have successfully possessed the minds and bodies of humans. Matthew takes over from Mark (Mark 1:34; 3:22–7; 5:1–20; 7:24–30; 9:14–29) and from Q (// Luke 11:14–15, 17–23) a number of texts which describe Jesus exorcising these unclean spirits (Matt. 8:16, 28–34; 9:32–4; 12:22–30; 15:22–8; 17:14–21). This task of exorcism is carried on by the disciples when Jesus sends them on their mission. According to the Q account of the mission charge, the disciples are instructed by Jesus to preach the kingdom and heal the sick (Luke 10:9). Matthew multiplies the instructions and adds that the disciples must also raise the dead, cleanse lepers and cast out demons (10:8; cf. 11:5).[5] Yet despite the success of the exorcisms of Jesus and the disciples, the evangelist is quite adamant that they constitute only a series of minor victories in the overall cosmic conflict. The final and decisive defeat of Satan and his contingent of demons will not take place until the eschatological judgement (cf. 25:41 and see further chapter 6). Consequently, they are still a force to be reckoned with until that time. This point is emphasised in the final clause of the Lord's Prayer which calls for constant deliverance from the evil one (cf. 13:19). We shall see in chapter 4 that Matthew believed that the threat posed to the righteous by the supernatural forces of evil would intensify considerably in the future.

This dualism on the cosmic level is found as well on the human level and the evangelist firmly agrees with the schemes in Revelation and the Qumran scrolls that there is a firm link between the two. The most precise statement of this theme appears in one of the gospel's most important apocalyptic-eschatological sections, the interpretation of the parable of the tares in 13:36–43. It is generally accepted that Matthew himself created this pericope outright and

---

[5]   See Davies and Allison, *Matthew*, II, p. 170; Schulz, *Q*, p. 407; Gnilka, *Matthäusevangelium*, II, p. 360; Gundry, *Matthew*, pp. 184–5 and Hoffmann, *Studien*, pp. 275–6.

there is no valid reason to suspect otherwise.[6] In explaining the parable of 13:24–30, the Matthean Jesus presents a completely dualistic perspective of the whole cosmic order. The Son of Man (i.e. Jesus himself) sows the good seed which represents the sons of the kingdom, while the weeds which arise amidst the seed are the sons of the evil one (οἱ υἱοὶ τοῦ πονηροῦ) and are sown by the enemy who is none other than the devil (verses 37–9a). Needless to say the former group is earmarked for salvation and the latter for eternal punishment as the later part of the tradition makes clear. At the harvest the wicked will be burned, while the righteous will shine like the sun in the kingdom of their father (verses 40–3a). According to this scenario, there is no middle ground in the cosmic conflict between Jesus and Satan and their respective human supporters; one is either a son of the kingdom or a son of the evil one and there is no third category. It has not escaped the attention of scholars that this contrasting terminology is close in meaning, if not in wording, to the Qumran dualistic categories, the sons of light and the sons of darkness.[7] By using such language Matthew deliberately relates the dualism of the human sphere to the cosmic battle which is being fought between Jesus and Satan. The human world is fundamentally divided into good and evil, and each group is aligned with its cosmic or supernatural counterpart. This text is further comparable to the Qumran schema in its affirmation that each group owes its origin to the leading players in the cosmic conflict. In 1QS these figures are Michael and Belial who rule respectively the spirits of truth and the spirits of falsehood, while for Matthew it is Jesus Son of Man, the leader of the heavenly angels, who sows the good seed and the devil who creates the weeds.

The evangelist gives further expression to this theme in the Q tradition of the return of the unclean spirit (Matt. 12:43–5//Luke 11:24–6). This pericope narrates the tale of an evil spirit which left its home in the body of a man but later desired to return there.

---

[6] See the impressive list of peculiarly Matthean features in the interpretations of both the parable of the tares (13:36–43) and that of the net (13:49–50) compiled by Jeremias, *Parables*, pp. 81–5. Those accepting this view include Davies and Allison, *Matthew*, II, pp. 426–7, 442; Luz, *Matthäus*, II, pp. 338–9, 357; Gundry, *Matthew*, pp. 271–4, 279–80 and Beare, *Matthew*, p. 311. Other views concerning the origin of this material will be considered in chapter 5.

[7] See the discussion of Davies, *Sermon*, p. 232. Both Schenk, *Sprache*, p. 120 and Kingsbury, *Parables*, p. 96 note the developed dualism in the language of this pericope, though neither mentions any resemblance to the Qumran literature.

Upon its return it finds its previous home cleaned out and put in order. The demon then brings seven more demons who are worse than itself and they all take up residence in the man. The passage concludes with the solemn words that the last state of that man will be worse than his original state (when only one demon possessed him); Matthew appends an application at the end of the pericope, 'so it will be also with this evil generation' (verse 45b), which aligns the present passage to the sign of Jonah pericope which precedes it (cf. 'an evil and adulterous generation' in 12:39). Apart from this redactional conclusion, a comparison of the two synoptic versions shows that Matthew has closely followed the wording of Q. He does, however, make one further editorial change, which perhaps elaborates what was implicit in the Q tradition, but which certainly conforms this material to his own dualistic perspective. In verse 44b (//Luke 11:25), the evangelist accepts the Q reference that the demon returns to its previous home only to find it swept and put in order, but he inserts the extra information that it was also empty (σχολάζοντα).[8] Most commentators agree that this addition, in conjunction with the fact that the man is later possessed again, serves to provide a warning that the vacuum left by the evil spirit should have been filled. Were the individual not aligned with or influenced by the evil forces (Satan and his demons), then he should have been aligned with the powers of good (Jesus and God) since this would have made repossession impossible. By this seemingly insignificant addition, the evangelist thus makes the important point that neutrality, i.e. emptiness, is not an option in the cosmic conflict; non-alignment with the cause of Jesus means ultimately taking the part of Satan. As with 13:36–43, the dualism of the human world merges completely with the dualism of the super-natural world.[9]

It was noted previously that this Matthean theme of wicked humans acting at the behest of Satan has affinities with the schemes in the Qumran scrolls and the book of Revelation, but it also appears in the first epistle of John. This text states that whoever

---

[8] Schulz, *Q,* p. 477; Davies and Allison, *Matthew*, II, p. 361; Gundry, *Matthew*, p. 247; Beare, *Matthew*, pp. 283–4.

[9] The advanced dualism here is acknowledged by Gnilka, *Matthäusevangelium*, II, p. 649. Gnilka makes the further point that this is the only text in the gospel which specifies that evil spirits are responsible for human sin; *Matthäusevange-lium*, II, p. 647. So too Davies and Allison, *Matthew*, II, p. 361 n. 113. But this view completely overlooks Matthew 13:36–43 which makes precisely the same point.

commits sin is of the devil, who has committed sin from the beginning (3:8), and it contrasts the children of God and the children of the devil (3:10; cf. also John 8:44; Acts 13:10). The author urges his readers to love one another and not be like Cain who was 'of the evil one' (ἐκ τοῦ πονηροῦ, 1 John 3:12; cf. Matt. 5:37) and murdered his brother because his deeds were evil and those of his brother were righteous. Hence, for this writer as well the cosmos is strictly divided into good and evil, a division which can be traced back to creation. He is also in no doubt that human evil, as exemplified by the murder of Abel by Cain, has its origin in Satan.[10] Parallels have been rightly drawn between this concept in 1 John and the dualistic scheme of Qumran,[11] but both Matthew and Revelation are comparable in this respect.

The point was made in chapter 1 that those who resort to apocalyptic eschatology generally tend to juxtapose and thereby contrast the two opposing groups which comprise the human world. Matthew is no exception to this rule and it is probably fair to say that he does so more than any other New Testament author. As we find in many apocalyptic-eschatological texts, the gospel of Matthew uses a variety of comparative terms. We have already noted the evangelist's contrast between the sons of the kingdom and the sons of the evil one, but we also find the comparison between righteous and doers of lawlessness (13:41–3), righteous and cursed (25:37, 41), wise and foolish (7:24–7; 25:1–13),[12] and faithful and wise and wicked (24:45–51).[13] The most prominent and important antithetical terms which Matthew uses, however, are good (ἀγαθός) and wicked (πονηρός). In some cases he has taken the contrast directly from Q. For example, in 12:34–5 (//Luke 6:45) we meet the comparison between the good (ἀγαθός) man who produces good and the evil (πονηρός) man who produces evil. The

---

[10] See Smalley, *1, 2, 3 John*, pp. 168, 180, 184.

[11] Smalley, *1, 2, 3 John*, p. 168. A further close parallel between 1 John and the Qumran scrolls appears in the related theme of the two spirits in the Community Rule and 1 John 4:1–6 where the author speaks of the spirit of truth and the spirit of error.

[12] The pair of contrasting terms in 7:24–7 is clearly attributable to Matthew. It is accepted by all scholars that the concrete descriptions of the two builders as φρόνιμος and μωρός are Matthean touches; see Gnilka, *Matthäusevangelium*, I, p. 280; Schulz, *Q*, pp. 313–4; Luz, *Matthäus*, I, p. 412; Davies and Allison, *Matthew*, I, p. 721 and Gundry, *Matthew*, pp. 134–5.

[13] Matthew adds 'wicked' (κακός) in v.48 (so Gundry, *Matthew*, p. 496 and Marguerat, *Le Jugement*, p. 531 contra Schulz, *Q*, p. 272), thereby highlighting the contrast which is already present in the Q narrative.

ἀγαθός/πονηρός contrast appears again in the Q parable of the talents (Matt. 25:14–30//Luke 19:11–27) which refers to the good (and faithful) servants (Matt. 25:21// Luke 19:17; Matt. 25:23 with no Lucan parallel) and the wicked (πονηρός) servant (Matt. 25:26// Luke 19:22). All the remaining instances of the contrast between the good and the evil are the result of Matthean redaction. In Matthew 5:45b (//Luke 6:35b) we meet a double contrast, evil and good (πονηρός and ἀγαθός) and righteous and unrighteous (δίκαιος and ἄδικος), and it is agreed that these are secondary to the non-dualistic Lucan terms ungrateful and evil (ἀχάριστος and πονηρός).[14] The same antithetical terms are found at the conclusion of the parable of the wedding feast where the servants gather both good and wicked in order to fill the hall (22:10). The Lucan parallel knows of no such distinction between the guests (Luke 14:23) and most scholars ascribe the difference to Matthew's redaction.[15] In the material dealing with the metaphor of trees and their fruit (Matt. 7:17–18 and 12:33//Luke 6:43), Matthew expands his source and specifically uses the ἀγαθός/πονηρός terminology; a good tree (δένδρον ἀγαθὸν) produces fine fruit (καρποὺς καλοὺς) and a bad tree (σαπρὸν δένδρον) produces evil fruit (καρποὺς πονηροὺς).[16] As a variant on the ἀγαθός/πονηρός contrast, Matthew also juxtaposes the righteous and the wicked (δίκαιος/ πονηρός) in the parable of the net (13:49).

We should not interpret these references to contrasting groups on the human level merely in terms of a moral division within humanity. Rather, all these texts serve to highlight Matthew's dualistic view of the cosmos which he constructed in 13:36–43. The question of morality or ethics is merely one aspect of the conceptual framework in which Matthew's dualistic terminology works. The righteous are good only in so far as they have aligned themselves with Jesus and his forces in the cosmic struggle. On the other hand, the wicked are evil not just because they act immorally, but because their immorality betrays their allegiance to Satan. Matthew's constant use of πονηρός as a descriptive term for the wicked clearly points in this direction. As followers of the evil one (ὁ πονηρός),

---

[14] See Davies and Allison, *Matthew*, I, pp. 554–5; Gundry, *Matthew,* p. 98 and Gnilka, *Matthäusevangelium*, I, p. 188. Luz, *Matthäus*, I, p. 306 n. 7 is slightly more tentative on the issue.

[15] So Schulz, *Q,* p. 397; Gnilka, *Matthäusevangelium*, II, p. 236; Gundry, *Matthew*, p. 438 and Beare, *Matthew,* p. 436.

[16] For Matthew's expansion of Q here, see Gundry, *Matthew*, p. 130; Luz, *Matthäus*, I, pp. 401–2 and Schulz, *Q*, pp. 317–18.

those who are opposed to God can themselves be designated wicked or evil (πονηρός). These texts thus reinforce the notion in Matthew 13:38 that those who take the part of Satan are indeed sons of the evil one. It ought to be noted at this point that Matthew's many references to 'this evil (πονηρός) generation' (11:16; 12:39, 41, 42, 45; 16:4; 17:17; 23:36; 24:34), which in almost every case he took from his sources, fit very neatly into this dualistic scheme. The generation which rejected and murdered the messiah must be considered as working in the service of Satan.

Matthew's advanced dualism finds further explicit expression in the Matthean pericope concerning the two ways (7:13–14) which derives ultimately from Q (//Luke 13:23–4). According to the Lucan parallel, Jesus tells his disciples to enter (the eschatological banqueting hall) by the narrow door, for many will try to enter but will not be able. The Matthean text, on the other hand, reflects a totally dualistic perspective. It speaks not of one point of entry, in this case gates rather than doors, but of two which lead to two different destinations. One gate is wide and the way to it is easy. This gate leads to destruction and many will enter it. By contrast, the other gate is narrow and the way to it is hard. The narrow gate leads ultimately to salvation (life) and those who find it will be few. Probability favours the hypothesis that Matthew has expanded the original Q pericope and contrasted the two gates and the two ways rather than the alternative view that Luke has abbreviated it.[17] The two gates presumably represent the respective entrances to the consummated kingdom of God and to Gehenna, the place of eschatological punishment. That Matthew considered the latter place to possess a gate is clear from 16:18 which refers to the gates of Hades (πύλαι ᾅδου). We may surmise from this that the evangelist accepted that a gate also led to the place of eschatological salvation. The idea of the end-time residence of the righteous being entered by a gate (or gates) is found in both Jewish and Christian apocalyptic literature (4 Ezra 7:6–8; Rev. 22:14; cf. also 21:12–13, 15, 21).[18] On the other hand, the combination of the two gates, one leading to salvation and the other to destruction, is comparatively

---

[17] In agreement with Luz, *Matthäus*, I, pp. 395–6 and Gundry, *Matthew*, pp. 126–7. On the other hand, Schulz, *Q*, pp. 309–11 argues unconvincingly for the originality of the Matthean text and the redactional nature of the Lucan parallel. Matthean priority is also affirmed by Guelich, *Sermon*, p. 385. The middle position is adopted by Gnilka, *Matthäusevangelium*, I, pp. 268–9 who argues for both Matthean expansion and Lucan contraction of the original Q pericope.

[18] For non-apocalyptic texts, see Jeremias, 'πύλη', p. 923.

rare in the literature of Matthew's time.[19] Matthew's use of this double imagery is a direct result of his adoption of the concept of the two ways and his insertion of it into this Q passage; the two ways must lead to two different destinations.

It was noted in chapter 1 that this notion of the two ways has its roots in the Old Testament but underwent considerable development in conjunction with the development of Jewish angelological and demonological traditions. In the Testaments of the Twelve Patriarchs and the Qumran literature, the clearest examples of this process, the two ways had been subsumed under the further dualistic concept that the cosmos is engaged in a fierce struggle between the powers of good and the forces of evil. We obviously find this development in Matthew as well. While Matthew 7:13–14 itself has no mention of this cosmic battle, it is clearly presumed because of the prominence of this theme elsewhere in the gospel. In the light of 13:36–43 and other passages, Matthew's concept of the two ways in 7:13–14 involves more than making moral decisions. In the final analysis it means taking either the part of God or the part of Satan in the supernatural conflict. Thus the two ways tradition in the gospel can be compared favourably with the specific doctrine of the two spirits in the Testaments of the Twelve Patriarchs and the Community Rule from Qumran.[20]

The evangelist gives point to his scheme of human dualism by emphasising that just as there are only two ways of human existence, the way of God or the way of Satan, so too is there no middle ground at the time of the judgement. One is earmarked either for punishment or for salvation and there is no category in between. This point is made right throughout the gospel, but it is most clearly delineated in a number of unparalleled pericopae. In 12:36–7 Matthew stresses that individuals will be either justified or condemned on the basis of their words. The description of the last judgement in 25:31–46 states that an individual will be placed at either the left hand or the right hand of the eschatological judge (verse 33), and then given eternal punishment or eternal life (verse 46). According to the parable of the tares and its interpretation (13:24–30, 36–43), there are only two categories, wheat and weeds, the former being saved and the latter being burnt (cf. 3:12). Precisely the same point is made in the related

---

[19]   So correctly Luz, *Matthäus*, I, p. 396.
[20]   So too Sabourin, 'Apocalyptic Traits', p. 22. The opposite view is expressed by Suggs, 'The Christian Two Ways Tradition', pp. 63–4 who sees no relationship at all between the notion at Qumran and this Matthean text.

parable of the net and its interpretation in 13:47–50; there are only
two types of fish, good and bad. These eschatological passages
illustrate clearly the fundamentally dualistic outlook of the evangelist. Since there is no middle path in human life, there is certainly
no third option at the judgement.

The advanced dualism of Matthew's gospel, though quite clearly
and consistently presented, is often overlooked by Matthean scholars. Perhaps the reason for this is that New Testament scholarship
in general has focused primarily on the dualism of the Johannine
literature. As is well known, the gospel of John and the first epistle
of John are intensely dualistic and employ a variety of contrasting
images – light/darkness (e.g. John 1:8; 3:19–21; 8:12; 9:5; 12:35–6,
46; 1 John 1:5–7; 2:8–11), flesh/spirit (e.g. John 3:5–6; 6:63), spirit
of truth and the spirit of error (1 John 4:1–6) to choose only three
such features. Parallels between the dualism of the Johannine
writings and the Qumran scrolls have long been drawn and
exhaustively examined.[21] This concentration on the Johannine
literature has perhaps helped to turn attention away from other
New Testament documents, including the gospel of Matthew. Yet
in its own way, the gospel of Matthew is no less dualistic than any
of these texts. While its dualism is perhaps not so obvious as that of
the Johannine literature, and its range of dualistic categories is not
so extensive, the perception of the cosmos it advances is no less
dualistic than its Johannine counterparts. The division of all
creatures, angels and humans, into two opposing camps, which is
also found in 1 John and the Apocalypse, has very clear parallels
with the dualism which operated at Qumran. In fact, by plainly
affirming that the human world and the angelic world are subsumed under the one cosmic dualistic scheme, Matthew betrays a
more developed dualism than many of the apocalyptic-eschatological schemes which were discussed in chapter 1! This point has
been rather neglected in the study of Matthew's gospel, but it must
be given the attention it deserves.

On the other hand, those scholars who have noted Matthew's
developed dualism have been less than comfortable with it. More
than one scholar has attempted to dissociate this gospel theme from
the viewpoint of the evangelist. The following words of F. W. Beare
in relation to Matthew 13:36–43 may serve as an illustration of this
reaction;

---

[21] See most recently, Painter, *Quest for the Messiah*, pp. 30–5.

> The picture is pure myth – human beings are...seen as...belonging to one of two classes, according to their origin in the Son of Man or in the devil. This is surely a conception of man which is quite alien to Jesus or to the Bible generally. Can it be that Matthew himself really thinks of mankind in these terms, or has he borrowed some alien myth without realizing its implications?[22]

Beare's comments raise some very pertinent issues. His point that this Matthean theme stands against the biblical view in general might hold true in terms of the Old Testament, which does not by and large contain a strong demonological tradition, but it hardly applies to the New Testament which took shape in an environment which emphasised the dualistic nature of the cosmos. As noted above, there are close conceptual and/or terminological parallels between the gospel, the first Johannine epistle and the Christian Apocalypse. Beare also raises the question whether Matthew really thought in these terms, or whether he had adopted an alien myth without realising the implications of doing so. This issue requires a few words as well, in so far as it directly affects our understanding of Matthew's apocalyptic eschatology in general and not just our approach to his advanced dualism. To begin with, there is no good reason to doubt that the evangelist completely accepted the reality of the situation as depicted in 13:36–43. This dualistic perspective is not an alien myth (whatever that means!), but belongs to a particular Jewish (and Christian) world view of the evangelist's day, and was clearly accepted by many of his contemporaries. That Matthew adopted it should occasion no surprise. We noted in chapter 2 that this world view arises in and responds to a certain social setting, and we shall examine in Part III how this applies to the evangelist and his community.

No doubt some scholars would argue that the evangelist could not have accepted the cluster of unappealing apocalyptic-eschatological features in 13:36–43, such as its marked dualism or its reference to the burning of the wicked. Beare's suggestion that Matthew might not have understood the implications of using this material provides one attempt to eliminate such uncomfortable themes from the overall viewpoint of the evangelist. Yet any claim of this sort entails the proposition that Matthew readily adopted language and concepts which had accepted meanings at that time

---

[22] Beare, *Matthew*, p. 312.

but wished to use them in a manner contrary to their normal usage. While this is not in itself impossible, it does need to be demonstrated and not merely assumed. In terms of the evangelist's understanding of 13:36–43, a passage he either created or subjected to heavy redaction, the onus of proof clearly rests with those who would argue that Matthew did not really refer to the dualistic nature of the cosmic order and the fiery fate of the wicked, despite writing about them both here and elsewhere in his gospel. The danger of this practice, of course, is that it runs a very real risk of tearing the evangelist from his historical and cultural context and fashioning him in our own image. We might not today accept the world view of this Matthean pericope and, like Beare, we might even disapprove of it, but we must never presume that Matthew considered matters in the same way. Modern exegetes must be prepared to accept that Matthew, as a child of his time, held a different set of beliefs from our own. Value judgements that such a vision of reality is unbiblical or mythical, or apologetically motivated attempts to divorce the evangelist from an unattractive world view, only serve to hinder rather than assist our understanding of Matthew and his intentions.

2. Determinism

Just as Matthew adopted a developed dualistic perception of the cosmos, so too does he accept that God has determined in advance the course of history up to and beyond the turn of the eras. This mechanistic view of history is expressed in a good number of texts. One clear example is 22:14, the logion which concludes the parable of the man without the wedding garment, 'For many are called, but few are chosen (or elected; ἐκλεκτός)'. This saying bears a striking resemblance to 4 Ezra 8:3, 'Many have been created, but few will be saved'. Underlying both texts is a strictly deterministic world view; God has deemed in advance that only a minority of people will be saved at the eschaton.

It was noted in chapter 1 that many of the apocalypses used the historical review to reinforce their convictions concerning the determined nature of history. This device was made possible by the pseudonymous aspect of the genre which placed the prophecies on the lips of an authoritative figure of the ancient past. The Qumran community, on the other hand, expressed its determinism in a different way. Since it did not compose an apocalypse and thus could not make use of the historical review, it used the *pesher* method of interpretation to show that the Old Testament prophecies were now meeting their fulfilment in the life of the Qumran community. This scheme of prophecy and fulfilment also presumes that the events of history are determined in advance. When we turn to the gospel of Matthew, we find a similar scheme to that which operated at Qumran. This is only to be expected. Matthew composed a gospel whose narrative was set a mere fifty years earlier than his own time, so he too could not avail himself of the full benefits of the historical review which the apocalyptic genre afforded. But he compensates for this by emphasising that the words of the prophets found their fulfilment in the life and mission of Jesus.

As is well known, the fulfilment of prophecy by Jesus played an important role in early Christianity. We know from 1 Corinthians 15:3–7 that from the earliest times Christians had seen in the death and resurrection of Jesus the fulfilment of past prophecies. As time progressed similar claims were made for other aspects of Jesus' life, and the fulfilment of scripture plays its part in both Mark and Q (see below) and in the gospel of John (cf. John 12:38; 13:18; 15:25; 17:12; 18:9, 32; 19:24, 28, 36, 37). It is equally well known that no New Testament author is more interested in this particular subject than the writer of Matthew. He specifies time and again that the prophecies of the Old Testament were fulfilled in the life of Jesus and incidents related to it. Some of this material derives from Matthew's major sources. Thus the appearance of John the Baptist as the prophesied forerunner of Jesus is found in both Mark and Q and adopted by Matthew (Matt. 3:3//Mark 1:3; Matt. 11:10//Luke 7:27). Mark provides a further three instances of prophetic fulfilment which Matthew incorporates into his gospel. In Matthew 15:7–9 (//Mark 7:6b–7), Jesus suggests that the unbelieving scribes and Pharisees fulfil the prophecy of Isaiah 29:13, while Matthew 21:42 (//Mark 12:10–11) claims that the rejection but ultimate vindication of Jesus fulfils Psalm 118:22–3. According to Matthew 26:56 (//Mark 14:49), Jesus claims that his arrest must take place to fulfil the scriptures, though neither evangelist cites the Old Testament text in question. This tradition clearly impressed Matthew for he inserts a further reference to this particular fulfilment of prophecy (26:54).

Matthew's keen interest in this theme is not restricted to those cases where he followed his sources. It is further evidenced in the ten so-called 'formula quotations' which are unique to his gospel

(1:22–3; 2:15; 2:17–18; 2:23; 4:14–16; 8:17; 12:17–21; 13:35; 21:4–5; 27:9–10). These citations of scripture are all introduced by a set 'formula', ἵνα πληρωθῇ τὸ ῥηθὲν διὰ τοῦ προφήτου λέγοντος (with minor variations), and applied to a given event in the life of Jesus (or an event related to it). Scholars agree that the evangelist himself was responsible for all instances of this formula. By adding this material, Matthew spells out for his readers that certain happenings in the time of Jesus which he found in his sources were all prophesied by the Old Testament prophets. Most of these fulfilments of prophecy concern Jesus directly – his virginal conception (1:22–3), his return from Egypt (2:15), his exorcisms (8:17) and so on – but the slaughter of the innocents (2:17–18) and the purchase of the potter's field with the 'blood money' of Judas (27:9–10) are two exceptions to this rule. No doubt Matthew's major purpose in highlighting the fulfilment of prophecy on these occasions was to validate the status of Jesus as messiah and son of God, but underlying this validation is the prior conviction that history as a totality is foreordained and unchangeable. Not even powerful historical figures like Herod the Great can alter the set course of history. Despite his best efforts to do so, Herod only succeeds in fulfilling another ancient prophecy (2:1–18) and so becomes a pawn in a process which God has fixed and which no human can change.

At this point it is appropriate to draw some comparisons between Matthew's employment of the formula quotations and the *pesher* technique at Qumran. There is a clear distinction in the application of each scheme of prophecy and fulfilment which can be attributed to the different genres involved. The *pesher* method adopted at Qumran involves an exegesis of a continuous prophetic text, while the evangelist composes a narrative and inserts at certain points in the story that the Old Testament prophecies have been fulfilled in the life of Jesus.[23] But these differences in the application of the Old Testament prophecies should not blind us to the complete agreement between them that God has fixed the course of history and revealed it to certain favoured individuals. The importance of this agreement between Matthew and the Qumran community should not be overlooked. In each case we have authors who embraced apocalyptic eschatology but did not compose an apocalypse. Yet both compensated for the lack of availability of the

---

[23] Stanton, *Gospel for a New People*, p. 350.

historical review by focusing on the fulfilment of the Old Testament prophecies to express their beliefs in the determined nature of history.

While the fulfilment of the Old Testament prophecies in the life of Jesus is an important Matthean theme, it comprises just one aspect of the evangelist's deterministic convictions. Matthew also emphasises that Jesus possesses knowledge of the future, and this theme is perhaps of even greater importance. The evangelist follows his sources in providing for his readers concrete examples of Jesus accurately prophesying the future. He predicts his own suffering, death and resurrection (16:21; 17:22–3; 20:18–19//Mark 8:31; 9:31; 10:33–4), his betrayal by Judas (26:21–5//Mark 14:18–21), the denials by Peter (26:34//Mark 14:30) and the destruction of Jerusalem (22:7) and its temple (24:2//Mark 13:2). Needless to say, Matthew makes clear in the course of his narrative that all these prophecies came to pass as predicted. Once again the fulfilment of these prophecies, while affirming the special status of Jesus and his relationship with God (cf. 11:25–7), presumes the mechanistic nature of the historical processes. The corollary to Matthew's deterministic view of history, and his depiction of Jesus' being privy to the course of future events, is that one can have implicit faith in the prophecies of Jesus which have not yet been fulfilled. One can be totally confident that those predictions of Jesus concerning the eschaton will just as surely meet with fulfilment as those prophecies which have already come to pass. This is an important point. As we shall see in subsequent chapters, the end-time prophecies of the Matthean Jesus are in reality the eschatological speculations of the evangelist himself. Hence, it is fair to say that one purpose of Matthew's deterministic scheme is to lend credence to his own end-time speculations. In this sense, there is not so great a difference between Matthew's use of determinism and that which we find in the historical review of the apocalyptic genre. Both the evangelist and the apocalyptist place a number of prophecies on the lips of a past authoritative figure whose future predictions (from the standpoint of the reader) must be treated with the same respect as those which have already met with fulfilment. By doing so, they lend an authority to their own vision of the future which it otherwise might not have. Consequently, Matthew's deterministic view of history provides the context in which his eschatological material is to be read. His readers are to believe that the future will unfold precisely as Jesus predicted.

While Matthew has a wholly deterministic view of the broad sweep of history, his position on the individual level is far less strict and upholds the concept of free will and the correlative idea of human responsibility for sin. As noted in chapter 1, this apparent inconsistency between historical determinism and individual free will is found in many of the apocalyptic-eschatological schemes of his day. Just as those schemes emphasise the possibility of repentance in order to join or remain within the elect community, so too does Matthew. In 18:15–17 the evangelist stresses that sinful community members should be given a number of chances to repent of their wrongdoings. Moreover, his many exhortations to moral behaviour, which will concern us in chapter 9, only make sense on the presumption that his readers enjoy free will in making moral decisions. This theme of free choice and repentance is also prominent in Matthew's story. John the Baptist urges his listeners to repent (3:2), to bear fruit befitting repentance (3:8) and offers baptism as a means of repentance (3:11). In similar vein, Jesus opens his ministry with the call to repentance (4:17) and criticises those cities which did not repent after witnessing his mighty works (11:20–4). These texts suffice to demonstrate that on the individual level Matthew accepted the notion of free will and human responsibility for individual action. The Jewish maxim that all is foreseen but freedom of choice is given applied just as much to this Jewish author as it did to other Jewish authors of the time.

3. Conclusions

In this chapter we have analysed the gospel of Matthew in terms of the two components which provide the framework for the end-time speculations in apocalyptic eschatology. It was found that the gospel adopts a completely dualistic perspective. The supernatural world is divided into two opposing groups, the heavenly angels led by Jesus Son of Man and the fallen angels who are commanded by Satan. Matthew is just as clear that the human world is similarly divided and that there are only two ways of human existence. Each group within the human sphere is directly associated with its supernatural counterpart; the righteous have their origin in Jesus, while the wicked are aligned with Satan. For Matthew there is no neutrality in this cosmic battle for supremacy. One stands in one camp or the other and there is no middle ground. In terms of the second theme, it was argued that the gospel of Matthew is strongly deterministic with regard to the course of history. The fulfilment of the Old Testament prophecies in the life of Jesus and the fulfilment of Jesus' own prophecies presuppose the notion that God has set the historical processes in motion and that they cannot be changed. This notion of absolute determinism provides the context for the gospel's eschatological material; the future will unfold as predicted just as surely as the past had done. On the individual level, the evangelist adopted a softer line and emphasised the concept of free will and human responsibility for sin.

4

ESCHATOLOGICAL WOES AND THE COMING OF THE SON OF MAN IN MATTHEW

Having examined in the previous chapter the two conceptual elements which provide the framework for Matthew's scheme of apocalyptic eschatology, we are now in a position to begin our study of Matthew's eschatological material. As noted in the previous chapter, Matthew upholds the notion of the two ages (cf. 12:32); the present age will come to an end and be replaced by a new era. This chapter will be concerned with the initial phase of his eschatological scheme, his description of the end-time woes and the arrival of Jesus the Son of Man as a saviour figure at the end of the age. While Matthew has taken from Mark and Q the specific idea that Jesus would return as Son of Man, the notion that Jesus would return in glory at the end of the present era was universal within early Christianity and is either affirmed or presumed right throughout the New Testament. While the origins of the notion of 'the second coming' are not absolutely clear, this doctrine presupposes the fundamental Christian conviction that Jesus had been resurrected from the dead and now resided in heaven. But as much as Matthew shared in common with other Christians the belief in the return of Jesus, it will become clear that the evangelist had his own thoughts concerning the significance of this event.

In the course of his narrative, Matthew often refers to the coming of the Son of Man without mentioning the events which precede it. Only in the apocalyptic discourse, specifically in 24:4–31, does Matthew treat together the signs of the end and the arrival of the Son of Man whose arrival they herald. Consequently, this section of the gospel assumes great importance for our reconstruction of the evangelist's particular apocalyptic-eschatological scheme. Our discussion in the present chapter will examine first Matthew's identification of Jesus with this Son of Man who signals the turning of the ages, and then move on to Matthew's allusions to and general descriptions of this event. Next we shall turn to the important section of the apocalyptic discourse which sets the arrival of the Son of Man within the evangelist's scheme of eschatological woes and signs of the end.

1. Jesus as the Son of Man

The figure whom Matthew expected at the end of the age is consistently called the Son of Man, but the evangelist makes it clear to his readers that this figure is none other than Jesus himself. The identification of the end-time Son of Man and Jesus is pointedly made in those Marcan and Q texts in which Jesus at the time of his ministry refers to himself as the Son of Man. Matthew adopts from Mark the view that Jesus was both the authoritative Son of Man (Matt. 9:6//Mark 2:10; Matt. 12:8//Mark 2:28) and the suffering/ resurrected Son of Man (Matt. 17:9//Mark 9:9; Matt. 17:22//Mark 9:31; Matt. 20:18//Mark 10:33; Matt. 20:28//Mark 10:45; Matt. 26:24//Mark 14:21; Matt. 26:45//Mark 14:31). From Q the evangelist took over a number of traditions which speak of the rejection (not suffering) of the Son of Man during his mission (Matt. 8:20// Luke 9:58; Matt. 11:19//Luke 7:34; Matt. 12:32//Luke 12:10). Matthew's adoption of this material serves many christological and theological purposes, but one of these is to identify the coming Son of Man with the rejected but vindicated Jesus of Nazareth.[1] Further identification of the two is made in the apocalyptic discourse. At the very beginning of this speech, Matthew rewrites the Marcan version of the disciples' question so that they now ask about the coming of Jesus and the end of the age, 'Tell us ... what will be the sign of your coming (τὸ σημεῖον τῆς σῆς παρουσίας) and of the close of the age' (Matt. 24:3 and Mark 13:4). Since Jesus then relates the end events in terms of the arrival of the Son of Man, the reader is meant to infer that it is Jesus himself who returns as Son of Man and that the disciples knew this when they posed the question to Jesus.

The bridge between the past and future phases of Jesus' activity as Son of Man is provided by Matt. 26:64. This text emphasises his present exalted status as Son of Man in the interim between his resurrection and his return in glory. Here Matthew drew from Mark 14:62 the statement of Jesus at his trial that his interrogators will see the Son of Man seated at the right hand of power (i.e. God)

---

[1]   A similar point is made by Marguerat, *Le Jugement*, pp. 69–71.

and coming with the clouds of heaven (26:64). This Marcan tradition is a combination of Psalm 110:1 and Daniel 7:13. The second of these texts requires further comment. Daniel 7:13–14 describes one like a son of man who travels on the clouds of heaven towards the heavens in order to accept his kingdom. It is not clear whether the figure in this text represents an individual, the messiah for example, or whether, as is more probable, he symbolises the people of Israel as a whole. No matter which exegesis is more appropriate, it is clear that by the time of Mark this text had undergone substantial reinterpretation by virtue of its association with Psalm 110:1. In Mark 14:62, the Son of Man no longer travels on the clouds towards heaven in order to be glorified and to claim his kingdom. Rather, he is already exalted and sits at the right hand of God (Ps. 110:1), and his journey with the clouds is not towards heaven but away from heaven towards the earth at the eschaton (cf. Mark 13:26). Thus, in distinction to Daniel 7:13, this Marcan text deals with two separate events, the enthronement or exaltation of the Son of Man after his resurrection and his return on the clouds of heaven. The enthronement itself is not described, but it is clearly presumed; for the Son of Man to leave the right hand of God at his parousia, he must have been exalted to that position previously.[2] Be that as it may, in Mark the emphasis falls upon the return of the Son of Man at the end of the age. His very public return will be witnessed by those who tried him.

Matthew accepts this basic idea and intensifies it. In a minor redactional change, he conforms the Marcan text more closely to the LXX version of Daniel by altering the Marcan 'with' (μετά) the clouds of heaven to 'upon' (ἐπί) the clouds of heaven. More significantly, Matthew inserts the words 'from now on' (ἀπ' ἄρτι) just prior to the prophecy of Jesus which predicts that the Jewish leaders will see the Son of Man. The addition of these words has the effect of bringing forward the time of their seeing the Son of Man; they will not see him just at the parousia (so Mark) but 'from now on'. In the context of the gospel narrative ἀπ' ἄρτι does not refer to the time of speaking but is a clear reference to the resurrection and its aftermath. By redacting in this manner, Matthew makes the point that immediately (or perhaps almost immediately in view of 28:16–20) after his resurrection Jesus will be

---

[2] So correctly Lindars, *Son of Man*, p. 110 and Hooker, *Son of Man*, pp. 166–7, pace Tödt, *Son of Man*, pp. 39–40 who argues that the text does not speak of Jesus' exaltation prior to the parousia.

seated at the right hand of God.[3] As noted above, such a notion is implied in the Marcan text but Matthew spells it out just to be sure. On his view, the risen Jesus who has been given all authority (28:18) is now seated at God's right hand. As the second half of this verse explains, it is this very figure who will return at the eschaton on the clouds of heaven.

2. General references to the arrival of the Son of Man

Excluding Matthew 24:30-1 which will concern us below, Matthew refers to the future coming of the Son of Man on a further seven occasions (10:23; 13:41; 16:27-8; 24:27, 37, 39, 44). These logia do little more than refer to this event in a very general way. In none of them is there a concrete description of his arrival, nor is there any attempt to relate the coming of the Son of Man to other eschatological events. The unparalleled 10:23 merely specifies that the missionaries whom Jesus sends out will not have gone through the towns of Israel before the Son of Man's arrival. This tradition has more to do with Matthew's general timing of the event than with anything else, and we shall examine it in more detail in chapter 7 below. The text of 13:41 mentions that at the close of the age the Son of Man will send his angels to gather from his kingdom all the evildoers. Four further general references to the coming of the Son of Man appear in the Matthean apocalyptic discourse. All four traditions derive from Q. In 24:44 (//Luke 12:40) Matthew presents a pericope which affirms only that the hour of the arrival of the Son of Man will be totally unexpected. The remaining three texts are perhaps of more interest. Two of these are found in the comparison between the coming of the Son of Man and the flood of Noah (Matt. 24:37-9) which begins and concludes with a reference to the Son of Man. The Lucan version of this tradition expands the comparison to include the destruction of Sodom, an element which might not have stood in Matthew's recension of the sayings source (Luke 17:26-30).[4] The point of this tradition in both versions is the

---

[3]   So Lindars, *Son of Man*, p. 121; Hooker, *Son of Man*, p. 167; Gundry, *Matthew*, p. 545; Hill, *Matthew*, p. 347 and Senior, *Passion Narrative*, pp. 178-83.

[4]   It is probable that had this material stood in Matthew's recension of Q, the evangelist would have adopted it. The reference to the destruction of Sodom by fire and sulphur would have appealed to Matthew since he views the eschatological fate of the wicked in similar terms. That the extra reference to Lot and Sodom was added by Luke himself or was already present in his version of Q is accepted by Schulz, *Q*, pp. 279-80; Gnilka, *Matthäusevangelium*, II, p. 234 n. 4;

same as in Matthew 24:44//Luke 12:40; the arrival of the Son of Man will be totally unexpected. Just as the victims of the flood (and the citizens of Sodom) were caught unawares in the course of their daily activities, so too will be the present generation when the Son of Man arrives. In the final text, 24:27 (//Luke 17:24), the emphasis is not on the unexpectedness of the arrival of the Son of Man, but on its very public nature. His appearance will be as a lightning flash which lights up all the sky.

In the last three sayings (24:27, 37, 39), Matthew uses a set expression in reference to the arrival of the Son of Man, οὕτως ἔσται ἡ παρουσία τοῦ υἱοῦ τοῦ ἀνθρώπου. The Lucan parallels offer a number of alternative expressions and there is no doubt that Matthew is responsible for the fixed form in his three sayings. As noted earlier, he inserted the reference to the coming (παρουσία) of Jesus in 24:3 (cf. Mark 13:4) and has done likewise to his Q material at these points.[5] This technical term for the return of Jesus at the eschaton is found only in Matthew of the gospels, but it has a very clear Christian background. It appears in this sense in the Pauline letters (1 Cor. 15:23; 1 Thess. 2:19; 3:13; 4:15; 5:23) and in other New Testament texts (Jas. 5:7–8; 2 Pet. 1:16; 3:4; 1 John 2:28). What makes this reference different in Matthew is that it now applies to the coming of Jesus *the Son of Man*. The significance of this point will become clear in due course.

The final text which mentions the arrival of the Son of Man, Matthew 16:27–8, is important in so far as it specifies the role of the Son of Man upon his return. This logion is an edited version of Mark 8:38–9:1. In Mark 8:38 Jesus affirms that whoever is ashamed of him (and his words) in his generation, the Son of Man will in turn be ashamed of him when he comes in the glory of his father with the holy angels. The arrival of the Son of Man here is depicted in different terms from Mark 14:62. There is no mention of the clouds (of heaven) as the vehicle of transport, and the angels are said to accompany Jesus at the time of his return. Matthew basically takes over this description (16:27a), though he changes the Marcan 'holy angels' to his favoured 'his angels'. Where Matthew does not follow the Marcan text in this pericope is the section which deals with the function of the Son of Man upon his return.

Schweizer, *Matthew*, pp. 459–60 and Lührmann, *Redaktion*, pp. 75–83. For the alternative view that Matthew omitted this material on the grounds of redundancy, see Gundry, *Matthew*, p. 493.

[5] See Tödt, *Son of Man*, pp. 87–8 and Schenk, *Sprache*, p. 18.

In Mark this figure is said only to be ashamed of those who were ashamed of him and there is no indication that he acts as the judge. In fact there is no Marcan text which depicts the returning Son of Man in this capacity. His role in 8:38 is more along the lines of an advocate at the eschatological tribunal over which God presumably presides.[6] This tradition finds a parallel in the Q material of Matthew 10:32–3//Luke 12:8–9, and a few words about this passage are appropriate here. According to the Lucan version, the Son of Man is said to acknowledge or deny individuals before the angels of God in return for their acknowledgement or denial of Jesus before men. The scenario is patently eschatological and the Son of Man clearly acts as an advocate at the court of judgement in which the holy angels play a leading part.[7] It is generally accepted that this Lucan tradition reflects the Q archetype and that Matthew has edited it in two significant ways.[8] First, he omits the Son of Man reference and replaces it with the first person pronoun. This does not change the sense of the passage, since for Matthew Jesus is the Son of Man anyway. But it does have the effect of avoiding the combination of Son of Man and the concept of eschatological advocacy. For Matthew, as we shall see in the next chapter, the Son of Man is the judge at the final court and not merely an advocate. Secondly, Matthew replaces 'before the angels of God' with 'before my heavenly father'. His motivation here is obviously to maintain the status of Jesus within the divine hierarchy. In Matthew's view the angels belong to the Son of Man and are consequently lower down the rung of authority. It would hardly be appropriate for the Son of Man to plead a case before them!

Just as Matthew subjects this Q material to redaction, so too at 16:27 does he extensively edit Mark 8:38a. He omits all the material pertaining to reciprocal shame because he had used the Q parallel

---

6   Some scholars deny this and have no hesitation in stating that Mark 8:38 portrays Jesus as the judge. So Hooker, *Son of Man*, p. 119. On the other hand, Lindars, *Son of Man*, pp. 50–1 and Higgins, *The Son of Man in the Teaching of Jesus*, p. 82 argue that both functions are in view in this text; the Son of Man will act as prosecutor and judge. Since neither view has any real support in the verse itself, or the remainder of Mark for that matter, it is permissible to question whether this Marcan text has been read on its own terms or whether it has been interpreted on the basis of other New Testament texts which depict Jesus as the judge.

7   So most scholars; Tödt, *Son of Man,* pp. 44, 56; Lindars, *Son of Man*, p. 50 and Higgins, *Jesus and the Son of Man*, p. 59.

8   On Matthew's redaction of this tradition, see Tödt, *Son of Man*, pp. 89–90; Schulz, *Q*, pp. 68–9 and Gundry, *Matthew*, pp. 198–9.

earlier in his narrative, but of far more importance is his redaction in the second half of the verse. Here, and in distinction to the Marcan text, the evangelist spells out precisely the function of the Son of Man at his parousia; he returns to repay (ἀποδίδωμι) every one for what they have done. In other words the Son of Man returns as the judge who will bestow rewards or punishments according to an individual's deeds.[9] By this addition in 16:27 Matthew clarifies the judicial function of the Son of Man. In Matthew he is no mere advocate (despite the implications of 10:32–3!); he is the judge. In the next verse, Matthew 16:28//Mark 9:1, Matthew effects further changes on his source. Where the Marcan Jesus pronounces that some standing here will not taste death before they see the kingdom of God come with power, the Matthean version has Jesus state that they will not taste death before they see the Son of Man coming in his kingdom (cf. 13:41; 20:21). With this editorial change Matthew keeps the focus firmly on the figure of the Son of Man. He comes in *his* kingdom, not the kingdom of God, and his arrival signals the eschaton and the judgement.

3. Matthew's eschatological scenario

The seven texts discussed above and Matthew 26:64 all refer to the arrival of the Son of Man at the end of the age, but none of them puts this event into any historical or chronological framework. They are completely silent about the eschatological events which must precede the return of Jesus as judgemental Son of Man. For this information we need to examine the initial section of the apocalyptic discourse. In 24:4–31 Matthew details not merely the arrival of the Son of Man, but the events which precede and herald this event. This section of the gospel is equivalent to the eschatological woes and signs of the end which are normally a part of Jewish apocalyptic-eschatological schemes and which provide information on the timing of the end. Matthew's particular scheme is based upon the scheme in Mark 13, though the evangelist has edited this material to conform it to his own interests and concerns, and it predicts a breakdown of both the social order and the natural order prior to the coming of the Son of Man.

In 24:4–14, which is a heavily edited version of Mark 13:3–8, 13,

---

[9]   Marguerat, *Le Jugement*, p. 93.

the Matthean Jesus sets out a timetable of the end. The events which must happen prior to the arrival of the Son of Man are stock Jewish apocalyptic-eschatological woes with a distinctively Christian flavour – the coming of false Christs, wars among nations, famines and earthquakes, the universal rejection of the righteous, constant betrayal, the appearance of false prophets and the increase of lawlessness. This material is of crucial importance in determining Matthew's timing of the end. We shall therefore examine this section in greater detail in chapter 7 when we turn to the evangelist's temporal end expectations. Of more interest in the present context is Matthew 24:15–28, the following section of the discourse which specifically relates to the final events in Judea. This is an extremely important component of Matthew's overall concept of the last events and its significance is not sufficiently appreciated. Yet this material refers to nothing less than the full-scale attack upon the righteous by the forces of evil as the final event of history. It describes therefore the beginning of the final war between the righteous and the wicked which is also a prominent theme in both Revelation and the Qumran scrolls.

The best place to begin the discussion of this theme is not with the apocalyptic discourse but with Matthew 16:18. In this redactional verse, the Matthean Jesus blesses Peter and proclaims him to be the rock upon which his church (ἐκκλησία) will be built. Jesus then tells Peter that not even the gates of Hades (πύλαι ᾅδου) will be able to prevail against it. There have been many suggested interpretations of 'the gates of Hades', some more probable than others. In their recent commentary, W. D. Davies and D. C. Allison identified and assessed no less than twelve interpretations of this term. At the end of their detailed analysis, they found themselves in agreement with the proposal of J. Jeremias that the 'gates of Hades' refers to the final attack upon the righteous by the powers of evil who will gather in and advance from the underworld. They argue that Matthew is representing a tradition which has close affinities with the material in Revelation (6:8; 9:1–11; 11:7; 20:7–8) and 1QH 6:22–9 from Qumran.[10] Although the evidence they adduce is convincing enough, it can be strengthened. It will be shown below that Matthew depicts the arrival of Jesus the Son of

---

[10] Davies and Allison, *Matthew*, II, pp. 630–44 and Jeremias, 'πύλη', pp. 924–8. Oddly enough, Davies and Allison do not mention the very text which provides the most information on the Qumran community's beliefs about this final conflict, the War scroll.

Man in military terms; he arrives at the end of the age with his angelic army and military paraphernalia. Such a militaristic representation of his arrival only makes sense if the evangelist envisaged that a full-scale (but one-sided) war was being fought on earth at the time of the parousia and that the Son of Man and his forces were to enter the conflict. We should expect that this eschatological battle between the righteous and the demonic powers to which 16:18 refers would receive some mention in Matthew's apocalyptic discourse, and this is indeed the case. The section in question is 24:15–28 which is dependent upon Mark 13:14–21. Let us examine briefly this Marcan pericope.

Mark 13:14 advises the gospel readers that when they see the abomination of desolation (τὸ βδέλυγμα τῆς ἐρημώσεως) set up where it ought not to be, then those in Judea should flee to the mountains. The meaning of this reference for Mark is disputed and to some extent is dependent upon one's dating of this gospel. Some scholars argue that the abomination of desolation is meant to refer to the temple's destruction which the Marcan Jesus had earlier prophesied in 13:2.[11] On this view, this verse thus demonstrates that Mark wrote either in the year 70 or shortly after it. Other scholars, however, interpret the phrase quite differently. They maintain that the evangelist's ungrammatical use of the masculine participle ἑστηκότα relating to the neuter βδέλυγμα suggests that Mark identified the abomination with a specific individual rather than with an event. It is argued that Mark identified this person with the antichrist,[12] the eschatological adversary of Christ who receives explicit mention in 1 John 1:18, 22; 4:3, but who is clearly depicted elsewhere in the New Testament. He figures as the beast who serves Satan in Revelation and is there explicitly linked with the myth of the returning Nero. A different account of the antichrist is reflected in the second epistle to the Thessalonians. This pseudo-Pauline letter speaks of 'the man of lawlessness, the son of perdition' (2:3) who works in the service of Satan (2:9) and who will take his seat in the temple proclaiming himself to be God (2:4). On this alternative reading of Mark 13:14 where the abomination represents the antichrist, the gospel can be dated prior to the destruction of the temple, in

[11] See, for example, Pesch, *Markusevangelium*, II, pp. 291–2 and, more tentatively, Geddert, *Watchwords*, pp. 206–7.

[12] So Streeter, *Four Gospels*, pp. 492–3; Marxsen, *Mark the Evangelist*, pp. 180–2 and Gaston, *No Stone on Another*, pp. 27–8.

which case the prophecy of its demise in verse 2 was unfulfilled at the time of writing.

For our purposes, it matters little which of these views applies to Mark, but the second of them is perhaps the more probable. Our interest lies with the meaning of the abomination of desolation at the Matthean stage of the tradition. How did Matthew understand this phrase? There is strong scholarly support for the view that Matthew, despite the fact that he used the more grammatically correct neuter participle (ἑστός) in reference to the abomination, identified the abomination with the antichrist.[13] In support of this interpretation is his alteration of the unclear Marcan statement of the location of the abomination. Where Mark writes that the abomination will stand 'where it ought not to be', Matthew significantly omits this clause and replaces it with 'in the holy place'. This is an almost certain reference to the Jerusalem temple or, more accurately in the time of Matthew, a reference to the temple ruins. The evangelist uses 'the holy city' of Jerusalem (4:5; 27:53) and the holy place would naturally be its temple. Matthew's association of the abomination with the temple thus agrees closely with the portrayal of the antichrist in 2 Thessalonians. We may infer from this that Matthew knew of this particular antichrist tradition and so identified the abomination with this evil eschatological figure. Whether or not the evangelist went further and identified the antichrist with Nero, as does the author of Revelation, is not clear from the extant evidence.[14]

In any event, the appearance of the antichrist in Jerusalem poses such a threat to the righteous in Judea that they must flee at once (24:16–20//Mark 13:14b-18). This advice is far different from that of the Qumran War scroll where the sons of light are

---

[13] So Gnilka, *Matthäusevangelium*, II, pp. 322–3; Gundry, *Matthew*, p. 482; Beare, *Matthew*, p. 468 and Hill, *Matthew*, p. 321. Other interpretations of this motif will be considered in chapter 7.

[14] Streeter, *Four Gospels*, pp. 516–20, 523 argues that Matthew did have in mind Nero as the antichrist, but his evidence is not convincing. On the basis of a sole Syriac manuscript, he takes 'in the holy place' to be a later explanatory gloss and not as an original part of the gospel text. In this case the location of the antichrist is not tied to the temple precincts but is left open. Since Streeter argues that the gospel was written in Antioch on the Orontes, where the *Nero redivivus* myth was prominent, he maintains that it is probable that the evangelist incorporated this myth into his antichrist tradition. The major problem with this interpretation, of course, is that the single variant manuscript to which Streeter appeals cannot carry the weight he places upon it.

encouraged to engage the forces of evil and much of the document is devoted to the preparations for this battle. The arrival of the antichrist will occasion tribulation which has no parallel in the history of the world (24:21//Mark 13:19). Significantly, Matthew qualifies the Marcan θλῖψις with μεγάλη and so intensifies the nature of this tribulation. This redaction fits in well with the notion of a full-scale assault by the forces of evil against the righteous as depicted in 16:18. The coming of the antichrist will witness the ascension of the demonic powers from the underworld. The righteous have no option but to flee and to await the arrival of the Son of Man. False Christs and false prophets will attempt to lead them astray by suggesting that he has arrived in the wilderness or the inner rooms (24:23–6), but Matthew stresses that the arrival of the Son of Man will be unmistakably public and perceivable by all. It will be as a flash of lightning which lights up the whole sky (24:27).

The final verse of this section of the apocalyptic discourse (24:28) is notoriously difficult to interpret. Matthew uses a Q tradition which is found in similar wording in Luke 17:37b and which reads, 'Wherever the corpse (πτῶμα) is, there the eagles (ἀετοί) will be gathered together.' This logion is usually interpreted along the lines of the preceding verse; just as the gathering of eagles (or vultures) signifies the presence of a corpse, so will the return of the Son of Man be obvious to all. While this exegesis suits the immediate context and is certainly plausible, the wider context of the final eschatological war (24:15–28) suggests a rather different interpretation in terms of Matthew's understanding. The eagle was the symbol on the Roman banner and was for this reason used in some apocalyptic-eschatological circles to symbolise the Roman Empire (cf. 4 Ezra chs 11–12). It is conceivable that Matthew read this Q reference to the eagles in a similar way, and so interpreted the gathering of the eagles as a reference to the Roman army. The allusion to the corpse (cf. 'body' in Luke) would then naturally refer to the antichrist whose presence signals death and destruction and not to the temple ruins as some scholars have suggested.[15] If this understanding of the text is appropriate for Matthew, then it is clear that he envisages in the last days an unholy alliance between the Romans and the antichrist and his supernatural forces of evil. This idea of a coalition between the demonic and human powers at

[15] Brown, 'The Matthean Apocalypse', p. 12.

the very end of the age also features prominently in Revelation and the Qumran scrolls.

The proposed interpretation of Matthew 24:15–28 in terms of the eschatological conflict is considerably strengthened by the material which immediately follows this section. Matthew follows Mark in affirming that immediately after the tribulation occasioned by the appearance of the antichrist a series of cosmic signs will occur; the sun will be darkened, the moon will fail to give light, the stars will fall from heaven and the powers of the heavens will be shaken (Matt. 24:29//Mark 13:24–5). All these cosmic signs stand firmly within the Jewish apocalyptic-eschatological tradition and signify the beginning of the breakdown of the existing cosmic order. They act as the prelude to the arrival of the Son of Man. Where the Marcan text recounts the arrival of the Son of Man and the angels immediately following the cosmic signs in 13:24–5, Matthew decides not to follow his source at this point. He inserts two further events which will accompany the appearance of this saviour figure. After the powers of the heavens have been shaken, the sign (σημεῖον) of the Son of Man will appear in heaven (24:30a) and the tribes of the earth will mourn (24:30b). Both these Matthean additions are crucial and require further discussion.

The exact meaning of the sign of the Son of Man which will appear in heaven is disputed. One popular view is that this sign refers merely to the appearance of the Son of Man; his visible arrival is the sign of the Son of Man.[16] This interpretation, however, seems to be ruled out by the fact that the sign of the Son of Man precedes his actual appearance. Another view is that Matthew had in mind here another cosmic phenomenon such as a comet or a star,[17] but this is no more than a guess. The most probable explanation is that the sign of the Son of Man is a military standard or ensign which heralds the arrival of the Son of Man and his angelic host.[18] We know from Matthew's redaction in 26:53, where the Matthean Jesus refers to twelve legions of angels, that

---

[16] So Gundry, *Matthew,* p. 488; Tödt, *Son of Man,* p. 80; Lindars, *Son of Man,* pp. 128–9 and Hare, *Son of Man,* pp. 172–3.

[17] Beare, *Matthew,* p. 471.

[18] So Glasson, 'Ensign of the Son of Man', pp. 299–300. Glasson's view is supported by Schweizer, *Matthew,* pp. 455–6; Hill, *Matthew,* p. 323 and tentatively Gnilka, *Matthäusevangelium,* II, pp. 329–30. A slight variation on Glasson's view is given by Higgins, who accepts that the sign of the Son of Man is his ensign but argues that it might have had the symbol of the cross emblazoned on it. See his *The Son of Man in the Teaching of Jesus,* p. 119. Earlier Higgins had accepted the patristic interpretation that the sign was itself the cross (not just a

the evangelist conceived of the heavenly host in military terms. That the sign in 24:30a represents a military standard is further suggested by Matthew's addition in the following verse of the reference to the trumpet call which acts as a signal to the angels to gather the elect (24:31). In Jewish eschatological thought the trumpet and the military ensign are often correlated. They play an important part in the prophetic tradition in reference to the day of the Lord when God will punish the enemies of Israel (e.g. Isa. 18:3; Jer. 6:1; 51:27) and appear together in the tenth benediction of the *Shemoneh Esreh*. Perhaps of more importance in terms of Matthew is the fact that the standard and the trumpet have an important role in the military battle depicted in the Qumran War scroll (1QM 2:15–4:17).

Matthew's dual insertion of the standard and trumpet motifs at this point therefore indicates his intention to portray the arrival of the Son of Man in terms of a military campaign. For Matthew, the return of Jesus and his angels will be like the arrival of a mighty, heavenly army. The Matthean Jesus had experienced partial success against Satan and his agents during his earthly mission (see chapter 3) and would return with his army of angels to complete the task. This representation of the arrival of the Son of Man makes little sense unless the evangelist believed that he would be opposed by an enemy military force, and this lends considerable strength to the interpretation of 24:15–28 as the first phase of the eschatological battle. The scenario envisaged in 24:30–1 is of a full-scale response to the all-out assault of the evil forces against the righteous and has clear parallels with the tradition in Revelation 19:11–19. According to this text, Jesus returns upon a white horse accompanied by the armies of heaven (τὰ στρατεύματα ἐν τῷ οὐρανῷ) and faces and defeats the assembled armies of the beast.

We may now turn to Matthew's second addition to the text of Mark, the reference to the mourning of the tribes of the earth. This text lends some support to our interpretation of Matthew 24:28 which argued that the human powers, the Romans, aligned themselves with the demonic forces led by the antichrist. With the arrival of the Son of Man, the human forces realise their mistake and mourn their fate because of their certain defeat. It is generally recognised that this text is an allusion to Zechariah 12:10. Another section of this prophetic text is cited in John 19:37, 'they shall look

symbol on a banner); *Jesus and the Son of Man*, pp. 108–14. While Higgins' later thesis is possible, it is incapable of demonstration.

upon him whom they have pierced', in reference to the spearing of Jesus on the cross. Both these elements appear in Revelation 1:7 which, interestingly enough, combines the allusion to Zechariah with a reference to Daniel 7:13, 'he is coming with the clouds of heaven, and every eye will see him, every one who pierced him, and all the tribes of the earth will wail on account of him'. Since Matthew follows his reference to Zechariah 12:10 with a description of the Son of Man which he took from Mark but which ultimately goes back to Daniel 7:13 (see further below), we have here yet another possible point of contact between the traditions which the author of Revelation used and the sources available to Matthew. Unlike Mark but like the seer, Matthew knew of a tradition which combined Zechariah 12:10 and Daniel 7:13 and consequently appended the text of Zechariah to the Marcan citation of Daniel. We should not, however, lose sight of the difference between Matthew 24:30b and Revelation 1:7. In the latter, and in Zechariah 12:10–14 for that matter, the mourning is initiated by regret as the tribes look upon the one who has been pierced. The author of Revelation thus uses this text to recall the crucifixion of Jesus. This seems not to be the meaning in Matthew since he fails to include the reference to piercing. We may infer from this that Matthew did not wish to focus on the past crucifixion of Jesus at this point; his immediate concern was the future arrival with power and great glory of Jesus the judgemental Son of Man.[19] That all the tribes of the earth are able to witness it confirms its universal visibility (cf. 24:27) and they mourn because of the ensuing judgement they will face as confederates of the antichrist (cf. 25:32, 41).

Having inserted these two motifs, thereby giving a military flavour to the return of Jesus the Son of Man, Matthew returns to the text of Mark in describing his actual arrival. Like Mark 14:62, the coming of the Son of Man in Mark 13:26 is depicted in terms which recall the one like a son of man in Daniel 7:13–14; he will be seen coming in (ἐν) clouds with great power (μετὰ δυνάμεως πολλῆς) and glory (δόξης). He will then send out the angels and gather his elect from the ends of the earth. Matthew 24:30c follows Mark 13:26 for the most part but contains a number of redactional changes as well. Matthew omits Mark's ἐν which refers to the

---

[19]   In agreement with Tödt, *Son of Man*, p. 81 and Burnett, *Jesus-Sophia*, p. 343, contra Higgins, *Jesus and the Son of Man*, pp. 112–13 who suggests that the sign of the Son of Man, the cross in his understanding, replaces the reference to piercing.

clouds and substitutes ἐπί in conformity to the Greek version of Daniel 7:13 (cf. the same in Matt. 26:64//Mark 14:62). For the same reason he qualifies the clouds with τοῦ οὐρανοῦ which also appears in the text of Daniel. A further redaction sees the transposition of πολλῆς from its position in Mark qualifying 'power' to where it now qualifies 'glory'. The reason behind this alteration is not clear, but it might be tied up with Matthew's perception of the Son of Man presiding over the judgement while sitting upon his throne of glory (cf. 19:28; 25:31).

More significant is Matthew's redaction in 24:31 (//Mark 13:27). He accepts the Marcan reference that the Son of Man will send out a group of angels, but specifies by inserting αὐτοῦ that the angels belong to the Son of Man. It was noted previously that the close relation between Jesus the Son of Man and the holy angels is a particular concern of the evangelist. Unlike Mark, where the Son of Man himself gathers his elect (the singular ἐπισυνάξει), in Matthew this task is performed by his angelic underlings (ἐπισυνά-ξουσιν). Another important addition Matthew makes to his source is that the angels are despatched with a loud trumpet call (μετὰ σάλπιγγος μεγάλης). The Pauline tradition also knows of a trumpet call signalling the return of Jesus (1 Thess. 4:16; 1 Cor. 15:52 cf. Rev. 11:15), but Matthew's association of the trumpet with the sign or standard of the Son of Man gives this motif an overt military sense which it does not have in these Pauline passages. For the remainder of the pericope, Matthew follows Mark in meaning if not in wording. The elect will be gathered from the four winds, from one end of heaven to the other (cf. 'the ends of the earth to the ends of heaven' in Mark).

Matthew 24:29–31 thus complements the earlier material in 24:15–28. Each section describes different aspects of the final eschatological war between the righteous and the powers of evil. The initial material refers to the great tribulation of the eschatological battle brought about by demonic agents of Satan (cf. 16:18) and perhaps their human allies from which the righteous are advised to flee. The later section points to the arrival of the Son of Man as the military commander of the angelic forces who arrives from heaven to engage the armies of the wicked and relieve the plight of the elect. That Matthew should have adopted this myth should occasion no surprise. His advanced concept of cosmic dualism, which he shares with Revelation and the Qumran scrolls, provides the foundation for such a view. The cosmos is currently engaged in a huge battle for supremacy which will intensify in the future to the advantage of the evil forces. Only the appearance of the Son of Man and his heavenly army can correct this situation and save the human righteous. Unlike Revelation and the Qumran War scroll, however, Matthew never describes the final conflict between the heavenly saviour figure and his evil opponents. Either his interest in this myth does not extend that far, or it might be the case that he expects an immediate surrender of the armies of the antichrist. In favour of this second possibility is 24:30b which describes the mourning of the tribes once they see the military ensign of the Son of Man. Whatever the case might have been, Matthew is more interested in depicting the victory of the Son of Man in terms of the final judgement. As we shall see in subsequent chapters, it is only at this point in Matthew's apocalyptic-eschatological scheme that the Son of Man's victory is complete.

4. Conclusions

To summarise the results of this chapter, it is clear that much of the primary phase of Matthew's eschatological scheme was drawn from his Christian sources. He upholds the universal Christian doctrine that Jesus would return at the end of the age, and he follows Mark and Q in describing Jesus in this role as Son of Man. Jesus was the Son of Man during his historical mission, is now the Son of Man at the right hand of God and will return in glory as the Son of Man. The coming or parousia of Jesus which is affirmed in many strands of the New Testament is specifically applied by Matthew to the arrival of the Son of Man. The evangelist's description of the arrival of this figure on the clouds of heaven with power and glory derives from his Marcan source and reflects an early Christian interpretation of Daniel 7:13–14.

Matthew often refers to the arrival of the Son of Man, but he only puts this notion into a meaningful framework in 24:4–31. Verses 4–14 spell out the eschatological woes which must occur prior to the arrival of the Son of Man, the breakdown of the social and natural orders, while verses 15–28 detail the appearance of the antichrist and the resultant eschatological conflict which this brings. While much of this scenario has been taken from Mark 13, Matthew intensifies it considerably. This intensification continues in the following verses which describe the arrival of the Son of Man as a military commander leading the armies of heaven. That Jesus would be accompanied by angels upon his return was a common notion in early Christianity, but only Matthew and Revelation depict them as heavenly soldiers and Jesus as their military leader. This myth of the final war which we find in different versions in Matthew and Revelation is likewise found in the Qumran War scroll where it receives its fullest expression. Much as we would expect, the Christian documents conform this battle scenario to their prior beliefs that Jesus would return in glory. Whereas the Qumran community expected the archangel Michael to lead the heavenly forces, this role now falls to the returning Jesus in Matthew and Revelation. In both these Christian texts and in distinction to other strands of the New Testament, it is emphasised that when Jesus returns he will do so *as a saviour figure who relieves the plight of the righteous in their darkest hour*. Like the author of the Apocalypse, the evangelist has conformed the Christian notion of the return of Jesus to an apocalyptic-eschatological perspective.

Unlike Mark and Q, which both describe Jesus as an advocate at the eschatological judgement, Matthew ascribes the role of judge to Jesus himself in his role as Son of Man. This is made clear in his redaction at 16:27 of Mark 8:38 and in other texts which we shall consider in the following chapter. This emphasis on Jesus the Son of Man as the overseer of the universal judgement perhaps explains why Matthew chose not to describe the battle between the forces of evil and the armies of heaven, if indeed he ever envisaged such a battle. Since Jesus comes primarily to judge, Matthew's eschatological chronology moves directly from the arrival of the Son of Man to the event of judgement. We shall proceed similarly in the following chapter.

5

THE JUDGEMENT IN MATTHEW

As many scholars have noted, the judgement by Jesus the Son of Man is one of the most important elements in Matthew's gospel. In this chapter, we shall examine Matthew's particular concept of Jesus the Son of Man as judge and how it relates to both Jewish and Christian apocalyptic-eschatological schemes. Prior to our consideration of this theme, it is necessary first to detail two eschatological events which, according to the evangelist's end-time chronology, must take place prior to the judgement. These events are the general resurrection of the dead and the recreation of the cosmos, both of which are common themes in apocalyptic eschatology.

1. The resurrection of the dead and the recreation of the cosmos prior to the judgement

The belief in the concept of resurrection, while very common in Judaism (see chapter 1), was almost axiomatic in early Christianity. The fundamental notion of the first Christians was that Jesus had been raised from the dead and that the end of the age would witness the general resurrection (cf. John 5:28–9; Rom. 6:5; 1 Cor. 15; 1 Thess. 4:13–18; Heb. 6:2; Rev. 20:4–6). Matthew is no exception to this general rule. He refers to the resurrection of Jesus (28:1–10) and even recounts a prior case of resurrection in rewriting the Marcan account of the death of Jesus (Mark 15:37–9). After Jesus yields his spirit in Matthew's version, a number of significant events take place. Matthew follows Mark in describing the tearing of the curtain of the temple (Matt. 27:51a//Mark 15:38), but he then writes freely by referring to an earthquake which is so violent that it opens many of the tombs of the saints and leads to their resurrection (27:51b-3).[1] This material is clearly dependent upon Ezekiel 37:12–13 and Zechariah 14:4–5 and perhaps even Daniel 12:2 as well.[2] Despite being raised, the bodies of the saints venture out of their tombs only after the resurrection of Jesus (27:53). Matthew here has obviously attempted to preserve the Christian tradition of the primacy of Jesus' resurrection (cf. Rom. 8:29; 1 Cor. 15:20; Col. 1:18; Rev. 1:5).

Matthew never concretely describes the general resurrection of the dead as the prelude to the universal judgement, but there is no doubt that he accepted the idea.[3] Two pericopae which Matthew took from his sources refer explicitly to this subject. First, in the Q passage at 12:41–2 (//Luke 11:31–2), the Matthean Jesus pronounces that the men of Nineveh and the queen of the south will rise at the judgement to condemn the wicked. The second text is 22:30 (//Mark 12:25) where Jesus announces that the righteous will be like angels in their resurrected state (ἐν τῇ ἀναστάσει). Both texts thus patently refer to the general resurrection of the dead without actually describing the event. That the evangelist and his readers took for granted this particular theme is evidenced by Matthew's omission of Mark 9:10 at the conclusion of the transfiguration narrative. According to the Marcan text, the disciples questioned or debated the meaning of Jesus' reference to the rising of the dead which occurs in the preceding verse. Matthew drops this tradition on account of its irrelevance for his readers; the concept of resurrection was clearly familiar to them.

Also to take place at some point between the arrival of Jesus the Son of Man and his execution of the judgement is the regeneration or recreation of the cosmos.[4] Matthew refers to the beginning of the collapse of the present cosmic order in 24:29 as one of the signs

---

[1] Most scholars accept that Matthew 27:51b-3 is pure Matthean redaction, though based upon wider Old Testament and apocalyptic-eschatological themes. This consensus, however, has been challenged by D. C. Allison who argues, quite unconvincingly in my opinion, that the evangelist has used a source which he redacted in only a minor way. See his *End of the Ages*, pp. 41–6.

[2] For the view that Ezekiel 37:12–13 alone underlies this material, see Senior, *Passion Narrative*, p. 320; Schweizer, *Matthew*, p. 515 and Hagner, 'Apocalyptic Motifs', p. 62. Other scholars correctly note the influence of Zechariah 14:4–5; so Allison, *End of the Ages*, pp. 43–4 and Gnilka, *Matthäusevangelium*, II, p. 477. Gundry, *Matthew*, pp. 576–7 argues that Daniel 12:2 is also referred to in this material.

[3] So correctly Milikowsky, 'Which Gehenna?', p. 248 n. 27.

[4] A much more detailed account of this issue can be found in Sim, 'The Meaning of παλιγγενεσία'.

preceding the arrival of the Son of Man. More importantly, in Matthew 19:28 the Matthean Jesus speaks of the new creation (παλιγγενεσία) in which the Son of Man will sit on his glorious throne and the disciples will judge the twelve tribes of Israel.[5] The Q parallel in Luke 22:28–30 uses an alternative expression, 'in my kingdom' (verse 30). There is some dissension over which evangelist is responsible for the redaction. Despite the fact that παλιγγενεσία is found just this once in Matthew's gospel, the majority of scholars accept that it is redactional in this single usage. It is usually argued that this expression serves to compensate for Matthew's omission of the Marcan 'the age to come' in the following verse (Matt. 19:29//Mark 10:30; cf. Matt. 12:32 for a similar expression).[6] Of greater importance than the issue of the redactional status of παλιγγενεσία is the question of its meaning in the context of the gospel.

The word παλιγγενεσία had a wide range of meanings in the time of Matthew.[7] It was used by the Stoics to describe the renewal of each age in the endless cosmic cycle. In the writings of Philo it denotes either the restoration of life or the renewal of the world after the great flood, while Josephus uses it to describe the reconstitution of the people after the Exile. The author of the Christian epistle of Titus employs the term in reference to rebirth after baptism (3:5). Matthew's usage in 19:28 is clearly eschatological and points to the recreation of the cosmic order after its prior destruction.[8] Unlike the Stoic idea where this renewal occurs time and again, the recreation of the cosmos in the gospel is a single end-time event. Not all scholars, however, agree with this interpretation of παλιγγενεσία. Some would argue that the word is merely the Matthean equivalent of the Marcan 'the age to come' which it replaces; it possesses only

---

5   The order of events in Matthew, recreation then judgement, agrees with the scenario in 4 Ezra 7:30–44 but is against the order of Revelation where the recreation (chapter 21) follows the judgement (chapter 20).

6   Those scholars who support Matthean redaction at this point include Gnilka, *Matthäusevangelium*, II, p. 170; Gundry, *Matthew*, p. 392; Schweizer, *Matthew*, pp. 389–90; Lindars, *Son of Man*, p. 125; Schenk, *Sprache*, p. 18 and Burnett, 'παλιγγενεσία in Matt. 19:28', p. 64. For the alternative view that Matthew has reproduced the text of Q, see Schulz, *Q*, p. 331 and Friedrich, *Gott im Bruder?*, pp. 58–9. According to Marguerat, *Le Jugement*, p. 463, παλιγγενεσία stood in Matthew's recension of Q.

7   For detailed discussion, see Büchsel, 'παλιγγενεσία', pp. 686–9.

8   In agreement with Gnilka, *Matthäusevangelium*, II, p. 172 and Beare, *Matthew*, pp. 398–9.

temporal significance and thus has no connotation of cosmic destruction and renewal.[9] In support of this claim, it is argued that while Matthew speaks often enough of the consummation of the age, he never refers to the end of the world. With no mention in the gospel of the prior destruction of the cosmic order, παλιγγενεσία can hardly be taken as referring to its recreation.[10] Yet there are solid grounds for disputing this claim. Apart from 24:29, Matthew refers twice more to the eschatological destruction of the existing cosmos. The texts in question are 5:18 (//Luke 16:17) and 24:35 (//Mark 13:31) which both speak of the present heaven and earth passing away.

Matthew 24:35 appears in the apocalyptic discourse and reads, 'Heaven and earth will pass away but my words will not pass away.' The point of this text is conveyed in the contrast of the two subjects; while the words of Jesus are eternal, the present cosmic order is temporary. The reference to the passing of heaven and earth in 5:18 must be taken in the same way. This logion states, '...until heaven and earth pass away, not an iota, not a dot, will pass from the law, until all is accomplished'. Since the passing of heaven and earth is tied up with the end events (Matt. 24:35), the meaning of this saying appears to be that the law remains valid only up to the time of the eschaton.[11] If we take together 5:18 and 24:35, and the similarity in wording suggests that we should, then Matthew is making the overall christological point that while the law is not eternal, the words of Jesus are. One set of teaching will survive the destruction of the cosmos and one will not. These two texts thus confirm the interpretation of παλιγγενεσία in terms of cosmic renewal. In specific agreement with his two major sources, and in general agreement with the wider apocalyptic-eschatological tradition, Matthew does speak of the destruction of the

---

[9] So, with varying nuances, Schweizer, *Matthew*, pp. 389–90; Lindars, *Son of Man*, p. 125; Sabourin, 'Apocalyptic Traits', p. 27; Burnett, 'παλιγγενεσία in Matt. 19:28', pp. 63–5 and Schenk, *Sprache*, p. 18.

[10] So Schweizer *Matthew*, p. 390 and Burnett 'παλιγγενεσία in Matt. 19:28', pp. 61–2.

[11] See Davies and Allison, *Matthew*, I, pp. 490–1, 494–5 and literature cited there for full discussion of this point; cf. also Schulz, *Q*, pp. 115–16 and Luz, 'Die Erfüllung des Gesetzes', pp. 417–18. Luz has since rejected this exegesis and now holds the alternative view that the passing of heaven and earth is a roundabout way of saying 'never'; the law thus remains valid forever. See Luz, *Matthäus*, I, p. 237. This interpretation of the phrase runs against its normal meaning (so Schulz, *Q*, p. 115) and makes nonsense of the contrast in 24:35. We shall return to Matthew's view of the law in chapter 8 below.

existing cosmic order at the eschaton. In view of this, παλιγγενεσία in 19:28 must be taken as representing the correlative notion
of the creation of a new heaven and a new earth. The eschaton
witnesses the passing of the impermanent and imperfect creation
and its replacement by an eternal and perfect order in the new
age. It is only after this has been accomplished that the judgement
can take place.

2. The judgement of the Son of Man

2.1 Matthew's terminology

Matthew's references to the event of judgement are both many and
widely distributed throughout his gospel. The sheer number of
these allusions testifies to the importance of this theme in the
evangelist's theology. Matthew uses a wide variety of terms and
symbols in referring to the judgement. Two of these he took directly
from Q, 'the coming wrath' (Matt. 3:7//Luke 3:7) and simply 'the
judgement' (Matt. 12:41–2// Luke 11:31–2). A favourite term of the
evangelist is 'the day of judgement'. This expression is found twice
in the Q passage where Jesus pronounces woes on a number of
Galilean cities (Matt. 11:22–4//Luke 10:12–15). While Luke uses
two different terms, 'on that day' (10:12) and 'in the judgement'
(10:14), Matthew twice uses the combined form 'on the day of
judgement' (11:22, 24). The same expression is found again in 10:15
where this Q material is employed a second time (cf. Luke 10:12)
and it appears also in 12:36 where it has no synoptic parallel. It is
generally agreed that all instances of this phrase are redactional.[12]
The term was seemingly widespread in both Judaism and early
Christianity; it is found in Jubilees 4:19; 4 Ezra 7:113; Psalms of
Solomon 15:12; 2 Peter 2:9; 3:7 and 1 John 4:17.

Another common phrase which Matthew uses is 'on that day'
(7:22; cf. 1 En. 45:3; Luke 17:31; 21:34; 2 Thess. 1:10; 2 Tim. 4:8) or
a variant of this expression (24:36//Mark 13:32; 24:50//Luke 12:46
and 24:42). The phrase is often found in the Old Testament
prophetic literature in reference to the day of the Lord (e.g. Isa.
10:20; Hos. 1:5; Amos 9:11; Zech. chs. 12–14) and passed into both
Judaism and Christianity from there. Yet another expression
favoured by Matthew for the end-time judgement is 'the end of the
age' (combining συντέλεια and αἰών) which is inserted redaction-

---

12 Schenk, *Sprache*, p. 324 and Schulz, *Q,* pp. 360–1.

ally at 24:3 (cf. Mark 13:4) and appears without parallel in 13:39, 40, 49 and 28:20. This term also enjoyed wide currency in apocalyptic-eschatological circles (1 En. 16:1; 2 Bar. 13:3; 19:5; 21:8; 27:15; 29:8; T.Levi 10:2; T.Ben. 11:3; T.Mos. 12:4) and occurs elsewhere in the New Testament only at Hebrews 9:26 (but cf. 1 Cor. 10:11). Of particular interest as a parallel to Matthew's usage is 4 Ezra 7:113, 'the day of judgement will be the end of this age'. Matthew also makes use of the simpler form 'the end' (τὸ τέλος; 10:22; 24:6//Mark 13:7; 24:13–14//Mark 13:13) which is often found in other early Christian texts (1 Cor. 1:8; 15:24; 2 Cor. 11:15; Phil. 3:19; Heb. 3:6, 14; 6:8, 11; 1 Pet. 4:7, 17; Rev. 2:26).

The evangelist also favours the symbol of the harvest to allude to the coming age and its attendant judgement. This motif appears in the Q account of the preaching of John the Baptist (Matt. 3:12// Luke 3:17). Here John prophesies that the eschatological judge will arrive with his winnowing fork in hand to clear the threshing floor, gather his wheat and burn the chaff. Precisely the same symbolism appears in the interpretation of the parable of the tares in 13:36–43. In this text the harvest symbolises the close of the age; the reapers represent the angels and the weeds to be burnt stand for the wicked. A slightly different use of the harvest imagery is found in Matt. 9:37–8 (//Luke 10:1–2) where the harvest represents the mission of the disciples. Yet even here the symbol has eschatological and judgemental overtones, since an individual's response to the mission dictates his or her ultimate fate (cf. 10:15, 40–2). In a scenario which coheres well with Matthew's dualistic perspective, the disciples begin a processing of harvesting which will conclude with the angels at the eschaton.[13] The Old Testament prophetic books supply the background for this particular metaphor. The harvest symbol is used there either as a metaphor for God's abundant future blessings (e.g. Amos 9:13–15) or for his judgement (e.g. Jer. 51:33; Joel 3:13). In the later apocalyptic-eschatological tradition the harvest is used in both senses, depending upon the goodness or otherwise of the persons involved (cf. 4 Ezra 4:29–39; 2 Bar. 70:1–2). It is in this sense that Matthew understood the term; at the harvest one receives either eternal reward or everlasting punishment (13:41–3). The harvest as a symbol of the eschaton appears elsewhere in early Christian tradition in Mark 4:26–9 and Revelation 14:14–20.

---

[13] So correctly Schweizer, *Matthew*, p. 234.

2.2 Jesus the Son of Man as the judge

Many early Christians, including Matthew, accepted that the returning Jesus would preside over the judgement. The early church believed that a number of functions which were the preserve of God in the Old Testament had been handed over to the risen Lord, including the role of eschatological judge (cf. John 5:22; Acts 10:42; 17:31; Rom. 2:16; 2 Cor. 5:10; 2 Thess. 1:8–9; 2 Tim. 4:1). This view, however, was by no means universal in the early church. Neither Mark nor Q suggests that Jesus performs this function. As noted in the previous chapter, both documents imply that Jesus will take the role of advocate while God himself will sit in judgement (Mark 8:38; Luke 12:8–9). This seems to be the scenario in the judgement scene of Revelation 20:11–15. God sits upon his great white throne (cf. 4:2–11) and judges individuals on the basis of what is written in the book of life, otherwise known as the book of the Lamb (i.e. Jesus; cf. 21:27). In this document Jesus appears as the advocate at the court of judgement (3:5).

While Matthew agrees with one stream of Christian tradition that Jesus himself will take charge at the final judgement, only in his gospel is there special emphasis that Jesus will preside *as Son of Man*. The closest New Testament parallel to this theme is found in John 5:27, 'and he [God] has given him [Jesus] authority to execute the judgment because he is the Son of Man (ὅτι υἱὸς ἀνθρώπου ἐστίν)'. This is immediately followed in verses 28–9 by material which refers to the future resurrection of the dead, thereby combining the twin apocalyptic-eschatological themes of resurrection and judgement. Some scholars have argued that the anarthrous construction in verse 27, which is unique in Johannine references to the Son of Man, suggests that the term is used here in a non-titular sense and ought to be translated simply as 'man'; Jesus is not given the authority to judge because he is the Son of Man, but because as a man (word made flesh) he is qualified to judge all humans. This interpretation emphasises those statements in the gospel which appear to put the judgement fully within the context of realised eschatology; the very appearance of the incarnate Jesus brings judgement into the world (cf. 3:19–21; 9:39; 12:31) and one is saved or condemned on the basis of one's response to the revelation he brings.[14] Other scholars, however, view the matter differently. Not

---

[14] See most recently, Hare, *Son of Man*, pp. 90–6 and literature cited there.

only do they take υἱὸς ἀνθρώπου as a title, but they argue that it refers to Jesus' role as judgemental Son of Man at the eschaton. The absence of the articles is normally explained on the grounds that the evangelist has deliberately conformed the reference to the text of Daniel 7:13. On this reading, John retains the traditional Christian future aspect of the judgement and merges it with his developed realised eschatology; Jesus the Son of Man has brought judgement into the world and will ratify this process as judge at the end of the age.[15] In view of the eschatological material which follows verse 27, this second interpretation is the more likely of the two. Consequently, it must be concluded that John accepted the view of Jesus as judgemental Son of Man which we find also in Matthew.

Be that as it may, the Matthean material dealing with this theme is far more plentiful and detailed than its Johannine counterpart. Apart from the texts which describe the arrival of the Son of Man at the parousia, there are two further texts which depict Jesus the Son of Man presiding over the eschatological tribunal. In both these traditions, Jesus the Son of Man is described as sitting on his throne of glory. The texts in question are Matthew 19:28 and 25:31. Both references are commonly but not universally ascribed to the hand of Matthew. Matthew 19:28, as we saw above, derives from a Q tradition which is represented as well by Luke 22:28–30. Matthew's version reads, 'in the recreation, when the Son of Man shall sit on his glorious throne (ἐπὶ θρόνου δόξης αὐτοῦ)', while the Lucan text has no reference to the Son of Man and presents the eschatological scenario in terms of the traditional motif of the messianic banquet, 'so that you may eat and drink at my table'. Both texts agree that this material has judgemental overtones because they proceed to mention the role of the disciples in judging the twelve tribes of Israel. There is no good reason to suspect Lucan redaction at this point since Luke normally retains future Son of Man sayings from his sources. On the other hand, Matthew's emphasis on the judgemental role of the Son of Man renders it probable that he is responsible for the alteration of Q here. At least this is the view of

---

[15] For comprehensive discussion, see Moloney, *Johannine Son of Man,* pp. 79–86 who is followed by Lindars, *Son of Man,* pp. 153–5. On the relationship between realised eschatology and future eschatology in the Johannine gospel, see Brown, *Gospel according to John,* I, pp. cxv–cxxi and Barrett, *Gospel according to St. John,* pp. 67–70. Both commentators interpret the Son of Man in 5:27 in a titular sense and view the judgement he initiates as future (Brown, *Gospel according to John,* I, p. 215; Barrett, *Gospel according to St. John,* p. 262).

most scholars.[16] Matthew 25:31 appears at the beginning of the unique tradition of the final judgement (25:31–46). This verse reads, 'When the Son of Man comes in his glory, and all the angels with him, then he will sit upon his glorious throne.' A minority of scholars argue that Matthew composed the whole pericope in 25:31–46[17] but, as we shall see shortly, it is far more probable that we are dealing with Matthean redaction of source material. In view of this, most commentators affirm that the evangelist composed verse 31 as an introduction to the traditional material in order to align it to his peculiar conception of the judgemental role of the Son of Man.[18] This view is supported by the fact that this verse bears a number of similarites to 16:27 and 24:30–1, Matthew's redacted versions of Mark 8:38 and 13:26 respectively; in all three texts the Son of Man comes in glory accompanied by an angelic host.[19]

[16] So Gundry, *Matthew*, p. 392; Gnilka, *Matthäusevangelium*, II, p. 170; Lindars, *Son of Man*, pp. 124–6; Friedrich, *Gott im Bruder?*, pp. 59–60, 65; Brandenburger, *Das Recht des Weltenrichters*, pp. 41–2 and Catchpole, 'Son of Man in Heaven', pp. 373–7. The view that the Matthean text is original here is advanced by Strecker, *Weg*, p. 109 and Schulz, *Q*, p. 331. According to Marguerat, *Le Jugement*, p. 463, the two versions of Q differed at this point and Matthew adopted this reference to the Son of Man on his glorious throne from his particular recension.

[17] So Gundry, *Matthew*, pp. 511–16 and Cope, 'Matthew xxv:31–46', pp. 32–44.

[18] Gnilka, *Matthäusevangelium*, II, p. 368; Schweizer, *Matthew*, p. 475; Tödt, *Son of Man*, p. 73; Brandenburger, *Das Recht des Weltenrichters*, pp. 45–51; Broer, 'Das Gericht', pp. 276–7 and Zumstein, *La Condition*, pp. 327–8. Both Friedrich, *Gott im Bruder?*, pp. 14–20, 111–37 and Catchpole, 'Son of Man in Heaven', pp. 383–7 argue rather unconvincingly that the verse is traditional, and supplied the background for Matthew's redaction at 19:28. The opposite conclusion is reached by Marguerat, *Le Jugement*, p. 463 n. 50 who argues that the traditional saying in 19:28 supplied the model for Matthew's redaction in 25:31.

[19] In view of the similarity between the Son of Man in 25:31 and the Son of Man in redacted Matthean passages, it is rather surprising that Catchpole, 'Son of Man in Heaven', p. 385 claims that the depiction of this figure in 25:31 is non-Matthean and thus pre-Matthean. Catchpole bases this claim on his assumption that the Son of Man in 25:31 is an exclusively heavenly figure who has not suffered hardship. Since in Matthew the Son of Man is one who experiences hardship and suffering (e.g. 8:20; 17:22; 20:18–19), the glorious heavenly being in 25:31 cannot be squared with the evangelist's view of the Son of Man. This fails to consider, however, that the Son of Man in Matthew's gospel acts in different capacities at different stages of his career. In his earthly mission, he is a suffering and rejected figure who must die and be raised to life, whereas in his future role at the end of the age he acts as the eschatological judge. The bridge between the two stages of the Son of Man's career is provided by 26:64. It should also be said that if the portrayal of the Son of Man in 25:31 does not correspond with the suffering Son of Man texts, then neither do any of those Matthean passages, traditional or redactional, which present this figure in terms of future glory. On Catchpole's criteria, Matthew's redaction of Mark 8:38 at 16:27 is non-Matthean as well! A similar criticism of Catchpole is made by Hare, *Son of Man*, p. 177.

The cluster of ideas here in 19:28 and 25:31, Jesus as Son of Man presiding over the judgement on his throne of glory, is attested nowhere else in early Christianity. John 5:27 mentions the Son of Man in a judgemental context, but fails to mention that he sits upon a throne of glory. Other texts mention that Jesus is awarded a throne, either the throne of David (Luke 1:32; Acts 2:30) or a share in the throne of God (Rev. 3:21), but in none of these cases is there reference to the Son of Man or to the judgement. We do find in the Pauline epistles the idea of Jesus sitting upon the judgement seat of God (Rom. 14:10; 2 Cor. 5:10; cf. Rom. 2:16), yet this is only a partial parallel to the Matthean concept since there is no mention of the Son of Man. For a close parallel to the Matthean portrayal of the Son of Man in 19:28 and 25:31 we have to look further than the early Christian literature.

As is well known, the portrayal of the Son of Man in these Matthean texts is strikingly similar to the depiction of the Son of Man in the Parables of Enoch. In this Jewish text, the Son of Man is also said to sit on the throne of glory and preside over the eschatological judgement. The document specifies that the throne belongs to God, the Antecedent of Time (1 En. 47:3; 60:2), and is given to his Elect One for this very purpose (51:3; 61:8; 62:2). A number of passages describe this Elect One sitting upon this throne (45:3; 55:4; 62:3), while others refer to the one upon the throne by another name, the Son of Man (62:5; 69:27, 29). Since this particular individual is often referred to as *that* Son of Man, it seems clear that he is intended to be identified with the Danielic one like a son of man. This figure has now developed from a corporate figure (so Daniel) to a pre-existent agent of eschatological judgement (1 En. 45:3). Because the portrayal of the Son of Man as the end-time judge on the throne of glory is found only in Matthew and the Parables of Enoch,[20] the

---

[20] The closest parallel in Jewish literature is found in the Testament of Abraham where the righteous Abel sits upon a throne of glory and acts as the final judge (Rec. A chs. 12–13). Originally, this text might well have referred to the Son of Man. As the son of Adam, Abel is of course the son of man. If a semitic original underlies the extant Greek recensions, then it is possible that the translators misunderstood the reference and identified this figure with Adam's righteous son. All this is uncertain, however, since there is no proof that Greek was not the original language of composition. For the view that the text did not originally speak of the Son of Man, see Nickelsburg, 'Eschatology in the Testament of Abraham', p. 36.

interesting possibility of a direct relationship between them must be considered.[21]

Such a relationship has been argued in detail by J. Theisohn who concludes, primarily on the basis of the throne of glory motif, that the evangelist was dependent upon the material which we find in 1 Enoch 37–71.[22] Theisohn does not go so far as to affirm that a literary relationship existed between these documents, but postulates instead that Matthew may have been influenced by this Enochic text through oral traditions.[23] A number of later scholars have followed Theisohn's analysis at this point,[24] and it is difficult to dispute that there was some contact between these two texts. Yet not all scholars would agree with this conclusion. E. Brandenburger makes much of the fact that a number of Matthean motifs have no parallel in the Parables of Enoch; the Son of Man sits on *his* throne of glory (*the* [God's] throne of glory in the Parables), and he comes in glory with his angels (concerning which 1 Enoch is silent).[25] But these elements can be attributed to Matthew's adaptation of the Enochic Son of Man to his own Christian point of view. That Jesus was awarded his own glorious throne (not necessarily the throne of God) was well established in early Christianity, as too was the belief that he would return in glory accompanied by (his) holy angels.[26] What ought to be read out of these differences between the Son of Man in Matthew and the Son of Man in the Parables of Enoch is that the evangelist edited his Jewish sources just as he

[21]   The precise relationship between these documents is one of the factors affecting the dating of the Parables. There are no unambiguous internal indications of its date, and the absence of copies from the Qumran library has only served to complicate the issue rather than shed light on it. In any event, most scholars date it somewhere in the first century CE, earlier in the century if the Qumran evidence is not taken as significant and later in the century if it is. For respective defences of each position, see Collins, *Apocalyptic Imagination*, pp. 142–3 and Knibb, 'The Date of the Parables of Enoch', pp. 345–59. The issue of the date of composition need not be settled here, for it is clear that the author of the Parables, like Matthew, was dependent upon much earlier traditions.

[22]   Theisohn, *Richter*, pp. 152–82. The first part of Theisohn's discussion establishes the close parallels between the Son of Man in Matthew 19:28 and 25:31 and the Son of Man in Enoch (pp. 152–61), while the latter section deals with Matthew's redaction of the two pericopae in question (pp. 161–82).

[23]   Theisohn, *Richter*, p. 161.

[24]   See, for example, Geist, *Menschensohn*, p. 207, and for an earlier statement of this position, Tödt, *Son of Man*, p. 223. Gnilka, *Matthäusevangelium*, II, pp. 172, 370–1 notes the parallels between Matthew and the Parables of Enoch but does not argue for direct dependence.

[25]   Brandenburger, *Das Recht des Weltenrichters*, pp. 42–3.

[26]   So Theisohn, *Richter*, p. 160, at least with regard to the Son of Man sitting upon *his* throne of glory.

edited his Christian traditions. Having said this, however, it is fair
to say that Theisohn claims too much with his suggestion that
Matthew was *dependent* in any sense upon 1 Enoch 37–71. If
textual dependence is ruled out, as Theisohn agrees, then there is no
reason to postulate a direct relationship at all. Theisohn seems to
believe that the oral tradition which influenced Matthew must have
derived from the written Parables of Enoch, but there is no
necessity to suppose this. It is just as likely, if not more so, that the
evangelist and the author of the Parables had access to a common
Son of Man tradition which each utilised in his own way. Matthew
would have added his Christian motifs, while the editor of the
Parables would have made his own editorial adjustments; the
merging of the figure of the Elect One with the figure of the Son of
Man, which is not found in Matthew, could well be one example.
At any rate, this hypothesis would explain both the similarities and
differences between these documents in terms of their respective
representations of the Son of Man.

The scholarly debate concerning the precise relationship between
Matthew and 1 Enoch 37–71 has suffered from an inflexible
posture on both sides; either Matthew knew the Parables of Enoch,
even in oral form (so Theisohn), or he was totally independent of
this text and its traditions (so Brandenburger). One side has
exaggerated the parallels, while the other has focused too much on
the dissimilarities. Since any reasonable solution to the problem
must take into account both phenomena, the middle position that
both authors had access to a common Jewish source seems to be
the most acceptable.[27] This Jewish tradition had presumably transformed the corporate one like a son of man in Daniel into *the* Son
of Man, the (pre-existent?) eschatological judge who would preside
over proceedings upon the throne of glory.

None the less Theisohn attempted to bolster his argument that

---

[27] Burnett, *Jesus-Sophia*, pp. 374–5 n. 4. This also seems to be the position of Hare,
Son of Man, pp. 164–5. Even so, Hare plays down the closeness of the texts by
suggesting that each author used 'common motifs' of Jewish apocalyptic eschatology. But the fact that this view of the Son of Man is confined to these
documents demonstrates that we are not dealing with a common apocalyptic-
eschatological tradition; rather, the theme of the Son of Man sitting on a glorious
throne overseeing the judgement was comparatively rare in apocalyptic circles!
The fact that this tradition was adopted by Matthew and the author of the
Parables demonstrates that this relatively rare motif appealed to their respective
eschatological conceptions. Marguerat also denies the direct dependence of
Matthew upon the Parables (*Le Jugement,* p. 106), and claims that the figure of
the judging Son of Man came to Matthew via Q in 19:28 (see note 16 above).

the Parables of Enoch itself (not its sources) directly influenced Matthew by arguing for such influence with regard to the material in Matthew 13:36–43, 49–50.[28] Theisohn argued that the true apocalyptic-eschatological sections of these passages, Matthew 13:40–3, 49–50, were redacted versions of a small Jewish *Vorlage* which was influenced by the Parables of Enoch and which contained the following elements – the sending of avenging angels at the end of the age, their separation of the wicked from the righteous, the former cast into a fiery furnace and the latter then shining like the sun.[29] Theisohn's case for a link between the Parables and these Matthean texts rests primarily upon two expressions in the gospel, ἡ κάμινος τοῦ πυρός and οἱ δίκαιοι ἐκλάμψουσιν ὡς ὁ ἥλιος, which he considers derive ultimately from the Enoch tradition. The first expression is found in 1 Enoch 54:6, while the second can be readily compared with 1 Enoch 38:4; 39:7; 50:1 and 58:3.[30]

Although Theisohn's arguments have been accepted by some scholars,[31] there is need in this case to exercise some caution. A number of pertinent objections have been raised against Theisohn's thesis.[32] To begin with, there is no evidence whatsoever to support the existence of his hypothetical source containing such a cluster of motifs. Certainly no one section of the Parables reflects such a grouping of these themes; they are in fact spread right throughout the document. Moreover, Theisohn fails to substantiate any firm link, either direct or indirect, between this Matthean material and the Parables. Neither the notion of the punishment of the wicked by fire (or specifically in a fiery furnace), nor the idea that the righteous will shine is confined to these two documents. As we noted in chapter 1, both concepts are very common apocalyptic-eschatological notions. We shall say more about these themes in Matthew in the next chapter. In view of these observations, there is no necessity to posit the dependence of Matthew 13:40–3, 49–50 on this Enoch tradition. If the evangelist did compose these verses, and this was accepted in chapter 3, then he clearly dipped into a pool of

---

[28]   Theisohn, *Richter*, pp. 182–201.
[29]   Theisohn, *Richter*, pp. 187–91.
[30]   Theisohn, *Richter*, pp. 192–200.
[31]   So Gnilka, *Matthäusevangelium*, I, pp. 499–500. Friedrich holds the singular view that all of Matthew 13:36–43, apart from verses 36–7a, 43b, is pre-Matthean (*Gott im Bruder?*, pp. 66–86) and he accepts Theisohn's basic argument of the influence of the Parables on this material (pp. 86–7).
[32]   For further detail, see Hare, *Son of Man*, pp. 152–3 and Knibb, 'The Date of the Parables of Enoch', p. 357.

common apocalyptic-eschatological motifs which were available to him. While some of these traditions might have been shared by the circle which produced the Parables of Enoch, including the Son of Man tradition, there were doubtless non-Enochic sources as well. Consequently, Theisohn's attempt to prove the direct influence of the Parables on the gospel of Matthew must be considered unsuccessful. A far more likely proposition is that just as the evangelist had access to Christian apocalyptic-eschatological traditions, so too did he possess a number of Jewish apocalyptic-eschatological sources, some of which also found their way into 1 Enoch 37–71. Of no small importance in this regard is the figure of the judgemental Son of Man seated upon his glorious throne. Matthew's adoption of this particular tradition reveals further his special interest in the judgement and the figure who presides over it.

The presentation of the returning Jesus in Matthew is thus a perfect synthesis of his Jewish and Christian Son of Man sources, each of which was a reinterpretation of the one like a son of man in Daniel 7:13–14. He took from Mark and Q the theme that Jesus was the Son of Man who would return as Son of Man in glory and on the clouds of heaven at the end of the age, while from his Jewish traditions which he shared with the author of the Parables of Enoch, he adopted the expressly judicial function of this figure seated upon his throne of glory. It seems clear that such a merging was deemed necessary by Matthew since neither of these traditions told the full story. His Christian sources identified Jesus with the Son of Man who would come at the eschaton, but they failed to specify his judgemental role. On the other hand, his Jewish Son of Man sources testified that this figure does perform this eschatological function, but they obviously had no mention of Jesus. By combining all these elements, Matthew constructed a distinctive and powerful eschatological vision of the end and the key player in these events. The resurrected Jesus who now resides in heaven will arrive on the clouds of heaven accompanied by his angelic army and then take his seat on his throne of glory in order to preside over the final judgement.

2.3 The scene of judgement

Matthew presents a rather detailed description of the final judgement in 25:31–46 at the end of his apocalyptic discourse. Such a detailed depiction of the judgement occurs in many other apocalyptic-eschatological texts (Dan. 7:9–14; 1 En. 62:1–63:12; 90:20–7; 4 Ezra 7:32–43; Rev. 20:11–15). We have already considered the introduction in verse 31 and may now proceed to the remaining verses which describe the judgement scene. All the nations (πάντα τὰ ἔθνη) will gather before the Son of Man (verse 32a) and he will separate them as a shepherd separates sheep from goats, placing the sheep to his right and the goats to his left (verses 32b–3). This narrative material is then followed by dialogue. The Son of Man (the king) welcomes to his kingdom those to his right on the grounds that they treated him appropriately (verses 34–6). When the righteous question this (verses 37–9), the Son of Man responds by explaining that when they acted well toward one of the least of his brethren, they acted as such toward him (verse 40). The judge then speaks to those at his left hand and sends them to the fire which has been prepared for the devil and his angels (verse 41). In an antithesis to the dialogue of verses 37–9, they are condemned, their protestations notwithstanding, for failing to act accordingly to the least of the brethren mentioned previously (verses 42–5). The pericope ends on the solemn note that the wicked will go to eternal punishment and the righteous to eternal life (verse 46).

Despite a small number of commentators who ascribe the whole pericope to Matthew's hand (see note 17), it can be safely assumed that much of this material derives from the evangelist's special sources.[33] The extent and nature of the evangelist's redaction,

---

[33] Both Catchpole and Friedrich argue that the whole pre-Matthean passage, which includes verse 31, reflects the influence of 1 Enoch. Catchpole builds his case mainly on the basis of a close correspondence between the judge and certain humans, the treatment of the latter being the yardstick by which the wicked will be judged, which he finds in both Matthew 25:31–46 and 1 Enoch 62–3 ('Son of Man in Heaven', pp. 380–2). Yet such a correspondence between the righteous and the final judge, be it the Son of Man, God himself or any other figure, is central to almost every apocalyptic-eschatological scheme (so correctly Hare, *Son of Man,* pp. 176–7 who raises a number of further objections). Catchpole's argument also depends to a large extent on the integrity of Matthew 25:31–46 at the pre-Matthean stage, but it is much more probable that verse 31 is a Matthean addition (see also notes 18 and 19 above). It is significant that Catchpole says little about verses 32–3, the metaphor of the sheep and goats. This material has nothing in common with the Parables of Enoch and is most closely paralleled in the Animal Apocalypse which also uses animal imagery in its judgement scene. Though it is unlikely that these Matthean verses are directly influenced by this tradition (see Friedrich, *Gott im Bruder?*, pp. 142–3), there can be no doubt that the pericope as a whole reflects material from a number of sources. For his part, Friedrich cites a number of parallels between Matthew 25:31–46 and the whole of 1 Enoch including the Parables (pp. 150–64). He affirms that the cluster of motifs in the former is found *en bloc* only in the latter which leads him to the conclusion of further influence of Enoch on the pre-Matthean tradition (p. 163). Yet such a

however, is a matter of dispute. It has been suggested that Matthew brought together two independent traditions, the parable of the separation of the flocks in verses 32b–3 and the antithetical dialogues in verses 35–40, 42–5, and combined these to create his account of the universal judgement.[34] On the other hand, the vast majority of scholars consider this tradition to have been a unity at the pre-gospel stage which Matthew adopted and subsequently edited at certain points. The differences between these two general positions need not concern us here. Nor for that matter is it essential to pinpoint every editorial alteration by Matthew. Only two of his redactional changes need be mentioned in the present context.

In the dialogue section the judge is termed 'the king' (verses 34, 40). Although Matthew refers to the kingdom of the Son of Man (13:41; 16:28; cf. also 20:21), the unexpected presence of 'the king' in these verses stands in some tension with the Son of Man terminology in verse 31; the narrative moves abruptly and without explanation from the Son of Man to the king and this suggests that the latter motif stood in Matthew's source. Because the king normally represents God in the synoptic parable tradition, it is likely that at the pre-Matthean stage the king in this material stood for God. But by inserting the reference to the Son of Man in verse 31, Matthew dramatically alters the emphasis. The judge and king is no longer God but the Son of Man. Matthew completes this reinterpretation by adding 'of my father' to 'Come, O blessed' which the king utters in verse 34. These editorial insertions of the whole of verse 31 and the words in verse 34 together comprise an important indicator of Matthew's perception of the final judgement. It is not God the father but Jesus the Son of Man who functions as the eschatological judge.[35] The second important redaction which Matthew effects on this material is his addition of verse 32a, 'before him will be

claim is an exaggeration of the evidence. Many of the motifs he considers are found outside the book of Enoch and reappear in clusters in the Qumran texts. We might, on Friedrich's reasoning, conclude that the original speaker of the judgemental material in 25:31–46 (for Friedrich this is Jesus) also knew the Qumran scrolls. This pre-Matthean material is related to 1 Enoch (and to the Qumran literature for that matter) only in so far as it reflects the same general apocalyptic-eschatological world view. To say any more than this would be to exceed the evidence.

34 So Robinson, 'Sheep and Goats', pp. 225–37.
35 For similar views, see Robinson, 'Sheep and Goats', pp. 236–7; Marguerat, *Le Jugement*, pp. 492–4 and Zumstein, *La Condition*, pp. 333–4.

gathered all the nations'.[36] By this addition the evangelist makes explicit what was perhaps implicit in his source: namely, that the judgement will be truly universal. All nations, every single human being, will be gathered before the judgement throne of the Son of Man. The language of Matthew here is reminiscent of Joel 3:11–12 where all the nations (LXX, πάντα τὰ ἔθνη) will face the judgement of Yahweh. If Matthew has been influenced by this Old Testament text,[37] then he has again seen fit to ascribe God's judgemental role to the Son of Man. The universal aspect of the judgement in Matthew 25:31–46 is important and we shall return to this subject in chapter 9.

Matthew 25:31–46 is not the only Matthean pericope which offers a description of the judgement. A second description appears in 7:21–3 toward the end of the sermon on the mount. The parallel with Luke 6:46 and 13:25–7 shows that Matthew has taken this material from Q. In the Matthean version, the dialogue is between Jesus the judge and Christian false prophets (cf. 7:15–20) and not between the judge and the wicked in general as in 25:31–46. Essentially the passage makes the point that these false prophets, though professing to be proper Christians, will be denounced as false and excluded from the kingdom. There is no mention of the Son of Man in this passage, and the only christological title used is 'Lord' which forms part of the confession of the false prophets. Despite the absence of the Son of Man title in this passage, it is quite clear from the remainder of the gospel that here Jesus functions as judging Son of Man. As will be shown in more detail in chapter 9, the Son of Man is the judge of all humans, including the members of his church.

A third but very brief description of the judgement is found in Matthew 19:28 which states that the (twelve) disciples will sit on twelve thrones and judge the twelve tribes of Israel. A comparison with the Lucan parallel in 22:30 reveals that Matthew took this motif directly from his source. The idea that the righteous will participate in the end-time judgement is found in a number of early Christian

---

[36] So most scholars; Friedrich, *Gott im Bruder?*, pp. 256–7; Marguerat, *Le Jugement*, p. 490; Zumstein, *La Condition*, pp. 328–9; Gnilka, *Matthäusevangelium*, II, p. 368; Geist, *Menschensohn*, p. 207 and Broer, 'Das Gericht', pp. 277–8. Catchpole, 'Son of Man in Heaven', p. 389 argues that the evidence for Matthean redaction is inconclusive, but suggests that it hardly matters; with or without the reference to the assembly of all the nations, the emphasis lies with the universality of the judgement.

[37] So Gundry, *Matthew*, p. 511.

texts (1 Cor. 6:2–3; Rev. 20:4; cf. Rev. 3:21) as well as Jewish apocalyptic-eschatological documents (Dan. 7:22, 1 En. 95:3; 96:1; T.Ab. 13:6). That such a concept was adopted in some apocalyptic-eschatological schemes should occasion no surprise. Since the criteria for judgement are usually tied up with the treatment of the righteous, the belief that those who suffer should have a hand in the judgement of those responsible for their suffering is perfectly understandable.

There are then no less than three different accounts of the final judgement in Matthew and it is not clear how the evangelist related these to one another. Did he envisage one judgement for the church (7:21–3) and another for the gentiles (25:31–46) over both of which the Son of Man presides, and a third judgement of Israel by the disciples (19:28)? G. N. Stanton accepts that the evangelist might well have envisaged a number of different judgements,[38] and this is a possible interpretation of the evidence. On the other hand, it is just as likely that Matthew, who was by no means a 'systematic theologian', had not himself clearly worked out and assimilated the precise details of the judgement from the disparate traditions at his disposal. What was important to Matthew was that the judgement would take place and that the righteous would be rewarded and the wicked punished.

3. Conclusions

By way of summarising this chapter, a few important points need to be reiterated. Matthew accepts the usual apocalyptic-eschatological scenario that the new age will witness both the general resurrection of the dead and the recreation of the cosmic order. These events lead to the all-important universal judgement over which Jesus Son of Man will preside on his glorious throne. The evangelist's vision of the judgement and the figure who oversees it is a combination of his Christian and Jewish Son of Man sources. He follows Mark and Q in identifying Jesus with the Son of Man who comes in glory, but because these sources stop short of describing him as the final judge (which other Christian texts do), Matthew supplements them with a Jewish tradition which is reflected in the Parables of Enoch. The end result is a perfect synthesis of all the Son of Man material available to him. Jesus will return in glory on the clouds of heaven at the end of the age and

---

[38] Stanton, *Gospel for a New People*, p. 213.

will assume his throne of glory in order to preside over the universal judgement. A similar combination of elements appears in the gospel of John, although it is far less pronounced there than in Matthew. The evangelist betrays his special interest in the event of eschatological judgement by referring to it constantly using a variety of terms and metaphors, and also by describing it more than once. The universal judgement scene in 25:31–46 is especially important in this regard, since the whole process of judgement is described. As the final passage of Jesus' last discourse, this pericope assumes fundamental importance in the context of the gospel. It elaborates and confirms all the references to the eschaton which come earlier in the narrative, with regard both to the righteous and to the wicked. In short, it is the passage to which all the other eschatological pericopae point. In Matthew the Son of Man comes for the purpose of judgement (cf. 16:27), but the judgement has a specific purpose as well. It is here that the wicked receive their eternal punishment and the righteous receive their eternal reward. We shall examine what Matthew has to say about these subjects in the next chapter.

6

THE FATE OF THE WICKED AND THE FATE
OF THE RIGHTEOUS IN MATTHEW

In the previous chapters, it was argued that Matthew combined his Christian and Jewish sources to arrive at a distinctive portrayal of Jesus as the saviour figure, the Son of Man. The Son of Man will return in glory with his angelic army, and will then sit upon his glorious throne to preside over the final judgement. As the one who sits in judgement, it is Jesus the Son of Man who dispenses eschatological rewards and punishments. As we would expect from an author for whom the judgement is paramount, Matthew devotes a considerable amount of space to each category. In relation to this subject, it is important to note that there is no hint in Matthew that the wicked dead or the righteous dead receive a sample of their respective eschatological fates in the intermediate period between death and the final judgement. While such an idea is found in later Jewish apocalyptic eschatology and is prominent in other New Testament writings, particularly the gospel of Luke (16:19–31; 23:43),[1] it seems to play no part in Matthew's apocalyptic-eschatological scheme.[2] This means that all emphasis falls on the final judgement and its aftermath.

1. The fate of the wicked

Matthew has a good deal to say about the ultimate fate of the wicked. The picture he presents is not a pretty one and is in fact

---

[1]   For a recent discussion of this notion in the New Testament texts, see Osei-Bonsu, 'Intermediate State', pp. 169–94.

[2]   Osei-Bonsu, 'Intermediate State', pp. 171–3 argues that the intermediate state is implied in the Q tradition in Matthew 10:28 and Luke 12:4–5. Yet C. Milikowsky correctly shows that while the Lucan form of this tradition adverts to the intermediate state, the Matthean form does not; Matthew's version refers to the post-judgement punishment of the wicked. See his 'Which Gehenna?', pp. 242–3. It should never be ruled out that the evangelist accepted the common apocalyptic motif of the post-mortem but pre-judgement punishment of the wicked, but there is no concrete evidence that he did so.

among the most severe of the apocalyptic-eschatological schemes of his time. There are references of a general nature which state that the wicked will meet with condemnation (12:41–2), destruction (7:13) and eternal punishment (25:46), but more revealing than these are his specific statements about the fate of the wicked. One example of specific punishment is found in the parable of the good and wicked servants (Matt. 24:45–51), which the evangelist took from Q (//Luke 12:42–6). According to this text, the condemned will be cut in half (διχοτομέω) before sharing the lot of the hypocrites (verse 51). Precisely how Matthew took this reference is very difficult to say. Some scholars affirm that what is actually meant is no more than mere exclusion from the realm of the righteous. They point to a parallel text at Qumran, 1QS 2:16–17, which they believe clarifies the meaning of this tradition; '... God will set him [the wicked] apart for evil ... he shall be cut off from the midst of the sons of light ... his lot shall be among those who are cursed for ever'.[3] On this reading of the text, therefore, the master will arrive, separate the wicked from the company of the righteous and place him with other sinners. Other scholars reject this interpretation as an unnecessary refinement of the text. They argue that the passage represents in general terms the horror and harshness of the eschatological fate of the sinners.[4] Given that Matthew's views of the end-time punishment are extremely harsh, this second interpretation is clearly more likely than the first.

1.1 Punishment by eternal fire

Matthew's most constant conviction about the eschatological punishment of the wicked is that they will burn for eternity. This is an extremely common apocalyptic-eschatological theme, which is prominent in Jewish texts and in the Christian Apocalypse. But before we examine the Matthean references to this motif, it is instructive to analyse its occurrence in the New Testament texts outside the gospel and the Apocalypse. A survey of this nature demonstrates that the notion of the everlasting punishment of the wicked by fire was not widespread in early Christianity.

Leaving aside for the moment the Q account of the preaching of

---

[3] See Bonnard, *Matthieu*, p. 357. Cf. also Hill, *Matthew*, p. 325 and Sabourin, *Matthew*, II, p. 835.

[4] So Marguerat, *Le Jugement*, p. 534; Gundry, *Matthew*, p. 497 and Beare, *Matthew*, p. 479.

John the Baptist, which will concern us below, the clearest examples of this theme are found in Mark 9:43, 45, 47–8, Jude 7 and the epistle of James. In the first of these passages, the Marcan Jesus pronounces that it is better to lose a sinful limb or organ and receive salvation than to remain whole and face eternal punishment. Three parts of the body serve to illustrate this point. Mark 9:43 advises that it is preferable to sever a sinful hand and enter (eternal) life maimed than to go whole to Gehenna where there is unquenchable fire (τὸ πῦρ τὸ ἄσβεστον). The foot is the subject of verse 45 and here the Marcan Jesus suggests that it is better to lose one of these than to be thrown into Gehenna. Finally, verses 47–8 state that a sinful eye should be plucked lest one be thrown into Gehenna 'where their worm does not die and the fire is not quenched' (cf. Isa. 66:24). This idea also finds expression in Jude 7 which states that the destruction of Sodom and Gomorrah serves as an example of the (eschatological) punishment by eternal fire (πυρὸς αἰωνίου).[5] The epistle of James contains two references to this theme. In James 3:6 mention is made of the fire of Gehenna but not in the context of eschatological punishment. The author points out that the tongue can stain the whole body and is set on fire by Gehenna, thereby indicating that Gehenna is the source of evil speech. Precisely how this process operates is not made clear and is of little concern in the present context.[6] What is of importance is that the author of James seems to accept the traditional view of the fiery Gehenna. This is confirmed by James 5:3 where the author affirms that in the last days the gold and silver of the wealthy will eat their flesh like fire.

Other New Testament passages make reference to fire associated with the eschaton, but none of them clearly reflects the apocalyptic-eschatological notion of the eternal punishment of the wicked by fire. Both Hebrews and 2 Peter appear to reflect an alternative tradition which refers to the complete obliteration of the wicked by eschatological fire and not to their everlasting torment. Hebrews 10:27 specifies that any Christian who deliberately sins faces the prospect of judgement 'and a fury of fire which will consume the adversaries'. This text recalls Isaiah 26:11 which itself represents one stream of Old Testament thought that God will utterly destroy his enemies with fire (cf. Isa. 33:11–14; 66:15–16; Ezek. 38:22; 39:6; Joel 2:3; Mal. 3:19). The idea of eternal torment by fire is not in

---

[5]   For further detail, see the discussion of Bauckham, *Jude, 2 Peter*, pp. 54–5.
[6]   See the discussion of Davids, *James*, p. 143.

view in these Old Testament texts (contrast Isa. 66:24); the emphasis is on the complete obliteration of the enemies of God and his people. It is difficult to determine precisely how the author of Hebrews interpreted the eschatological fire of 10:27. Is it a fire of destruction after which the wicked do not survive, or is it a fire of eternal torment? It is possible of course that both ideas are in view, in which case the author envisages an initial conflagration and subsequent punishment by everlasting fire. Such a scenario is found in Revelation 20:9–10. A more likely possibility, however, is that the author of Hebrews took this text to mean the total annihilation of the wicked. This reading is supported by 10:39, 'But we are not of those who shrink back and are destroyed, but of those who have faith and keep their souls,' which implies strongly that by losing their souls the wicked are destroyed totally and face no further punitive measures; by contrast, those who keep faith retain their souls and so live on in the new age. The second epistle of Peter also seems to affirm the utter destruction of the wicked by fire. This document contains the (Stoic) notion of the end of the cosmos in a great conflagration (3:10–12) and specifies that the fire which is being stored until the day of judgement is for the destruction of the wicked (3:7). That the wicked do not survive in order to receive further punishment is suggested in verse 13, which affirms that in the new heaven and new earth only righteousness (the righteous) will dwell; the wicked presumably have no share at all in the new cosmic order. In any event, there is no mention of the punishment of the wicked after the conflagration.

There are three possible references to eschatological fire in the Pauline (and deutero-Pauline) literature, yet none of these clearly adverts to eternal punishment by fire. In Romans 12:19–20 Paul advises his readers to leave vengeance to God and cites Proverbs 25:21–2, 'but if your enemy is hungry, feed him; if he is thirsty, give him drink; for by so doing you will heap burning coals upon his head'. The idea of heaping burning coals on a person's head might reflect an Egyptian rite of repentance, but it is not known whether or not Paul was aware of this. If he was, then this reference to the coals should be taken in a positive sense; showing kindness to one's enemies will bring them to repentance. On the other hand, Paul might not have known of the background of this material and so interpreted it in the sense of eschatological punishment; showing kindness to enemies will increase their guilt and the severity of their (fiery) punishment when God exacts his revenge. While the issue is by no means clear cut, the majority of commentators opt for the former interpretation, usually in view of the positive tone of verse 21, 'Do not be overcome by evil, but overcome evil by good.'[7] If this is the correct understanding of this passage, and it is the more probable view, then Romans 12:20 cannot be understood as a reference to the fiery torment of the wicked.

The second Pauline text is 1 Corinthians 3:13–15. Like Romans 12:20, this pericope does not speak of eternal punishment by fire, though it does advert to an eschatological fire. The fire to which Paul refers is a testing fire at the eschaton; 'and the fire will test what sort of work each one has done' (verse 13b). The closest parallel to this notion appears in the Testament of Abraham 12:10–14; 13:11–14 where fire is the instrument by which the works of each soul are tested at the judgement. Paul affirms that if a person's works survive the fire, he will receive a reward (verse 14), and then specifies that if his works are burnt 'he will suffer loss, though he himself will be saved, but only as through fire' (verse 15). The precise meaning of this verse is not clear, but it might simply mean that the individual will be saved 'by the skin of his teeth'.[8] Be that as it may, since the person is eventually saved the idea of eternal punishment by fire is not suggested in this passage.

The final reference to eschatological fire in the Pauline corpus appears in 2 Thessalonians 1:7–8. In language echoing the coming of Yahweh in judgement in Isaiah 66:15–16, the author refers to the revelation of Jesus at his parousia in fire of flame (ἐν πυρὶ φλογός) to inflict vengeance on the wicked. Once again it is not certain just how the reference to fire ought to be taken. Does it belong with the statement of Jesus' appearance and thereby depict his parousia in terms of the Old Testament theophanies (eg. Ex. 3:2; 19:18; Deut. 3:2; Ezek. 1:13; Hab. 3:4; Dan. 7:9–10), or does it belong with the reference to vengeance and so indicate the nature of the eschatological punishment (as it does in Isa. 66:16)? In favour of the former interpretation is that verse 9, which deals with the fate of the wicked, speaks of the punishment of eternal destruction and exclusion from the presence of the Lord, but never mentions punishment by means of fire.[9] While it is true that this reference might presume

7 So Dunn, *Romans*, II, pp. 750–1; Stuhlmacher, *Römer*, p. 177 and, more tentatively, Ziesler, *Romans*, pp. 306–7. That Paul is speaking of eschatological punishment by fire is argued by Lang, 'πῦρ', p. 945.
8 See Lang, 'πῦρ', p. 944 and Conzelmann, *1 Corinthians*, pp. 76–7.
9 On the meaning of verse 9, see Marshall, *1 and 2 Thessalonians*, pp. 178–80. Significantly, Marshall does not mention the theme of everlasting torment by fire.

a fiery end to the wicked, any such reading must then take this motif in the same sense as Hebrews 10:27 and 2 Peter 3:7; the wicked will be utterly destroyed by eschatological fire, but they will not be punished forever by it. We must conclude, therefore, that there is no suggestion in 2 Thessalonians of eternal torture by fire.

The above review of the relevant New Testament passages outside Matthew and the Apocalypse which advert to eschatological fire yields the following results. Only three texts, Mark 9:43, 45, 47–8, Jude 7 and James 5:3, unequivocally attest that the wicked will burn forever as punishment for their sins. On the other hand, Hebrews, 2 Peter and possibly 2 Thessalonians, while mentioning that the eschaton will witness a punishment by fire, seem not to accept the notion of eternal torture by burning; rather, they appear to promote the idea of the total obliteration of the wicked in a conflagration which accompanies the parousia. A completely different view of the eschatological fire is found in 1 Corinthians. In this text the fire is a test of works and there is no hint that it is inflicted forever on the wicked. Finally, Romans 12:20 seems not to advert to eschatological fire at all. The results of the survey testify that this particular apocalyptic-eschatological theme was not universally adopted by the early Christians. The motif appears infrequently in the Christian literature and is hardly emphasised where it does occur. Mark and Jude contain a single allusion each, while James has a mere two references to this theme. It is within the context of the relative paucity of this motif in the New Testament (disregarding the Apocalypse) that we need to approach this subject in the gospel of Matthew. A review of the evidence reveals that Matthew does not simply affirm that the wicked will be punished by eternal fire. On the contrary, he fervently and constantly promotes it. In this respect he stands well apart from most of his Christian contemporaries with regard to this particular subject.

Matthew's gospel contains no less than seven references to the eternal torture of the wicked by eschatological fire. Only two of these texts derive from Mark or Q. In 18:8–9 Matthew takes up the single Marcan reference to the fiery punishment of the wicked (Mark 9:43, 45, 47–8). The evangelist characteristically abbreviates this material and combines the examples of the hand and foot into one double example. He retains the fire motif but writes 'into the eternal fire' (εἰς τὸ πῦρ τὸ αἰώνιον) in place of Mark's 'into Gehenna, into the unquenchable fire'. The example of the sinful eye is adopted by Matthew and again he retains but edits the fire reference. The rather verbose Marcan citation of Isaiah 66:24 is omitted and Mark's 'into Gehenna' is expanded to 'into the Gehenna of fire' (εἰς τὴν γέενναν τοῦ πυρός). The Q pericope containing this theme is that which represents the eschatological preaching of John the Baptist (Matt. 3:7–12//Luke 3:7–9, 16b–17). The message of the Baptist as preserved by the saying's source focuses primarily on the terrible punishment of the wicked, and there are three references to their punishment by (eternal) fire. The day of judgement (the coming wrath) is depicted metaphorically as an axe already poised to strike a tree. Any tree which fails to bear good fruit will be cut down and thrown to the fire (Matt. 3:10// Luke 3:9). John then speaks of his successor as the one who will baptise not with water, but with the holy spirit and with fire (Matt. 3:11//Luke 3:16). The preaching of the Baptist ends on a fiery note and in metaphorical terms. His successor will clear the threshing floor with his winnowing fork, gather the wheat into his granary and burn the chaff with unquenchable fire (πυρὶ ἀσβέστῳ; Matt. 3:12//Luke 3:17). This final reference to eternal fire implies the everlasting torture of the wicked and not the idea of their obliteration by eschatological fire. Apart from these statements of eternal punishment by fire which Matthew inherited from Mark and Q, one attributed to Jesus and one attributed to John the Baptist, no other statement of this kind in his gospel can be clearly attributed to a source. All the remaining references to this subject appear on the lips of Jesus and it is likely in each case that this material stems from the hand of Matthew.

The heavily apocalyptic-eschatological material in 13:36–43, 49–50 which, as noted in chapter 3, was probably composed by Matthew himself, contains two references to the everlasting burning of the wicked. In the interpretation of the parable of the tares, Matthew stresses that just as weeds are gathered and burned (13:40), so will the angels cast the wicked into the furnace of fire (εἰς τὴν κάμινον τοῦ πυρός; verse 42). The interpretation of the parable of the net says precisely the same thing. Just as the bad fish are thrown away, so will the angels throw the wicked to the fiery furnace (13:50). The two references to the furnace of fire have parallels in the wider apocalyptic-eschatological tradition (cf. 1 En. 54:6; 98:3; 4 Ezra 7:36) and the language might have been taken directly from Daniel 3:6 (εἰς τὴν κάμινον τοῦ πυρός τὴν καιομένην), even though this motif does not possess an eschatological sense in Daniel. Matthew's great judgement scene of 25:31–46 contains a specific reference to the punishment of the wicked by eschatological fire. Verse 41 affirms that the wicked will be sent 'into the eternal fire (εἰς τὸ πῦρ τὸ αἰώνιον) prepared for the devil and his angels'. This text is important in so far as it specifies with crystal clarity the evangelist's view that all the opponents of God, be they angelic or human, will share the same terrible fate. Since the phrase εἰς τὸ πῦρ τὸ αἰώνιον is also found in 18:8, Matthew's redacted form of Mark 9:43, it is probable that he is responsible for this reference to the eschatological fire.[10]

The final two instances of this theme appear in the sermon on the mount at 5:22 and 7:19. In the first of these texts, the Matthean Jesus speaks about the eschatological consequences of anger. He comments that anyone who is angry with his brother will be liable to judgement and that anyone who insults his brother will be liable to the council, and concludes with the warning that whoever says 'you fool' will be liable to the Gehenna of fire (εἰς τὴν γέενναν τοῦ πυρός). Whatever the origin of the third and final part of this verse, it is almost certain that the reference to the Gehenna of fire is redactional; the same expression was used by Matthew at 18:9 in his redaction of Mark 9:47–8.[11] With regard to 7:19, 'Every good tree that does not bear good fruit is cut down and thrown into the fire', there is general agreement that Matthew took this saying from his Baptist material in Q (cf. 3:10) and transferred it to the lips of Jesus at this point. The verse appears within a Q passage which spoke of the righteous and the wicked as good and bad trees respectively (Matt. 7:16–18//Luke 6:43–5), and has no Lucan parallel in this context. The evangelist obviously noted the aptness of the Baptist's words at this point and put them into the mouth of Jesus.[12]

In relation to this subject of the punishment of the wicked by eternal fire, it should not be overlooked that the gospel contains four unqualified references to Gehenna; that is to say, this location

[10] It is accepted as redactional by Marguerat, *Le Jugement*, p. 492; Gnilka, *Matthäusevangelium*, II, p. 369; Zumstein, *La Condition*, p. 331 and Broer, 'Das Gericht', p. 284.

[11] The whole section is deemed redactional by Davies and Allison, *Matthew*, I, p. 514 and Gnilka, *Matthäusevangelium*, I, p. 152. On the other hand, Luz *Matthäus*, I, pp. 252–3 believes that the sentence is traditional, but that Matthew is responsible for the τοῦ πυρός which qualifies Gehenna.

[12] So Davies and Allison, *Matthew*, I, pp. 710–11; Luz, *Matthäus*, I, p. 401; Schulz, *Q*, p. 318 and Marguerat, *Le Jugement*, p. 185.

is mentioned but nothing is said about its fiery character. While one of these derives from Q (Matt. 10:28//Luke 12:4–5), the other three are unparalleled (5:29–30; 23:15, 33) and all are most probably redactional. In the light of 5:22 and 18:9, let alone current usage in the wider apocalyptic-eschatological tradition, these passages presume the notion of the fiery furnace, despite their failure to mention it specifically. It is pertinent to mention at this point that Matthew also twice uses the synonymous Hades (11:23; 16:18) to describe this place of punishment.[13] If we add these four (or six) texts to the list of passages which specifically refer to the fiery fate of the wicked, then we have an impressive collection of references which is unequalled anywhere in the New Testament, including the Apocalypse. In fact few documents of the entire apocalyptic-eschatological tradition can compare with the amount of this type of material which is found in the gospel of Matthew. The evangelist's intense concentration on the punishment of the wicked by the fire of Gehenna entails that his other references to the judgement and its aftermath ought to be interpreted in these terms. In other words, when Matthew wrote of the destruction or everlasting punishment of the wicked, his intended readers were meant to identify these statements with the eternal fire of Gehenna.

Matthew's consistent view of eschatological punishment by eternal fire explains his omission of Mark 9:49, 'for every one will be salted with fire', his only identifiable omission of an eschatological fire tradition from his sources. This Marcan saying appears between and bridges the body/Gehenna material of 9:43, 45, 47–8 and two logia dealing with the subject of salt (9:50). Matthew omits the two salt sayings on account of their obscurity and uses a parallel Q tradition in the sermon on the mount (5:13//Luke 14:34–5). As for Mark 9:49, Matthew would have objected to it on two grounds. First, he would have disagreed with the general nature of the Marcan logion; for Matthew, only the wicked, not every one, will be subject to the fire. Secondly, since salt has purifying qualities, Mark 9:49 could be taken to mean that the fire acts as a purifying

---

[13] According to Jeremias, 'γέεννα', p. 658, the New Testament as a whole distinguishes between Hades and Gehenna, the former being the place of post-mortem punishment and the latter the place of punishment subsequent to the judgement. This very neat hypothesis, which tends to harmonise the evidence, was attacked by Boyd, 'Gehenna – According to J. Jeremias', pp. 9–12. Since Matthew seems to know of no punishment of the wicked immediately after death (see note 2 above), any such distinction between his usage of Hades and Gehenna is inappropriate.

agent as it does in 1 Corinthians 3:13–15 and the Testament of Abraham 12:10–14; 13:11–14. In Matthew, however, the fire is wholly punitive and has no purifying function whatsoever.

Though it might be tempting to do so, we should not attempt to disguise the full horror of this dominant Matthean theme. Like many of his contemporaries, Matthew accepted the reality of Gehenna as a place of eternal punishment and there is no reason to suspect that he intended his references to this location to be taken other than literally. And it is crucial that we understand precisely what the evangelist believed about this place of fire and the fate of the wicked there. What the notion of Gehenna entails is not a single flame licking an extended finger or toe on a temporary basis, but an all-consuming inferno which would encompass the whole body and put the condemned person in a state of perpetual agony. For Matthew, the eschatological fate of the wicked would be one of eternal torture by flames which would burn but not consume. The torturous nature of the end-time punishment of the wicked is evidenced in two further gospel passages and these must be given full weight.

At the conclusion of the parable of the unforgiving servant (Matt. 18:23–35), he who was forgiven his debt but failed to do likewise to others is ultimately handed over by his master to the torturers (οἱ βασανισταί). Matthew's own application of this parable in verse 35, 'So also my heavenly father will do to every one of you, if you do not forgive your brother from your heart,' puts this reference in an eschatological context. Most scholars interpret the motif of the torturers in the context of the gospel in terms of the horrible punishment which awaits the wicked.[14] The consigning of the wicked to the fires of Gehenna can thus be compared favourably with the handing over of a wayward servant to the torturers. That this is how Matthew envisaged the fate of the wicked is confirmed by examining the episode of the Gadarene demoniacs in 8:28–34 (//Mark 5:1–20). In the Marcan story the demons plead with Jesus not to torment or torture (βασανίζω) them by performing the exorcism (5:7). For Mark, the torture of the evil spirits results from their expulsion from the human body they now possess and their potentially homeless state thereafter. Matthew's redaction of this verse at 8:29 is rather striking and gives an entirely new meaning to the torture motif. The demons ask Jesus, 'Have you

---

[14] See, for example, Davies and Allison, *Matthew*, II, p. 803; Gnilka, *Matthäusevangelium*, II, p. 146 and Gundry, *Matthew*, p. 375.

come to torture us (βασανίσαι ἡμᾶς) before the time (πρὸ καιροῦ)?' There is no doubt that πρὸ καιροῦ here refers to the final judgement and its aftermath which, in Matthew, means consignment to the eternal flames (cf. 25:41). In the Matthean narrative, therefore, the supernatural demons of 8:28–34 are well aware of their ultimate fate and, quite naturally, express concern that this horrible punishment will be inflicted upon them by Jesus (the judge) sooner than they expected. Matthew thus gives the torture motif an eschatological sense which it did not possess in his Marcan source. This eschatological usage of the verb in 8:29 corresponds precisely with the meaning of the nominal cognate in 18:34.[15] According to Matthew, the punishment of the wicked will be torturous indeed.

This Matthean theme compares favourably with statements about the fate of the condemned in Revelation. According to Revelation 14:10–11, the worshippers of the beast will be tortured (βασανίζω) with fire and sulphur and the smoke of their torment (βασανισμός) will rise for eternity (cf. 20:15). A similar fate awaits Satan, the beast and the false prophet, all of whom will be thrown into the fiery lake where they will be tortured (βασανίζω) day and night forever (20:10). These two documents thus agree on the nature of the eschatological punishment; the wicked will be tortured forever in the flames of Gehenna (so Matthew) or the fiery lake (so Revelation). We find here yet another important parallel between these two Christian apocalyptic-eschatological authors. This agreement is even more significant in so far as there are almost no parallels to this particular motif in the remainder of the New Testament. The only comparable passage is the Lucan parable of the rich man and Lazarus (16:19–31). The former finds himself in Hades, the place of torture (βάσανος; verses 23, 28), where he suffers on account of the flames.

1.2 Other Matthean themes concerning the fate of the wicked

Matthew further stands in the apocalyptic-eschatological tradition by emphasising that the fiery place of torment is also characterised by complete and perpetual darkness. On three occasions he depicts the consignment of the wicked to the place of punishment in terms of being sent 'into the outer darkness' (εἰς τὸ σκότος τὸ ἐξώτερον;

---

[15] So correctly Gundry, *Matthew*, p. 159.

8:12; 22:13; 25:30) and it is universally agreed that each instance is redactional. This material should not be interpreted as an alternative tradition to the idea of the fiery Gehenna. The darkness indicates the separation of the wicked from the light of God and is simply another grim aspect of the place of torment. These passages serve in fact to reinforce just how well the evangelist knew the wider apocalyptic-eschatological tradition and how much of it he had absorbed.

Another uncomfortable but important theme concerns Matthew's preoccupation with the reaction of the wicked to their plight. They will weep in misery and gnash their teeth in rage once they realise the horrible and unchangeable circumstances in which they find themselves and the salvation they have lost. The evangelist originally found this reference to weeping and gnashing of teeth in Q (8:12//Luke 13:28; ἐκεῖ ἔσται ὁ κλαυθμὸς καὶ ὁ βρυγμὸς τῶν ὀδόντων), and it clearly appealed to him since he uses it on no less than five further occasions. Three of these are found in Matthean creations, the interpretations of the parables of the tares and the net (13:42, 50) and the parable of the man without the wedding garment (22:13b).[16] In the two other cases the evangelist has obviously inserted this phrase into his Q material. It is found without Lucan parallel as the conclusion to both the parable of the two servants (24:51) and the parable of the talents (25:30). Since Luke used this logion at 13:28, we may presume that he would have used it in each of these cases had it appeared in his recension of Q. It is essential to note that this quite unpleasant theme, which was clearly to Matthew's liking, finds few parallels in the contemporary apocalyptic-eschatological tradition where the terrible suffering of the wicked is more taken for granted than described. Consequently, Matthew oversteps a boundary which few of his contemporaries had crossed. This point is often overlooked but it is of the greatest importance when assessing the function of Matthew's apocalyptic-eschatological language. We shall return to this point in chapter 9.

2. The fate of the righteous

2.1 Matthew's terminology

As we might expect, the fate of the righteous is the converse of the lot of the wicked and Matthew uses common Christian words and

---

[16] For evidence of Matthew's composition of 22:11–13, see Sim, 'Matthew 22:13a and 1 Enoch 10:4a', pp. 8–9 and literature cited there.

phrases to express this in general terms. The righteous will receive rewards in heaven which can be described by the noun μισθός (5:12// Luke 6:23; 10:41–2//Mark 9:41; 20:28; cf. also Luke 6:35; John 4:36; 1 Cor. 3:8, 14; 9:17–18; 2 John 8; Rev. 11:18; 22:12) or by the verb ἀποδίδωμι (Matt. 6:4, 6, 18). In 12:36, 16:27 and 20:8, this verb is used in the extended sense of payment or repayment, either reward or punishment, at the time of the eschaton (cf. Rom. 2:6; 2 Tim. 4:14; 1 Pet. 4:5; Rev. 22:12). The evangelist also speaks of the related idea 'treasures in heaven' (6:20//Luke 12:33; 19:21//Mark 10:21; cf. 13:44–6) and uses the symbol 'life' (7:14; 18:8–9//Mark 9:43; 19:17) or 'eternal life' (19:16, 29//Mark 10:17, 30; 25:46), terms which are found throughout the New Testament but which are especially prominent in the Pauline and Johannine literature.

Matthew also depicts the fate of the righteous in the more concrete image of the eschatological (or messianic) feast of traditional Jewish (and Christian) expectation. This idea is most clearly expressed in the Q tradition in 8:11–12 (//Luke 13:28–9) which states that the righteous will recline at table in the kingdom of the heavens with Abraham, Isaac and Jacob. It is also suggested by those passages in which the kingdom is symbolically depicted as a wedding feast (22:1–14; diff. Luke 14:15–24) of which Jesus is the bridegroom (9:14–15//Mark 2:19–20; 25:1–13). The first of these themes is a development from the Old Testament notion that Israel is the bride of Yahweh (Isa. 62:4–5; Jer. 2:2; Ezek. 16:8; Hos. 3:20), while the notion of Jesus as the bridegroom was common in early Christianity (John 3:29; 2 Cor. 11:2; Rev. 19:7, 9; cf. Eph. 5:25–9). The state of the righteous in the eschatological age is specified in the beatitudes. As participants in the end-time banquet they shall be fully sated (5:6//Luke 6:21a) and comforted (5:4). They will inherit the earth (5:5), receive mercy (5:7), be called sons of God (5:9) and even see God face to face (5:8).

On the question of whether Matthew adopted the common apocalyptic-eschatological theme of the righteous residing in a new Jerusalem (so Revelation) with a new Temple (so many Jewish texts) there is no easy answer. It is often claimed that the words of the Matthean Jesus in 5:14, 'You are the light of the world. A city set on a hill cannot be hid', refer to the new Jerusalem which many texts say would be placed on a mountain and give light to the whole world.[17] Yet nothing in the pericope itself concretely points to the new

---

[17] This view was originally proposed by von Rad, 'The City on the Hill', pp. 232–42 and taken up by Campbell, 'The New Jerusalem', pp. 335–63. It is accepted by

Jerusalem. There is no definite article to indicate that only one city rather than any city was in mind, and the context of the saying points more toward an alternative reading. Just as any city cannot be hidden, and the light of any lamp should not be hidden (5:15), neither should the light of the disciples manifest through their works be hidden (5:16). All in all, if Matthew was referring in 5:14 to the eschatological Jerusalem, then he has placed this important concept in an odd context and expressed it in a most peculiar way.[18]

2.2 The righteous as angels

The evangelist is adamant that in the new age the righteous will become angels. According to Matthew 22:30, following Mark 12:25, the righteous will be like angels in heaven, a concept which is affirmed either explicitly or implicitly in many apocalyptic-eschatological texts. Unlike Mark, however, Matthew specifies precisely what this entails. In the parable of the man without the wedding garment in 22:11–13, the evangelist states that those admitted to the eschatological feast will wear a certain garment; the intruder is cast out by the attendants of the king because he has arrived at the celebration without the appropriate attire. It is most probable that the wedding garment represents the end-time garment of glory which many apocalyptic-eschatological texts equate with the garb of the angels. The righteous will thus be like angels in so far as they too will be dressed in eschatological or angelic garments.[19] Matthew specifies that they will also see God (5:8), a privilege of the holy angels (cf. 18:10), and this too suggests the angelic status of the righteous in the new age.

This theme is further evidenced in 13:43 where Matthew writes that the righteous will shine like the sun (οἱ δίκαιοι ἐκλάμψουσιν ὡς ὁ ἥλιος) in the kingdom of their father. Although it is often claimed that this text is based upon Daniel 12:3 (οἱ συνιέντες φανοῦσιν ὡς φωστῆρες τοῦ οὐρανοῦ), this is not certain. The verbal differences are quite extensive and the brilliance of the state of the elect in the new age is a very common motif in the apocalyptic-eschatological tradition. We shall return to the origin

Donaldson, *Jesus on the Mountain*, p. 117 (and see p. 256 n. 68 for other scholars holding this view).

[18] Davies and Allison, *Matthew*, I, p. 475; Luz, *Matthäus*, I, p. 223; Sabourin, *Matthew*, I, p. 355 n. 93 all argue against a reference to the new Jerusalem.

[19] That this is the best understanding of the garment motif, see Sim, 'Matthew 22:13a and 1 Enoch 10:4a', pp. 15–17.

of 13:43 shortly. For the moment it ought to be said that this verse must be taken in conjunction with the description of the angel at the empty tomb in Matthew 28:3. Matthew's source at this point, Mark 16:5–6, describes how the women who witnessed the crucifixion of Jesus entered the empty tomb and saw a young man dressed in a white robe who informs them that Jesus is risen. It is generally and rightly accepted that this figure is intended to be taken as an angel. Matthew adopts the general scenario, but elaborates it substantially. In 28:2 he describes the young man as an angel of the Lord (cf. 1:20, 24; 2:13) who descends from heaven amidst a great earthquake, and who rolls back the stone over the tomb and sits upon it. Matthew writes freely in the following verse and depicts the appearance of the angel in much greater detail than his Marcan source. He is described as having the appearance of lightning and wearing a garment white as snow. Most scholars accept that this description of the angel consists of a combination of elements which the evangelist took from the book of Daniel. The motif of the lightning recalls the account of the angel in Daniel 10:6 (cf. 2 En. 1:5; 19:1; Rev. 10:1), while the garment white as snow reflects Daniel's reference to the garb of the Ancient of Days in 7:9 (cf. too 1 En. 14:20; 71:1; T.Levi 8:2). This similarity between the brilliance of the angel at the empty tomb and the brilliance of the end-time state of the righteous in 13:43 confirms the point in 22:30; the righteous will be as angels in the eschatological era.

That these texts belong together receives confirmation in the transfiguration narrative (Matt. 17:1–9//Mark 9:2–10) which provides a bridge between them. Our interest lies with Mark 9:3 and Matthew's edited version of this tradition in 17:2. The Marcan verse states that when Jesus was transfigured his garments glistened with intense whiteness which no fuller on earth could reproduce. This material must be taken in an apocalyptic-eschatological context since, as we have seen, intense whiteness and brightness characterise the clothing of God and the holy angels. Yet Matthew clearly was not satisfied with the Marcan narrative at this point, for he intensifies considerably this particular section of the pericope. In Matthew's version it is not merely the garments of Jesus which undergo transformation, but his face as well (17:2). The face of Jesus shone like the sun (ἔλαμψεν τὸ πρόσωπον ὡς ὁ ἥλιος), while his clothes became white as light (τὰ ἱμάτια αὐτοῦ ἐγένετο λευκὰ ὡς τὸ φῶς). We shall take each motif in turn.

The reference to the alteration of Jesus' face is no doubt intended to recall the similar experience of Moses at Sinai (Ex. 34:29–30), but the fact that it shone like the sun is not found in that Old Testament text. This motif is paralleled, of course, in Matthew 13:43 and this correspondence between these two pericopae indicates Matthew's desire to present Jesus transfigured into his eschatological state of glory, a state which the righteous would also share in the eschaton; the transfigured Jesus thus prefigures not only his own eschatological (resurrected) state, but also that of all the righteous.[20] We find an interesting parallel to this description of Jesus in Revelation 1:16. According to this text, the face of Jesus shone like the sun in full strength (ἡ ὄψις αὐτοῦ ὡς ὁ ἥλιος φαίνει ἐν τῇ δυνάμει αὐτοῦ). In view of the close agreement between these passages, we may safely guess that Mathew and the author of Revelation had independent access to the same Christian tradition, one which depicted the face of the risen and glorified Jesus shining like the sun. If this is the case, then it becomes probable that this particular tradition and not Daniel 12:3 underlies Matthew's description of the righteous in 13:43.

Just as the transformed face of the Matthean Jesus signifies his eschatological state, so too does his altered clothing. Matthew abbreviates the pleonastic Marcan text and states simply that the garments of the transfigured Jesus became white as light. In the apocalyptic-eschatological tradition, light is an important characteristic of the end-time nature of the righteous, as is the theme of the brilliantly white eschatological or angelic robe. This reference to the garment of Jesus is similar to the redactional description of the angel in 28:3 whose attire was white as snow. Although Matthew has seen fit to use different comparative terms (light and snow), the whiteness motif remains the same and its brilliance is emphasised in each. His choice of φῶς in the transfiguration narrative might have been prompted by his later use of the adjective φωτεινή to describe the cloud from which God speaks (verse 5). In any event, it seems clear in view of the background of this theme that Matthew wished to emphasise that the risen or eschatological state of Jesus was also akin to the angelic state.[21]

---

20 So correctly Davies and Allison, *Matthew*, II, pp. 431, 696; Luz, *Matthäus*, II, p. 510; Schweizer, *Matthew*, pp. 348–9 and Sabourin, *Matthew*, II, pp. 701–2.

21 This does not mean, of course, that Matthew believed Jesus was merely transformed into an angel. The evangelist was of the view that Jesus far outranks the angels, coming second only to God in the divine hierarchy. As glorified Son of Man he sits at the right hand of God (26:64) and has total charge of the angelic retinue. While Matthew accepts that the eschatological existence of Jesus

Thus the description of the transfigured Jesus provides a bridge between the description of the righteous in 13:43 and that of the angel in 28:3 and shows that these texts belong together. In his eschatological state Jesus shines as the righteous will shine at the eschaton, and his transformed clothing is similar to that of the holy angels. In this way Matthew reaffirms his view that the righteous will be like the angels in the new age. This is an important point in so far as it concerns Matthew's concept of dualism. Just as all the wicked, both angels and humans, will be cast to the fiery furnace (cf. 25:41), so will all the righteous, both angelic and human, share the same state of blessedness. It demonstrates again the evangelist's all-embracing dualistic perception of the cosmos where only two modes of existence pertain, both in the present and in the new era.

There is no evidence that Matthew agreed with the Qumran notion that the righteous had already attained the angelic state. While it is true that the Matthean Jesus can say that his disciples are the light of the world (5:14a; cf. 4:16) and that they should let their light shine before men (5:16a), it is not a proleptic angelic existence which is at issue here. Rather, Matthew is thinking of the disciples standing out in the world by performing good works in accord with God's will (5:16b). Texts such as 13:43, 22:11–14 and 22:30, which place the transition from human to angelic state in the eschaton, demonstrate that the evangelist accepted the more common apocalyptic-eschatological line on this issue.

3. Conclusions

In this chapter, we have examined Matthew's convictions on the fate of the righteous and the fate of the wicked subsequent to the final judgement by Jesus the Son of Man. His views are by and large consistent on this matter and conform to the most common apocalyptic-eschatological scenario. The wicked will be consigned to Gehenna, the place of fire and darkness, where they will be tortured eternally by unquenchable fire as punishment for their sins. There they will weep and gnash their teeth as they realise their plight. In accepting and fervently promoting these notions about the fate of the wicked, Matthew stands apart from the majority of New Testament texts, with the sole exception of the author of the

approximates the angelic state, in so far as he is now part of the heavenly world, he is careful to ensure that this does not in any way compromise the status or authority of Jesus.

Apocalypse. With regard to the fate of the righteous, Matthew states that they will be given the eschatological garment of glory and be transformed into angels. In this state, they will partake of the eschatological banquet and live a life of perfect bliss in heaven with God forever. Matthew provides his readers with a glimpse of this magnificent end-time existence by depicting the transfigured Jesus in his eschatological glory.

That much of the material pertaining to these themes is redactional demonstrates their fundamental importance to the evangelist. This leads us to a further crucial point. It is precisely these two notions which give meaning and substance to Matthew's focus on the judgement. All his statements about this event, from general references to those descriptions of the Son of Man seated on his throne of glory, ultimately refer to the rewards or punishment his judgement brings. In other words, underlying every Matthean allusion to the judgement are the specific ideas that, amongst other things, the righteous will become angels and the wicked will burn for eternity. This extremely important point is not appreciated fully in Matthean scholarship. Normally the discussion of Matthew's eschatology centres on the fact that the evangelist accepts the idea of 'the judgement', which is referred to without qualification and is thereby depicted in rather colourless terms. Nothing is said of the aftermath of the event. It will be recalled from the Introduction that both Strecker and Marguerat justify this procedure on the grounds that Matthew has no consistent view of the end events. They infer from this that he was interested merely in the fact of the judgement and not concerned with its specific elements. Two points can be made in response to this argument.

The first is that Matthew was not a systematic theologian, so we should not expect a wholly coherent view on this matter. As a writer with access to many sources, Matthew used a wide variety of terms and metaphors to describe or allude to the process of judgement. Secondly, Matthew is not as inconsistent as Strecker and Marguerat claim. It was shown above that he is basically consistent in terms of the aftermath of the judgement – the wicked will burn forever and the righteous will be transformed into angels with the eternal life this brings. In view of this, we cannot dismiss these themes so easily. This is especially so in the light of the largely redactional nature of this material. If anything gives meaning to Matthew's emphasis on the judgement, then it is the very contrast between the beatific state of the righteous and the horrific fate of the wicked. Far from being irrelevant, this material assumes the greatest importance in Matthew's overall apocalyptic-eschatological scheme. The Son of Man does not merely come for the purpose of a colourless or banal judgement; he comes ultimately to bestow magnificent rewards and to inflict horrific punishments. This is precisely what 'the judgement' means. The material delineating the respective fates of the righteous and the wicked is therefore the climax of Matthew's particular scheme to which everything else points. By dismissing it as irrelevant, we run a very real risk of misinterpreting the evangelist's eschatological material.

7

THE IMMINENCE OF THE END IN
MATTHEW

The previous three chapters have detailed Matthew's end-time expectations, and this chapter will address the issue of the timing of these events. As noted in chapter 1, apocalyptic-eschatological schemes which accept the doctrine of the two ages almost without exception hold that the expected end events will occur in the imminent future. Since Matthew shows himself to be fully conversant with the other aspects of this perspective, we should expect that he too held fast to the imminence of the end. Yet any such suggestion would be firmly disputed by the majority of Matthean scholars. It was shown in the Introduction that a fundamental shift in scholarly opinion had occurred on the issue of Matthew's temporal end expectation. The earlier position of Streeter (and others) that Matthew's gospel strongly affirmed the impending arrival of the Son of Man had been displaced by the view of the early redaction critics which held that Matthew focuses more upon actions in the interim than upon the time of the end. While Streeter's position still has its proponents today, the view of Trilling, Strecker and Marguerat is still the more favoured hypothesis. The question of when Matthew expected the parousia is not just an academic question. It is an extremely important issue, since it directly affects our interpretation of the function of all the eschatological material which we have thus far surveyed. It will be argued in this chapter that the older view of the evangelist's temporal end expectations is the correct one and that the later alternative hypothesis fails to take into account the role of this theme in Matthew's overall apocalyptic-eschatological scheme. Since we are arguing against a well represented scholarly position on this issue, the argumentation in this chapter must necessarily be detailed. We shall begin the discussion with an analysis of the suggested arguments against an imminent end expectation in the gospel.

1. The arguments against an imminent end expectation in Matthew

The view that Matthew did not expect the arrival of Jesus the Son of Man in the immediate future, though widespread among Matthean scholars, is not as soundly based as is often supposed. It is built upon two general arguments, neither of which stands up to close scrutiny. One argument concerns Matthew's view of the church as an established institution, while the other bases its conclusion on a certain reading of the Matthean apocalyptic discourse. We shall take each of these arguments in turn.

1.1 Matthew's view of the church

This argument takes as its starting-point the fact that Matthew has a developed notion of the church. He is the only evangelist to use ἐκκλησία in a technical sense, he refers to the founding of the church as an institution (16:18–19; 28:19–20a) and he devotes a good deal of space to church regulations and discipline (18:15–35). The underlying idea here appears to be that such a developed notion of church organisation and discipline points toward the prolonged existence of the church, and this in turn precludes any belief in the imminence of the parousia.[1] The validity of this argument, however, should be strongly questioned. It relies on an unstated presupposition that groups anticipating the end (necessarily) tend to lose interest in mundane affairs generally and group discipline in particular. Yet there is no evidence at all from the time of the evangelist to support this premise. What evidence there is actually points to the opposite conclusion. In the writings from Qumran, where an imminent end expectation was a dominant belief, we find all the above-mentioned elements. This group described its founding as a separate sect, it was very rigidly structured and it was greatly concerned with matters of order and discipline. In terms of structure and discipline, the Qumran community appears to have been far more developed and rigid than the Matthean church. As shown in chapter 2, many apocalyptic communities, the group at Qumran included, tend to become more rigid in matters of discipline where the luxury of internal disobedience cannot be permitted. We shall see in chapter 9 how this

---

[1] Strecker, *Weg*, pp. 43–4; Kee, *Christian Origins*, p. 143 and Schulz, *Stunde*, p. 229.

applies to the Matthean community. While it would exceed the
evidence to appeal to the Qumran community to prove that
Matthew's church necessarily accepted the nearness of the parousia,
the Qumran evidence does falsify the premise upon which the
opposite argument is based.

A related argument which is sometimes put forward against
Matthew's near end expectation concerns 28:16–20, the final pericope of the gospel. The very last sentence which mentions the
abiding presence of Jesus, 'and behold, I am with you all the days
(πάσας τὰς ἡμέρας) to the close of the age', is considered to point
to the deferment of the end. The promise of Jesus to be with his
followers implies the continuing life of the church in the world.[2]
Yet it is quite clear that this verse by itself says nothing of the time
of the end. Its temporal meaning, either for or against an imminent
end expectation, must be determined by other indications in the
gospel.[3] The comforting promise of the risen Jesus to be with his
church as it carries out its mission in the face of persecution (see
further below and chapter 8) makes just as much sense in the
context of the nearness of the end as it does in the context of a
deferred parousia. We are permitted to conclude, therefore, that
nothing in Matthew's ecclesiology has a direct bearing on his
timing of the end.

1.2 The apocalyptic discourse

For many scholars, the evidence of Matthew's apocalyptic discourse, particularly the latter section, shows that Matthew did not

---

[2]   Strecker, *Weg*, p. 44; Schulz, *Stunde*, p. 229; Donaldson, *Jesus on the Mountain*,
pp. 166–7 and Meier, 'Salvation History in Matthew', p. 214. On the other hand,
Lohmeyer, *Matthäus*, p. 422 takes this verse as evidence of Matthew's near end
expectation.

[3]   The opposite is argued by Trilling who, following the earlier work of O. Michel,
argues that 28:18–20 is the key to the gospel and that the remainder of the
document must be interpreted in the light of it (*Wahre Israel*, p. 6). This leads
him to the conclusion that since this pericope is silent about the time of the end,
the emphasis in this passage, and thus the whole gospel, falls upon the strong
faith of the church in the present and not upon (temporal) apocalyptic speculation (*Wahre Israel*, p. 29). Without denying the importance of the final pericope
for Matthew, any suggestion that it must determine one's reading of the rest of
the gospel is clearly assigning it far too much significance. On Trilling's view,
Matthew's dualism and his views on the judgement and its aftermath must be
given secondary roles in so far as they do not receive specific mention in the final
passage. Any such reading of the gospel, however, would lead to severe distortion
of its message. Consequently, if there are temporal indications elsewhere in the
gospel, then Matthew 28:18–20 must be interpreted in the light of these.

accept the imminence of Jesus' parousia. There are in fact two separate arguments at issue here which need to be examined separately. One argument highlights the concept of the delay of the parousia to which Matthew refers in three parables dealing with the interim period between the resurrection and the parousia – the parable of the good and wicked servants (Matt. 24:45–51//Luke 12:41–6), the parable of the ten virgins (Matt. 25:1–13) and the parable of the talents (Matt. 25:14–30//Luke 19:11–27). It is argued that in these three pericopae the evangelist acknowledges that the end both has been delayed and will by implication be delayed further. The first two parables mention that Jesus, the master in one text and the bridegroom in the other, has been delayed (χρονίζω; 24:48; 25:5), which suggests that Matthew was well aware of the problem of the delay of Jesus' return. In the parable of the talents, he takes this a step further by indicating that Jesus will be delayed for some time to come. According to Matthew's version, the man who went away (i.e. Jesus) returned after a long time (μετὰ δὲ πολὺν χρόνον; verse 19). The Lucan parallel is different at this point and reads 'when he returned', which says nothing directly of the length of the man's absence. It is disputed whether Matthew's text at this point is redactional or original, but the former possibility is more likely.[4] Hence, it is argued that by this redaction Matthew indicates to his readers that Jesus has been delayed and will return not in the near future but only after a long period of absence.[5]

The problem with this argument is that none of these texts bears the weight which is placed upon them. Let us take first Matthew 24:48 and 25:5. While these texts certainly testify to Matthew's conviction that the parousia had been delayed, they tell us nothing about his future expectations. Contrary to the logic of the proposed argument, an awareness of an event's delay does not in any way imply or entail its further delay. Moreover, there is no contradiction between recognising such a delay and hoping for the event to happen in the near future. In other words, these texts do not necessarily indicate a deferral of the parousia from the standpoint of the author, nor are they inconsistent with an imminent end

---

4   Strecker, *Weg*, p. 44 and Gundry, *Matthew*, p. 504 assign these words to Matthew's redaction, while Schulz, *Q*, p. 290 and Gnilka, *Matthäusevangelium*, II, p. 358 consider them to have stood in Matthew's source.

5   See Bornkamm, 'End-Expectation', p. 23; Strecker, *Weg*, pp. 44–5; Schulz, *Stunde*, p. 229 and Meier, 'Salvation History in Matthew', p. 212 n. 19.

expectation. It might be argued that the reference to Jesus' return 'after a long time' in 25:19 is certain confirmation that Matthew had rejected the idea of an imminent parousia and deferred it to the distant future. Yet this interpretation has a hidden and fallacious assumption. It presumes that the fifty years or so which intervened between the resurrection and the composition of the gospel was not perceived by Matthew as 'a long time'. But on what grounds do we know this? Surely it is likely that the five decades waiting for the parousia, the whole period of the church's existence, would have been accepted by the Christians of Matthew's time as a very long time indeed. One suspects that scholars interpret this phrase from their modern perspective, where fifty years is not such a long period in the context of two millennia, but this clearly cannot be applied to the first-century Matthew. Consequently, while Matthew 25:19 says something about Matthew's perception of the length of time Jesus had been gone, it says nothing of a further postponement of his arrival. Like the two other texts, it is not inconsistent with Matthew's holding fast to an imminent end expectation.

The second argument based upon the apocalyptic discourse is broader in scope and more sophisticated in approach. This argument refers to the cluster of related material in 24:36–25:13 which stresses that the date of the parousia is unknown. At the beginning of this section, Matthew takes from Mark 13:32 a logion which specifies that no-one, apart from God himself, knows the day or the hour of the return of the Son of Man (24:36). The remainder of the material stresses this very point and in the process enjoins its readers to be watchful. Matthew 24:37–41 (//Luke 17:26–35) maintains that the Son of Man will come suddenly and catch people unawares. The evangelist appends to the end of this Q material a saying which he took from Mark 13:35, 'Watch, therefore, for you do not know on what day [diff. Mark 'when'] your Lord is coming' (verse 42). The two parables which follow, the thief in the night (24:43–4//Luke 12:39–40) and the good and wicked servants (24:45–51//Luke 12:41–6), also derive from Q and emphasise this theme. The first uses a traditional motif (cf. 1 Thess. 5:2–4; 2 Pet. 3:10; Rev. 3:3; 16:15) and claims that had the owner of a house known when the thief was coming, he would have watched and not let his house be burgled. Then follows the admonition that the reader must be ready, for the Son of Man (like the thief) will come at an unexpected hour. The parable of the two servants states that the master of the wicked servant will return when the servant least expects it and punish him. The concluding passage, the parable of the ten virgins (Matt. 25:1–13), describes five virgins who were prepared for the return of the bridegroom and five who were not. At the conclusion of this text, Matthew adds in verse 13, 'Watch, therefore, for you know neither the day nor the hour' (cf. 24:42).[6]

It is argued that in 24:36–25:13 Matthew is deliberately discouraging any speculation about the time of the end, either in terms of its imminence or in terms of its deferral. The evangelist is fully aware that the end has been delayed (24:48; 25:5, 19), but he does not perceive this in itself to be a problem. What does cause problems, from Matthew's point of view, is any speculation regarding the timing of the parousia. This applies equally to (apocalyptic) speculation which counts on its nearness and to the contrary belief which reckons with its continued deferment. The latter view especially can lead to moral laxness and the abuse of authority. In order to combat both beliefs, he focuses in this section on the fact that the time of the parousia is unknown and will therefore be sudden and unexpected. His exhortations to watchfulness therefore assume a paraenetic function, advising the reader to reckon continually with (but not count on) the arrival of the Son of Man and live a proper life accordingly. The emphasis falls more on one's actions in the present than on the timing of the end. In this way both an imminent and a prolonged expectation of the end play their part in the gospel and are pressed into the service of exhortation.[7] A number of points need to be made in response to this very widespread interpretation of 24:36–25:13.

The first is that there is no doubt that one purpose of this material is to exhort the readers to good behaviour in the period prior to the parousia; the parable of the two servants and the parable of the talents make this very point and it is clearly assumed in the remaining material. We shall return to this subject in chapter 9. What is not so certain, however, is that by emphasising this element Matthew intended to replace speculation about the time of the parousia. The common interpretation of those statements

6 So most scholars; Jeremias, *Parables*, p. 52; Marguerat, *Le Jugement*, p. 537; Gnilka, *Matthäusevangelium*, II, p. 348 and Zumstein, *La Condition*, p. 272.

7 This general view can be attributed, with some differences in detail, to Strecker, *Weg*, pp. 241–2; Marguerat, *Le Jugement*, pp. 521–44; Zumstein, *La Condition*, pp. 256–81 and Hahn, 'Die eschatologische Rede', pp. 120–23. Cf. also Bornkamm, 'End-Expectation', p. 23 and Schulz, *Stunde*, p. 229. These Matthean texts, along with other synoptic pericopae, are similarly interpreted by Grässer, *Parusieverzögerung*, pp. 77–95.

which affirm that the day and/or hour of the Son of Man's arrival is unknown reads far too much into this motif and is in fact based upon a false premise. The premise in question is that imminent eschatological schemes always nominate a certain day for the end events. Only on the basis of this assumption can it be argued that Matthew, by concretely rejecting the naming of a specific day, simultaneously rejected an imminent end expectation.[8] Yet there is no evidence whatsoever to support this premise. It will be recalled from chapter 1 that the apocalyptic-eschatological schemes of Matthew's time normally did not nominate a specific day for the arrival of the eschaton, even though the imminence of this event was clearly affirmed in other ways. The sole exceptions to this rule are the books of Daniel and Revelation. In view of this general reluctance to be precise about the time of the end, we may suppose that most writers would have agreed with Matthew that God alone knows the exact day and hour of the eschaton. Certainly their failure to nominate specific dates did not prevent them upholding the nearness of the events in question. While it might well be true that Matthew's emphatic insistence that the day of the parousia is unknown was intended to combat certain members of his church who were nominating precise dates, the rejection of this practice is in no way inconsistent with the evangelist himself expecting the imminent return of Jesus. There is a distinction between these two positions which should not be blurred.

This point has important repercussions for the correct interpretation of the exhortations to be prepared and to watch. As noted above, this is often interpreted in purely paraenetic terms where all emphasis falls on the present life of the reader. The reader should take care to live a proper Christian life at all times since the day of the parousia is unknown and one must not be caught unprepared. This position is reached, of course, because it is assumed that Matthew had done away with speculating about the time of the end. Yet if this assumption is not allowed to influence the interpretation of this material, and we are permitted to read these hortatory verses in terms of the general timing of the parousia, then it is clear that they enjoin the imminence of that event. Matthew is warning his readers to be watchful and to be prepared (by living a proper life) precisely because the end is near, even if its exact date is

---

[8]   This assumption is not confined to Matthean scholarship. It is found, for example, in the recent study of Mark 13 by Geddert. See his *Watchwords*, pp. 246–7.

unknown; it is the imminence of the event which leads to the calls for vigilance.[9] This point is in a sense conceded in the alternative exposition which claims that the imminence of the end still has a part to play in Matthew's gospel. In reality there is almost no difference between reckoning with the possibility that the end might come at any time and actually expecting it in the imminent future. Consequently, this argument against Matthew's acceptance of the imminence of the end actually speaks in favour of it. It is appropriate now to examine the further indications in the gospel which testify to Matthew's belief in the imminence of the parousia.

2. The evidence in favour of an imminent end expectation in Matthew

2.1 Matthew 16:28 and 24:34

Scholars who affirm a near end expectation in the gospel of Matthew usually appeal to three texts in support of this interpretation, 10:23, 16:28 and 24:34.[10] We shall examine 10:23 shortly and concentrate for the moment on the second and third of these texts. In Matthew 16:28, the redacted version of Mark 9:1, the Matthean Jesus proclaims that there are some standing here who will not die before they see the Son of Man coming in his kingdom. Matthew 24:34 is taken directly from Mark 13:30 and states that 'this generation' will not pass away until all the events mentioned previously in the apocalyptic discourse take place. Taken at face value, these two texts do seem to affirm the imminence of the end. It matters little whether Matthew applied the 'some standing here' and 'this generation' to the contemporaries of Jesus or to his own contemporaries; in either case the nearness of the parousia and not its deferral is clearly in view. These texts thus set a general (not precise) time for the arrival of the end. The parousia will occur before the present generation dies out. Those scholars who deny an imminent end expectation in Matthew approach these texts (and 10:23) in one of two ways. The first is to deny any significance to this material by claiming that Matthew has merely copied these texts from his sources.[11] For the reasons provided in the Introduction, this is not a legitimate response since we must take seriously

---

[9] So correctly Hagner, 'Apocalyptic Motifs', p. 76 and Lambrecht, 'Parousia Discourse', pp. 325–6.

[10] See, for example, Kümmel, *Introduction*, p. 118 and Fenton, *Matthew*, p. 21.

[11] So Schulz, *Stunde*, p. 229.

those texts which Matthew chose to retain intact from his source material. The second approach is to argue that, despite appearances, these passages do not in the context of Matthew carry the meaning of a near end expectation.[12] It is not necessary to discuss any of these alternative exegeses at this point. Rather, it is preferable to turn to other sections of the gospel which clearly express Matthew's view that the end was imminent. In the light of this evidence, it will become clear that Matthew 16:28 and 23:34 must be taken in terms of the imminence of the parousia.

2.2 The apocalyptic discourse

It will be recalled from our earlier discussion that most apocalyptic-eschatological schemes do not express a near end expectation by making concrete statements to this effect. A more common mode of expression is that of the historical review, the final sections of which detail the events leading up to the eschaton. This particular device was used to inform the readers precisely where they stood in relation to the end events. Matthew makes use of this technique in a limited way, primarily in the apocalyptic discourse, and a proper understanding of his usage reveals that he wished to inform his readers that the Son of Man was expected soon. We have already noted that the exhortation to watch in 24:36–25:13 itself involves this motif in general terms (cf. 24:34), but even more precise information is given in the earlier section of the discourse, particularly in verses 4–14. Prior to examining this material in detail, however, it is necessary to devote some attention to the preliminary question of the relationship between the destruction of Jerusalem and the apocalyptic discourse.

A number of scholars believe that the destruction of Jerusalem and its temple in 70 CE provides the key to the Matthean apocalyptic discourse. How much, if any, of this discourse directly concerns this event, and what is the relationship between it and the timing of the parousia? The answers to these questions depend almost entirely upon one's assessment of the double question of the disciples in 24:3 which prompts Jesus to speak about the end events. In Mark 13:3–4 the disciples ask Jesus, 'Tell us, when will this be, and what will be the sign when these things are all to be accomplished?' Since this double question immediately follows

---

[12] One example is Strecker, *Weg*, pp. 41–3.

Jesus' prophecy of the destruction of the temple (13:2), the first part
of it (at least) necessarily adverts to the time of the temple's
ruination and the following discourse addresses this issue. The
Matthean version of the disciples' question also follows Jesus'
words about the end of the temple (24:2) and retains the two part
structure. He reproduces the first question ('when will this be?') but
sharpens the eschatological orientation of the second with standard
Matthean language, 'and what will be the sign of your coming and
of the close of the age?'

Some scholars argue that by keeping the first question Matthew
by and large adopted the Marcan scheme; the following discourse
answers both the question about the destruction of the temple and
the inquiry about the coming of the Son of Man at the end of the
age. There is no consensus, however, about which sections of the
discourse respond to which question. According to S. Brown, the
whole section in verses 4–31 relates to the temple's destruction, and
the material which follows applies to the Son of Man.[13] On the
other hand, J. Lambrecht confines the material referring to the
temple's demise to 24:15–28, the material dealing with the 'abomination of desolation' in the holy place (the destruction of the
temple) and the flight of the righteous.[14] Neither view is convincing.
Brown's hypothesis in particular is hard pressed to substantiate
that 24:29–31, the verses which deal with the breakdown of the
cosmic order and appearance of the Son of Man, refer to a past and
not a future event.[15] Moreover, both Brown and Lambrecht face
the difficulty of Matthew's redaction of Mark 13:18 in 24:20. In this
verse the evangelist alters the Marcan 'pray that it (the tribulation)
may not happen in winter' to 'pray that your flight may not be in
winter or on a sabbath'. The addition of the sabbath reference
makes no sense at all if the flight is an event of the past and the day
of flight is already established; clearly here Matthew is thinking of
an event which has yet to take place.[16] This means that all the
material in the immediate context of this verse, Matthew 24:15–28,
seems to pertain to the future and not to the past. In view of this

---

[13] Brown, 'The Matthean Apocalypse', pp. 2–27. An earlier version of this
      interpretation was presented by A. Feuillet, 'Le Sens du Mot Parousie',
      pp. 261–80. Feuillet's analysis was accepted by Gaston, *No Stone on Another*,
      pp. 483–5.
[14] Lambrecht, 'Parousia Discourse', pp. 321–3. In agreement is Hahn, 'Die eschato-
      logische Rede', p. 119.
[15] For more detail, see Donaldson, *Jesus on the Mountain*, pp. 164–5.
[16] So correctly Hare, *Jewish Persecution*, pp. 177–8.

observation, these verses cannot be applied to the events of 66–70 CE. It will be recalled from chapter 4 that the event Matthew has in mind in this section is the eschatological war between the righteous and the forces of the antichrist which has not yet occurred. With the exclusion of this material from consideration, it becomes impossible to find any part of the apocalyptic discourse which gives *sustained treatment* to the destruction of the temple by the Romans. Many scholars therefore argue that Matthew did not concern himself with this question in chapters 24–5.

Those commentators who adopt this view claim that Matthew did not follow the Marcan setting of the apocalyptic discourse. They contend that the evangelist intended to align the material treating the destruction of the temple (24:1–2) with the discourse against the scribes and Pharisees in chapter 23. In doing so, Matthew separates completely the fate of the temple from the apocalyptic discourse. On this reading, the double question of Matthew 24:3 refers solely to the arrival of the Son of Man. The arguments upon which this hypothesis rests can be summarised briefly as follows.[17] Matthew structures his narrative and edits his Marcan material in order to present the prophecy of destruction in 24:2 as the climax of his carefully manufactured and polemical episode of Jesus in the temple (21:23–24:1).[18] He concludes the polemical discourse in chapter 23 with the Q logion in which Jesus states that the temple (your house) is forsaken and desolate (23:37–9//Luke 13:34–5). He then omits Mark's story of the widow's mite (Mark 12:41–4), and describes Jesus not just leaving the temple (so Mark) but moving away from it (24:1); the temple is thus forsaken and desolate by his complete absence from it. The following prophecy of its destruction (24:2), a past event for Matthew (cf. 22:7), serves as the appropriate conclusion by demonstrating how the temple is now abandoned by God and is ultimately destroyed by him as a result. Matthew 24:3 is then taken as the introduction of a completely new section of the gospel which deals only with the parousia and in which the temple plays no part. That Matthew focuses entirely on the end events and not on the temple is

---

[17] The most detailed defence of this thesis is found in Burnett's *Jesus-Sophia*, but unfortunately it is not presented as a unified whole. Rather, it is found piecemeal throughout his monograph. Of particular importance are pp. 18–24, 112–16, 152–65, 198–215. See also Gnilka, *Matthäusevangelium*, II, pp. 311–13 for a more recent statement of this view.

[18] For more detail on Matthew's redaction and purpose in this section, see Sim, 'Man without the Wedding Garment', pp. 167–9.

suggested by a number of editorial changes to the Marcan text. He omits Mark's reference that the temple was opposite Jesus as he sat on the Mount of Olives, and he sharpens considerably the eschatological focus of the disciples' question.

This view has much in its favour. It can be readily conceded that Matthew has structured and edited his sources in order to separate 24:2, the climax of Jesus' visit to the temple, from 24:3, the introduction to the apocalyptic discourse. Moreover, it is supported by the point made above that nothing in the apocalyptic discourse seems to provide a detailed description of the destruction of the temple, suggesting that the evangelist was not concerned with this event at this point in his narrative. Yet, despite its advantages, this hypothesis has difficulty with the first part of the disciples' question in 24:3 which Matthew copies from Mark. The immediate antecedent to 'when will this be?' is the prediction about the temple in 24:2, and this suggests that the evangelist did not totally omit the destruction of the temple from his apocalyptic discourse. The response by those who acknowledge this problem is to take the καί, which connects the two parts of the disciples' inquiry, not conjunctively as it is in Mark, but epexegetically instead. The question would then read, 'Tell us when will this be, that is (καί), what will be the sign of your coming and of the close of the age?'[19] This proposal is possible but not very likely for the simple reason that it cannot explain why Matthew chose to express himself at this point in such a convoluted and ambiguous manner. If his intention was to separate the prophecy of the temple's destruction from the apocalyptic discourse, then why did he not adopt the easiest solution and simply omit altogether the problematic first question and write only the second?

We are left then with a rather confusing situation. The setting of the apocalyptic discourse in 24:3 seems to demand that the destruction of the temple receives some mention in the speech which follows, and yet no section of the discourse provides a detailed description of this event. How are we to account for this anomaly? According to D. R. A. Hare, Matthew simply ignores the first question, since for him the fate of the temple is no longer tied up with the end events. The evangelist de-eschatologises the temple's destruction and so refuses to mention it in the material which describes the events leading up to and including the

---

[19] So Burnett, *Jesus-Sophia*, pp. 206–8 who acknowledges his debt to the earlier work of R. Walker on this issue.

parousia.[20] Yet this response too seems rather inadequate, since it also ascribes to Matthew an extremely odd treatment of his sources. Once again, we might ask why he did not simply omit the first part of the question and focus all attention on the second part.[21] We must conclude, therefore, that given Matthew's retention of the initial part of the disciples' question he does intend to treat the destruction of the temple in the apocalyptic discourse. But precisely where is this reference?

If, as argued above, 24:15–28 is excluded as a possibility, then the only candidate would seem to be the reference to wars between nations in 24:6–7a. It is inherently likely given the lack of alternatives that Matthew intended this material to refer to the Jewish war of 66–70 CE, which included the destruction of the temple. In this way, the prediction of the temple's demise does receive its fulfilment in the apocalyptic discourse, albeit in this rather indirect manner. But this immediately poses the further question; why does the evangelist treat this event so curtly? The answer lies in the overall purpose of the apocalyptic discourse which, as Matthew's alteration of the disciples' second question shows, was primarily to provide information about the return of Jesus the Son of Man. In itself the destruction of Jerusalem and its temple conveyed little information about this subject. As an eschatological event of the comparatively distant past, a decade or so from Matthew's time of writing, the fate of the temple was of little use in determining the time of the parousia. From Matthew's perspective, more current end-time events provided better information on this subject and he appropriately chose to focus on these. This is understandable, given that the primary purpose of the eschatological sections of the historical review is to pinpoint for the readers the present time within the series of events. The end of the temple is thus not so much de-eschatologised as placed in its proper eschatological perspective. This point will become clearer once we examine in detail Matthew's timetable of the end in 24:4–14.

Though it is not generally recognised, Matthew provides an explicit timetable of the end in 24:4–14. This section of the discourse is thus far more important for determining his temporal end expectation than the later section in 24:36–25:13 which, as we have seen, seems to dominate the discussion of this particular issue. Matthew 24:4–14 is reminiscent of the timetables which are found

[20] Hare, *Jewish Persecution*, pp. 178–9.
[21] See Burnett, *Jesus-Sophia*, pp. 203–4.

throughout the apocalyptic literature, although the time-frame is more limited. Here we have an authoritative figure of the past, whose other prophecies have come to fulfilment, making predictions about the events preceding the eschaton. Like the apocalyptists, Matthew uses this device to inform his readers exactly where they stand in relation to these eschatological events. Once we grasp Matthew's intentions in this section, we find that he vigorously affirms the imminence of the end.

Matthew 24:4–14 is a mixture of Marcan material (Mark 13:5–8, 13) and Matthean redaction. It is the latter material which provides the clues to his intentions. In verses 4–8 Matthew follows closely the Marcan text (Mark 13:5–8) in listing the signs which indicate the 'beginnings of the birth pangs'. False Christs will appear (24:5), there will be wars and rumours of wars (24:6), nations will rise against nations and kingdom against kingdom, and there will be famines and earthquakes (verses 7–8). After verse 8 Matthew drastically edits his source. He transposes the block of material in Mark 13:9–13 (minus verse 10) to the mission charge of chapter 10 (10:17b–22). This transposition need not concern us here, for it has no bearing upon the present discussion. It is none the less an important redactional procedure on the part of Matthew and we shall return to it in due course. More important at this point is the fact that in place of Mark 13:9–13 Matthew presents a freely written section for the remainder of his timetable. Some of this material he drew from the omitted Marcan section and heavily edited (cf. Matt. 24:9a//Mark 13:9a; Matt. 24:9b//Mark 13:13a; Matt. 24:13//Mark 13:13b; Matt. 24:14//Mark 13:10), while the rest is his own creation. That Matthew saw fit to edit Mark so drastically at this point is important. We must presume that in doing so he was creating a chronology of events which was both applicable and meaningful to the particular situation of his readers. This in itself severely weakens the alternative positions regarding Matthew's temporal expectations. Why would he so drastically and deliberately alter this material, if he either was not particularly interested in the timing of the end or had deferred it to the distant future?

The events expected after the initial 'birthpangs' in Matthew's revised timetable are as follows. The disciples (the church) will be delivered to tribulation and put to death (24:9a) and they will be hated by all nations for Jesus' sake (verse 9b). Following this many (Christians) will be scandalised and betray one another (verse 10).

Many false prophets will arise and lead many astray (verse 11), while most men's love will run cold because of the growth of lawlessness (ἀνομία verse 12). Matthew appends at this point the Marcan exhortation that the one who endures to the end will be saved (verse 13). This editorial section concludes with the statement that the gospel of the kingdom must be preached throughout the world as a testimony to all nations, and then the end will come (verse 14). Matthew 24:4–14, therefore, sets out in very precise terms the events leading up to the parousia. In other words it spells out Matthew's eschatological timetable. What needs to be determined now is at what point within this general period the evangelist places his own time. To put the matter another way, which events, if any, were past from the perspective of Matthew and which did he still expect?

One important attempt to answer this question is that of W. G. Thompson.[22] In attempting to pinpoint Matthew's historical perspective in 24:4–14, Thompson focuses on the comments in this section which accompany the prophecies and serve to interpret them. These comments are found in verses 6cd, 8, 13 and indicate, according to his analysis, that the accompanying prediction either has been fulfilled or is in the process of being fulfilled. Verse 6cd follows the prophecies of the appearance of false Christs and the occurrence of wars and rumours of wars. The statement 'for this must take place' (verse 6c) puts these events in the context of God's divine plan and implies, according to Thompson, that these occurrences have already taken place. The next clause, 'but the end is not yet' (verse 6d) confirms this in so far as it serves to correct a false interpretation on the part of Matthew's readers that the end has already arrived (pp. 248–9). The comment in verse 8 specifies that certain wars, earthquakes and famines comprise the beginning of the birth pangs or eschatological sufferings. The placement of these events in a concrete period in history suggests for Thompson that the period belongs to the past. The Matthean community could have looked back to the time of the Jewish war as ample fulfilment of these prophecies (p. 249). Finally, Thompson turns his attention to 24:13. This verse, which contains the advice 'But he who endures to the end will be saved', comes after the prediction of the external persecution and internal dissension and betrayal. With regard to this material Thompson writes, 'The proverbial tone suggests that

[22] Thompson, 'Historical Perspective', pp. 243–62.

this comment speaks directly to the present experience of the Matthean community' (p. 249).

Thompson continues his analysis by pointing out that no further comments are forthcoming with regard to the final two predictions of verses 14a and 14b. These prophecies state that the gospel must be preached throughout the world and only then will the end come. The lack of comment or interpretation here, explains Thompson, must be attributed to the fact that these predictions are still future for Matthew; explanatory comments are only permissible when the prediction either has been fulfilled or is currently being fulfilled (p. 249). In an important summary statement Thompson asserts (p. 250) that as the Matthean community listened to these words of (the Matthean) Jesus;

> ...they would understand that his predictions about tension between nations and kingdoms and about famines and earthquakes (vss 7–8) referred to events already experienced, that his description of hatred and opposition from without and of internal dissension and widespread wickedness within the community (vss 9–13) spoke to their present situation, and that his words about completing the mission to all nations and about the end of the age (vs 14) provided clear guidelines for the future.

This study of Matthew 24:4–14 by Thompson thus firmly puts the time of the evangelist and his community somewhere near the end of the eschatological timetable. The only eschatological event they still expected before the arrival of the end was the proclamation of the gospel throughout the world; all the others either had been fulfilled or were in the process of being fulfilled.

In my view Thompson's general argument is basically correct, but I would argue that he has not presented his case as strongly as it could be presented. What Thompson failed to emphasise in his analysis of this section was the significance of the false prophets in verses 11–12. This material requires detailed analysis. Matthew 24:11–12 reads, 'And many false prophets (ψευδοπροφῆται) will arise and lead many astray. And because lawlessness (ἀνομία) is multiplied, most men's love will grow cold.' The problem of false prophecy was common in early Christianity (e.g. 2 Pet. 2:1–2; 1 John 4:1–3; Rev. 2:20) and in some circles the arrival of false prophets was considered to be a sign of the end. This belief is reflected, for example, in Mark 13:22. Matthew 24:11–12, however, is not dependent upon Mark 13:22. Matthew reproduces this verse later in the discourse at 24:24. As noted earlier, verses 11–12 are entirely redactional. The fact that Matthew creates this second and seemingly unnecessary reference to false prophets, and inserts it into his manufactured timetable of the end-events, clearly indicates his interest in this particular eschatological sign. An obvious question now presents itself; why is Matthew so concerned to warn his readers of the appearance of false prophets in the end-time? Only one answer seems probable. Since the purpose of the eschatological timetable is to indicate where the readers stand in relation to the end events, we must suppose that Matthew's modification of his Marcan material at this point was designed to provide such a clue. This means the evangelist considered that these false prophets, whose presence signified the nearness of the end, would be known to his readers. In other words, these false prophets were active in his church.

This suspicion receives confirmation from Matthew 7:15–23. We may infer from this material that Matthew's church contained a number of charismatic figures whom he reckoned to be false prophets.[23] This section is a mixture of three disparate Q texts (cf. Luke 6:43–5, 46; 13:25–7) which Matthew introduces with a redactional statement warning of the dangers of false prophets (7:15). The purpose of this material is to direct a hostile attack on these pseudo-prophets. The passage opens with a warning to beware of false prophets who come in sheep's clothing but are actually ravenous wolves (7:15). This is followed by a statement of the means by which these false prophets may be identified. They can be easily detected by their deeds; a good tree bears good fruit while a bad tree bears evil fruit (verses 16–20). Matthew concludes this pericope on a note of judgement. Despite their claims to be good Christians, confessing Jesus as Lord as well as prophesying and performing mighty works in his name, they will be identified as false by Jesus at the final judgement; as workers of lawlessness (ἀνομία), they will receive his condemnation (verses 21–3). There can be little doubt that in this particular section Matthew is addressing a present problem in his church and not merely taking precautions against a possible future

---

[23] D. Hill argues against the consensus, and ultimately in unconvincing fashion, that Matthew 7:15–23 refers to two sets of opponents, false prophets in verses 15–20 and a group of unrelated charismatics in verses 21–3. See his 'False Prophets and Charismatics', pp. 335–40.

threat.[24] Two arguments can be marshalled in support of this statement. First, it is surely far more probable that such a bitter attack was motivated by actual experience rather than abstract speculation about the future. As we know from Matthew 23, Matthew had few qualms about denouncing in the strongest terms those whom he considered present threats to his church. The polemic in 7:15–23 should not be read any differently. We shall say more about this subject in chapter 8 when we examine Matthew's view of the Christian church as a *corpus mixtum*. Secondly, Matthew's intimate knowledge of these charismatics almost certainly suggests that he knows them first-hand. He knows that they confess Jesus as Lord and both prophesy and work miracles in his name. His knowledge of these opponents is so thorough that he can even suggest ways of identifying them. Clearly, such precise information regarding the activities of these prophets strongly implies that they were known personally to Matthew and his readers. The evangelist thus constructed 7:15–23 in direct response to the threat which this group posed to his community.

The issue to determine now is whether these false prophets are to be identified with the eschatological false prophets of 24:11–12. Many scholars have argued that the two groups ought to be identified,[25] and this supposition has much in its favour and little against it. Matthew offers no suggestion that he has two distinct groups of false prophets in mind. On the contrary, he explicitly states that both of them are characterised by lawlessness (ἀνομία). Matthew 24:11–12 states that on account of the activities of these people lawlessness will multiply, while Matthew 7:15–23 affirms that the present opponents are workers of lawlessness. This similarity in both function (false prophecy) and purpose (lawlessness) between these two groups implies strongly that Matthew drew no distinction between them. The false prophets currently causing trouble in his community are none other than the false prophets who were expected at the end of the age. This means the evangelist believed that he and his church were caught up in the events which were to precede the coming of Jesus the Son of Man.

Not all scholars would agree with this conclusion. D. Hill argues

---

[24] Strecker, *Weg*, pp. 137–8 n. 4 argues unconvincingly that Matthew was not reacting to real opponents, but was merely warning his readers not to be misled by false teachings.

[25] So Davies and Allison, *Matthew*, I, p. 705; Luz, *Matthäus*, I, p. 403; Gnilka, *Matthäusevangelium*, I, p. 274; Burnett, *Jesus-Sophia*, pp. 247–9 and Barth, 'Matthew's Understanding of the Law', p. 75.

that Matthew did not identify the two groups of false prophets. According to Hill, '...there is no certainty that the false prophets of 24, 11 are the same as those referred to in 7, 15: only the presence of the word ἀνομία in both texts ... offers a *prima facie* case for identifying them, as expected in the one case, and as present in the other'.[26] Yet surely it stands to reason that had the evangelist not wished these groups to be identified, he would have described them in different terms or provided some other clue that they represented two distinct groups. As it stands, what indication does Matthew give his readers that the present false prophets who are workers of lawlessness should be distinguished from the end-time false prophets who also contribute to an upsurge in lawlessness? This question is even more pointed in view of the fact that both pericopae are heavily redactional. The burden of proof rests with those who would deny the clear evidence of the two passages and seek to separate the groups in question.

A different attempt to show that Matthew distinguished between the false prophets of 7:15–23 and 24:11 is undertaken by D. Marguerat.[27] He claims that the trouble caused by the present false prophets prefigures or anticipates the danger which their future (eschatological) counterparts will bring. In support of his view that Matthew has in mind two distinct groups, Marguerat emphasises the use of the present tense in 7:15 (ἔρχονται) and the future tense in 24:11, 24 (ἐγερθήσονται). Though attractive on the surface, this argument breaks down under closer examination. Marguerat considers the tenses from the perspective of the author, i.e. Matthew. Thus the present tense in 7:15 is taken as referring to Matthew's time and the future tenses in chapter 24 necessarily advert to a future time. Yet this reading of the text is inappropriate. The tenses of all the verbs must be understood from the perspective of the speaker in Matthew's narrative, i.e. Jesus. From that perspective all the tenses, not just those in chapter 24, are actually future. The present tense in 7:15 is not intended to refer to the time of Jesus but to a future event and so should be taken as a futuristic present in the context of Matthew's story. This reading of the verbal tense agrees with the strictly future tenses found in the following sentences; 'you will know them by their fruits' (verses 16, 20). Marguerat's argument is thus based upon an inaccurate reading of

---

[26] Hill, 'False Prophets', p. 336 (original emphasis).
[27] Marguerat, *Le Jugement*, p. 188. Cf. also Schweizer, *Matthew*, pp. 185–6 and Hare, *Jewish Persecution*, pp. 144, 163.

the Matthean narrative. From the viewpoint of the speaker both references to false prophets allude to future events, but from the perspective of the author these events are now taking place. The Matthean Jesus predicts the arrival of false prophets in the Matthean community and the evangelist is keen to demonstrate the fulfilment of this prophecy.

One suspects that underlying the reticence of many scholars to identify the false prophets of chapter 7 with those of chapter 24 is the prior assumption that Matthew had either deferred the parousia or intended to tone down any speculation about the time of the end (see above). Given this presupposition, Matthew obviously could not have identified the troublemakers of the eschatological future with those of the present. But if we dispense with this premise and we approach the texts on their own terms, then nothing precludes the conclusion that Matthew did indeed see in the false prophets of his own day the expected eschatological foes. This conclusion adds extra weight to Thompson's thesis that, in terms of Matthew's eschatological timetable in 24:4–14, those edited verses which speak of trial and tribulation and the appearance of the false prophets (verses 9–13), are now a present reality for Matthew and his community.

If the above conclusion is correct, then Matthew's timetable has two implications. First, the events in the timetable which are said to precede the time of the false prophets, specifically the events listed in verses 4–10, must have been seen by Matthew as already having taken place. This is not a difficult proposition to accept. As Thompson claimed, the events of the Jewish war would have been sufficient fulfilment of the prophecies concerning wars and false messiahs. Moreover, famines and earthquakes were not uncommon in the ancient Levant and the evangelist would have had at his disposal a whole range of events which he could have easily identified as fulfilling these predictions. The prophecies of tribulation and murder had, from the evangelist's perspective, doubtless met with fulfilment. It will be argued in chapter 8 that Matthew's community had experienced persecution and that some of his community members had been killed. Secondly, and perhaps more importantly, the one sign of the end which had not yet been fulfilled was the proclamation of the gospel throughout the whole world. Did Matthew consider this prophecy to be close to fulfilment? If so, then it is clear that he held fast to the imminence of the parousia, since the end (τέλος) will come immediately after it. That Matthew did accept that this prophecy was close to fulfilment is very probable. As a result of the missionary endeavours of the early church, including the missionaries of Matthew's church (Matt. 28:18–20), the Christian message had spread quickly throughout the known world as it was defined in his day.[28] Confirmation that Matthew accepted the imminent fulfilment of this prophecy comes from verse 13 where he urges his readers to continue in the hope that those who endure to the end (τέλος) will be saved. These words of comfort are only meaningful if the fulfilment of this sign is well under way and parousia is considered to be very near. The mission discourse in chapter 10 plays a role in this regard and we shall return to this material shortly.

Having analysed Matthew's timetable of the end in some detail, we may now evaluate the remainder of the apocalyptic discourse. Matthew's timetable in 24:4–14 is followed by the extended section which details the eschatological war in Judea immediately prior to the end (24:15–28). If we correlate this event with those in the timetable, then it seems clear that the conflict will take place just as the fulfilment of the world-wide mission nears its completion. That Matthew expected at least some of his readers to witness these events in Judea is clear from verse 22 which he adopts from Mark 13:20. This verse contains words of comfort that for the sake of the elect the days of tribulation will be shortened (cf. 1 En. 80:2; 2 Bar. 20:1–2; 80:1). Had Matthew deferred the time of the end and not expected some of his readers to experience these events, then his reproduction of these consolatory words seems rather pointless. In 24:23–8, Matthew warns that as part of this great tribulation false messiahs and false prophets will arise pointing to the arrival of the Christ in a specific location. They are not to be believed because the arrival of the Son of Man will be fully public and witnessed by all (verse 27). The false prophets mentioned here are not to be identified with the false prophets of 24:11 (and 7:15–23); though of similar ilk, these prophets are both geographically and chronologically different from the others and operate only in Judea during the period of great distress. While it is true that these figures also perform great signs and wonders, they are not designated, unlike the false prophets of 7:15–23 and 24:11, workers of lawlessness.[29] In verses 29–31 Matthew follows Mark 13:24–27 in describing the

---

[28] This point was acknowledged as long ago as 1907 by Allen, *Matthew*, p. lxxxiv.
[29] So correctly Barth, 'Matthew's Understanding of the Law', p. 75 and Burnett, *Jesus-Sophia*, p. 268.

breakdown of the cosmic order and the arrival of the Son of Man. Once again he signifies his belief that some of his readers will witness these events by adding εὐθέως to the beginning of this section. The collapse of the cosmos will happen *immediately* after the tribulation of those days. Many commentators have correctly noted that this addition seems completely unnecessary unless Matthew affirmed the imminence of the end and expected his readers to witness it.[30]

After describing the arrival of the Son of Man in verses 29–31, Matthew again emphasises the impending nature of the parousia in verses 32–4 which he took from Mark 13:28–32. Just as one knows summer is near when a fig tree sprouts leaves, so will the readers know that the Son of Man is near when all these things take place (verse 32–3). Since the earlier eschatological timetable had conveyed that most of the events had already come to pass, the imminence of the end is once more affirmed. The following statement, that the present generation will not pass away before the fulfilment of these happenings, acts to reinforce this point (cf. 16:28 earlier in the narrative). The following section concerning the exhortations to watchfulness in 24:36–25:13 must be taken in this context of the nearness of the end. As argued earlier, this material in itself suggests such an understanding, but this is absolutely certain once we view this material in the light of the temporal notions in the earlier parts of the discourse. Matthew uses this material to exhort his readers to watch for the unknown but impending day and to live a proper Christian existence in the short time remaining. The final two pericopae, the parable of the talents and the description of the last judgement, are silent on the time of the end, but in view of the material which precedes them were intended to be taken in terms of its imminence.

2.3 The relevance of the mission discourse

Before leaving the subject of Matthew's beliefs about the time of the end, a few words concerning the mission discourse (9:37–10:42) are in order since the evangelist consciously correlates this speech with the apocalyptic discourse. The Matthean mission charge, which is a mixture of Marcan, Q and unique material, has always

---

[30] The imminence theme at this point is noted as well by Lambrecht, 'Parousia Discourse', p. 323; Gundry, *Matthew*, p. 487; Schweizer, *Matthew*, p. 455 and Streeter, *Four Gospels*, p. 521.

caused exegetical problems. On the one hand, since it confines the mission of the disciples to the Jews of Palestine (verses 5–6),[31] it seems to contradict the command to make disciples of all nations at the conclusion of the gospel (28:19). On the other hand, it contains a prophecy that the Son of Man will come before they have completed the mission (10:23b),[32] a prophecy which clearly did not come true during the lifetime of the historical disciples to whom this promise is made. Matthew's arrangement of this material also causes problems in so far as he transposes verses 17–22 from the Marcan apocalyptic discourse (Mark 13:9, 11–13) for reasons which are disputed.

The first thing to note is that the Matthean Jesus here speaks not to the historical disciples but to the later Matthean community. It is well known that the evangelist uses the motif of the disciples on two levels; these figures in the narrative refer both to the actual circle of Jesus' disciples and in an extended sense to the intended readers of the gospel. That Matthew here was thinking in terms of the extended sense, i.e. his community or at least its missionary elements, is confirmed by two considerations. First, only on this view is the prophecy of Jesus in 10:23b not falsified, whereas it clearly remains unfulfilled if the mission charge is applied to the historical disciples. Secondly, unlike Mark (6:30), Matthew does not relate the return of the disciples after the mission. In Matthew's narrative, the mission is open-ended and applicable to the present time.[33] This means that the evangelist in chapter 10 was enjoining a specific mission to the Jews which continues until the parousia.[34] Such an understanding of the text in no way contradicts the

---

[31] That this mission is limited geographically to the land of the Jews (i.e. Palestine) and does not include the Jews of the Diaspora is clear from the geographical statement in verse 5 where Samaria is mentioned and from verse 23 which refers to the towns of Israel. Either reference seems out of place if a world-wide mission to the Jews is in mind. So correctly Levine, *Salvation History*, pp. 50–1 and see literature cited there both for and against this hypothesis.

[32] For recent discussion of the many diverse views regarding the origin of this verse, see Davies and Allison, *Matthew*, II, pp. 187–9.

[33] For further arguments, see Brown, 'Mission to Israel', pp. 74–5. In view of this evidence the alternative interpretation that Matthew intended the mission discourse to apply only to the pre-easter period is simply untenable. For this exegesis, see Strecker, *Weg*, pp. 194–6; Trilling, *Wahre Israel*, pp. 81–2; and Meier, 'Salvation History in Matthew', pp. 204–5. It seems also to be represented in the literary-critical analysis of the mission discourse by D. Weaver. See her *Matthew's Missionary Discourse*, pp. 151–2.

[34] So correctly Brown, 'Mission to Israel', pp. 74–5; Davies and Allison, *Matthew*, II, p. 190; Gnilka, *Matthäusevangelium*, II, p. 379; Gundry, *Matthew*, pp. 194–5 and McDermott, 'Mt. 10:23 in Context', p. 235.

universal mission of 28:19. The risen and glorified Jesus commands his followers to make disciples of all nations (πάντα τὰ ἔθνη) which, as most scholars now accept, includes the Jews along with the other nations of the world (cf. 24:14; 25:32).[35]

It will be recalled from our earlier discussion that the final sign which requires fulfilment before the arrival of the Son of Man is that the gospel would be preached throughout the whole world (24:14). For Matthew this includes a mission to the Jews of Palestine, since he clearly ties in the exclusive mission to the Jews in chapter 10 with this final world-wide mission. He does so by including in both discourses the same words of comfort and the same promise of the imminence of the end. In 10:22b Matthew takes from Mark 13:13 the words of comfort which he also uses in 24:13, 'but he who endures to the end will be saved'. This is followed immediately by the promise in 10:23b that the missionaries who are to flee from persecution will not have gone through all the towns of Israel before the Son of Man comes. Precisely the same set of themes is found in 24:13–14. First comes the exhortation to endurance which is then followed by the promise that the end will come when the gospel has been preached throughout the whole world. The similarity between these pericopae almost certainly means that the evangelist intended them to be taken together. The mission discourse is thereby given an eschatological framework in Matthew which it did not possess in Mark. Since Matthew 'eschatologises' the mission charge, we can better understand his transposition of Mark 13:9–13 to 10:17–22. This material, which speaks of eschatological rejection and persecution of all Christians in the context of Mark, is now confined by Matthew to those missionaries who embark upon this final mission to the Jews. His transposition does not affect the eschatological timing of these events, but only those who are affected by them.[36] We shall see in the next chapter why the evangelist focuses on the suffering of these missionaries.

---

[35] See Meier, 'Nations or Gentiles', pp. 94–102. That the phrase in 28:19 excludes the Jews is argued unconvincingly by Hare and Harrington, 'Make Disciples of all the Gentiles', pp. 359–69. In agreement with the view of Meier are Stanton, *Gospel for a New People*, pp. 137–8; Gnilka, *Matthäusevangelium*, II, pp. 508–9; Gundry, *Matthew*, pp. 595–6; Sabourin, *Matthew*, II, p. 936 and Burnett, *Jesus-Sophia*, pp. 423–7. The position of Hare and Harrington is adopted by Schweizer, *Matthew*, p. 530.

[36] Cf. the comments of Davies and Allison, *Matthew*, II, p.182, 'nothing in chapter 10 tones down the eschatological nature of the Markan material'. So too Gundry, *Matthew*, pp. 193–4.

The inference to draw from all this is that Matthew believes the fulfilment of the prophecy of the gospel being preached world-wide in 24:14 requires a last mission to the Jews of Palestine. The mission discourse therefore seems to have been composed in order to urge or even legitimate one final mission to the Jews, a mission which up to now had not been a major success. Such a mission would have given Matthew's fellow Jews one last chance to accept the gospel before the arrival of the Son of Man. With the Jerusalem church fragmented and dispersed after the Jewish war, the evangelist probably reasoned that this duty fell to the next most prominent church in the region, his own church at Antioch. This understanding of the mission charge explains why the evangelist, writing in northern Syria, pays so much attention in 24:15–28 to the terrible events in Judea which precede the arrival of the Son of Man. It is those missionaries who preach the gospel in Judea during the final mission who are meant by 'those in Judea' in 24:16. They will be caught up in the appearance of the antichrist in the temple and the ensuing tribulation. But more important in the present context is that the imminent end expectation of the mission charge (10:23b) reinforces the temporal notion of the apocalyptic discourse. Both discourses make clear that the end will come while the final mission is in progress.

This interpretation of the Matthean mission discourse runs against the common understanding of it. It is usually accepted that Matthew's transposition of Mark 13:9–13 to 10:17–22 serves to 'de-eschatologise' the material in this section. Representative of this view is D. R. A. Hare who writes, '...Matthew has de-eschatologized the Marcan passage by removing it from its eschatological context; that which is described by Mark as pertaining to the period immediately preceding the Parousia has become for Matthew characteristic of a continuing situation'.[37] The problem with this interpretation is that it does not adequately account for the close relationship between verse 22b (from Mark 13:13) and verse 23b which, by analogy with 24:13 and 24:14b, must be taken together. Significantly, Hare does not refer at all to 10:22b in his discussion of this material. Yet this verse which reappears in the apocalyptic discourse is a firm indication that Matthew placed this Jewish mission into his scheme of the last events. Hare's discussion of 10:23b, on the other hand, makes the claim that Matthew

---

[37] Hare, *Jewish Persecution*, pp. 99–100. So too Strecker, *Weg*, p. 44; Burnett, *Jesus-Sophia*, pp. 273–5 and Schweizer, *Matthew*, p. 244.

adopted all of this verse because he found appropriate the persecution motif in the first half. He writes, 'The first half of the double logion suits Matthew's purpose admirably; the immediate context is concerned primarily with the fate of the missionaries...The context thus ignores 23b, which is concerned with the geographical and temporal limits of the mission.'[38] This argument presumes that Matthew adopted material with which he did not agree, a view which is inherently unlikely; the evangelist was free to omit verse 23b if it did not suit his purposes, but he made a conscious decision not to do so.[39] Thus in one fell swoop, Hare either ignores or plays down the two elements which place the mission charge in an eschatological context and promote the evangelist's view of the imminence of the parousia.

Other scholars also focus on the consolatory nature of 10:23 by arguing that the evangelist intends more to offer comfort to those who are on the receiving end of persecution and to exhort them to steadfastness than to make any definitive statement about the time of the end.[40] Yet it is obvious that we cannot so easily separate the two elements. It stands to reason that the consolatory aspect of this tradition is conveyed precisely by the temporal theme. What gives hope and encourages steadfastness is the information that the persecution will cease with the arrival of the Son of Man. Consolation without an imminent end expectation is no consolation at all! This is the point of 24:13–14 and we should not read Matthew 10:22–3 any differently. It is clear then that the plain temporal meaning of this verse cannot be so easily dismissed.[41]

The conclusion to draw from this short and necessarily brief excursus on the Matthean mission discourse is that it supports the temporal end expectation which Matthew sets out in 24:4–14. The gospel is now being preached throughout the world, including Palestine, which means that the end is looming ever nearer. Matthew stresses that the missionaries of this final call to Israel will meet with persecution and participate in the eschatological conflict, but that the Son of Man will arrive before they have completed their task.

---

[38] Hare, *Jewish Persecution*, p. 111. Cf. also the comment of S. H. Brooks that 10:23 stands 'in tension with Matthew's own eschatology', *Matthew's Community*, p. 54.

[39] So correctly Davies and Allison, *Matthew*, II, pp. 191–2.

[40] See, for example, McDermott, 'Mt. 10:23 in Context', pp. 235, 239–40; Geist, *Menschensohn*, pp. 231–8; Weaver, *Matthew's Missionary Discourse*, pp. 202–3 n. 140 and Bartnicki, 'Trostwort', pp. 311–19.

[41] So correctly Luz, *Matthäus*, II, p. 117. Cf. too Brown, 'Mission to Israel', p. 82.

3. Conclusions

In this chapter we have examined Matthew's temporal end expectations. It was demonstrated that the arguments which point to a deferred parousia for Matthew have no real basis in the evidence. They are based upon a lack of understanding of the general concept of apocalyptic eschatology and, as a consequence, tend to misrepresent the gospel texts on this issue. It was then argued that the evidence strongly supports the view that Matthew actively promotes an imminent eschatological expectation. The evangelist affirms the nearness of the parousia in a number of passages, but this theme is best represented in the apocalyptic discourse. The eschatological timetable which he constructs in 24:4–14 is of paramount importance in this respect and reveals that Matthew placed his own time toward the end of this end-time schedule. The one major unfulfilled prediction is that the gospel must be preached throughout the world but it was argued that Matthew probably considered that this was close to fulfilment. Of relevance here is the mission discourse which legitimates a final mission to the Jews of Palestine in fulfilment of this final prophecy and itself affirms the imminence of the arrival of the Son of Man. That Matthew expected his readers to witness the coming of this saviour figure is plainly suggested by a number of comments in both the apocalyptic and mission discourses which provide comfort in the face of distress: those who endure to the end will be saved (10:22b; 24:13), the days of tribulation have been shortened (24:22) and immediately after the tribulation the Son of Man will arrive (24:29). Such consolatory words lose their point if the evangelist had abandoned an imminent end expectation.

That Matthew so fervently promotes the impending arrival of the Son of Man should occasion no real surprise. Apocalyptic-eschatological schemes which emphasise the judgement and its aftermath almost without exception affirm that these events are to occur in the imminent future. Since Matthew also focuses on the eschaton and the punishments and rewards it will bring, his adoption of an imminent end expectation is perhaps to be expected. What is surprising with regard to this subject is the reluctance of many Matthean scholars to accept the evangelist's very clear statements on the imminence of the end.

SUMMARY OF PART II

In Part II we have attempted to reconstruct Matthew's particular apocalyptic-eschatological scheme. It is clear from the discussion that the evangelist embraces a comprehensive apocalyptic-eschatological world view which includes and emphasises all the eight major characteristics of this religious perspective. Some of these elements are attributable to his Christian heritage, while others stand more in line with Jewish apocalyptic eschatology. His interest in this religious perspective is apparent from his redaction of his Christian sources, his adoption of certain Jewish sources and his outright creation of important apocalyptic-eschatological pericopae (e.g. 13:36–43, 49–50).

The evangelist promotes a developed form of cosmic dualism. The cosmic order is involved in a desperate fight for supremacy. On the one side stand God, Jesus the Son of Man and his angelic forces, and on the other stands Satan and his retinue of fallen angels. The human world is also engaged in this conflict and all individuals must choose whether they take the part of the heavenly world or its demonic counterpart. There is no middle ground or neutrality in this battleground. As we find in the Qumran War scroll and Revelation, Matthew adopts other aspects of this perspective, notably the idea of the final war between these two opposing sides as the final event in history. The evangelist also emphasises the concept of historical determinism which is commonly found throughout both Jewish and Christian texts. Matthew's expression of this idea via the medium of a scheme of prophecy and fulfilment is taken basically from his Christian tradition, though he has seen fit to supplement and thereby intensify it with his addition of the formula quotations. These two themes of developed cosmic dualism and historical determinism provide the framework for Matthew's eschatological expectations.

Like most proponents of apocalyptic eschatology, Matthew

believes that the end of the age would be preceded by a number of tell-tale signs which herald its arrival. While he follows in part Mark's particular scheme, which itself shares affinities with the Jewish apocalyptic-eschatological schemes, he sees fit to update it where appropriate in order to let his readers know where they stand in relation to the end. His redaction of Mark at this point, and other indications in the gospel, testify plainly that he accepted that the eschatological woes were well advanced and that the new age would be introduced in the imminent future. The final event in history would be the eschatological war between the righteous and the combined forces of the human and angelic wicked which would take place in Judea. This attack would be repulsed by the arrival of a saviour figure, Jesus the Son of Man, who would return in glory and on the clouds of heaven accompanied by his heavenly forces. The Son of Man would then ascend his throne of glory in order to execute the final and universal judgement. The evangelist's distinctive portrayal of the Son of Man is a combination of his Christian synoptic sources and certain Jewish traditions which are also found in the Parables of Enoch. The climax of Matthew's eschatological scheme concerns the very purpose for which the Son of Man comes, the bestowal of rewards and punishments. After the general resurrection of the dead and the recreation of the cosmos, he will reward the righteous by granting them angelic status and eternal life in a peaceful, new creation, while the wicked will suffer horribly as they burn eternally in the fires of Gehenna and weep and gnash their teeth on account of their plight. The contrast between the supernatural world and the human world which holds prior to the eschaton now ceases to exist. The human righteous join their angelic counterparts, and the human wicked are delivered to the same place of fiery punishment as the demons whom they supported. The first of these themes is well represented in both Jewish and Christian apocalyptic eschatology, but the second finds its closest parallels in the Jewish tradition. With the notable exception of the book of Revelation, the consignment of the wicked to the fires of Gehenna is not particularly common in the early Christian literature.

It is clear from this reconstruction that the Christian gospel of Matthew ultimately stands firmly within the general Jewish (and Christian) apocalyptic-eschatological tradition which was analysed in Part I. Although Matthew made use of the gospel genre which he took from Mark, he has presented his story of Jesus within the framework of the distinctive religious perspective apocalyptic eschatology. The evangelist adopts a very developed scheme, particularly in terms of the theme of cosmic dualism, and it is noteworthy that the closest parallels to his apocalyptic eschatology are found in the respective sectarian schemes of the Jewish Qumran writings and the Christian Apocalypse. Such is the dominance of this vision of reality in Matthew that the gospel actually stands as one of the most comprehensive and clear examples of apocalyptic eschatology in the contemporary literature. On the basis of this, we are justified in viewing the Matthean community as an apocalyptic group. The recognition of this point emphasises all the more that apocalyptic eschatology and apocalypticism are not necessarily related to the apocalyptic genre and that there is a pressing need to revise the terminology associated with this religious perspective.

A number of questions remain unanswered, however. What prompted Matthew to adopt this religious perspective and promote it with such fervour? What led this evangelist to divide the cosmos into two fundamentally opposing groups and to portray the parousia and the final judgement in the terms he did? Why did he adopt such a vindictive and vengeful attitude toward those whom he considered to be the wicked. The strong affinity between Matthew's apocalyptic eschatology and that which appears in contemporary documents would seem to supply the key to this problem. We know from Part I that those Jews and Christians who embraced apocalypticism and its attendant symbolic universe did so in response to a current crisis, and this raises the possibility that the same general sociological principle might explain Matthew's actions in this regard. We shall explore this possibility in Part III.

PART III

The social setting of the Matthean community and the function of apocalyptic eschatology in the gospel of Matthew

It was demonstrated in Part II that Matthew had fervently embraced a developed apocalyptic-eschatological perspective. In Part III of this study we shall attempt to provide an explanation for this state of affairs. Given that such a pronounced apocalyptic-eschatological scheme does not arise in a vacuum but has a concrete social setting, precisely what conditions or circumstances prompted Matthew to construct his symbolic universe? To put this matter another way, does the gospel of Matthew provide any clues to the social situation of the author and his community and, if so, were these circumstances serious enough (or perceived to be serious enough) to warrant the embracement of apocalypticism by the evangelist and his group? In order to answer these questions, chapter 8 will offer a reconstruction of the Matthean community's historical and social situation. It will be argued that the Matthean community faced a number of related crises occasioned by the Jewish war, and that these provided sufficient cause for its adoption of apocalyptic eschatology. The following chapter will then attempt to identify the function of the gospel's apocalyptic eschatology within the context of that community's social setting as identified in chapter 8. How does the evangelist use his apocalyptic-eschatological material to respond to the problems occasioned by his group's social setting? By pursuing these particular questions, Part III builds upon our findings in Part II and completes the discussion of apocalyptic eschatology in Matthew's gospel.

8

THE SOCIAL SETTING OF THE MATTHEAN COMMUNITY

It will be recalled from chapter 2 that the situation of crisis, either real or perceived, which led certain Jewish and Christian groups to resort to apocalyptic eschatology, could take any number of forms. Some of those circumstances which were identified seem not to be applicable to Matthew and his group. Unlike the circles which produced the Parables of Enoch and the Epistle of Enoch, there is no hint that the Matthean community suffered economic oppression. On the contrary, a number of scholars have put forward the view that certain pointers in the gospel indicate that the Matthean community was comparatively wealthy.[1] Moreover, the crisis of the destruction of Jerusalem and its temple, which prompted a number of apocalyptic-eschatological works, was not directly the situation of crisis which motivated Matthew to write his gospel in the manner he did. The evangelist, like the authors of 4 Ezra, 2 Baruch and the Apocalypse of Abraham, saw these events as God's punishment for the sins of his people (22:7), but in distinction to these Jewish writers, he is not moved to ponder the injustice of the situation. For Matthew, the destruction of Jerusalem and its temple was God's appropriate and just response to the rejection of his messiah by his people.

The social setting of the Matthean community, like that of the book of Revelation, is rather a complex one which involves a number of historical and social factors working in unison. Of most importance are the effects of the Jewish war on the Matthean community. It will be argued in the present chapter that a whole combination of factors which emerged in the aftermath of the events of 66–70 contributed in large part to the

---

[1] So Beare, *Matthew*, p. 11; Kingsbury, *Matthew as Story*, pp. 152–3 and Crosby, *House of Disciples*, pp. 39–43. Hare's study of the persecution theme in the gospel reveals no evidence of economic oppression. See *Jewish Persecution*, p. 125.

Matthean community's sense of crisis. These factors led to conflict with the Jewish world, the gentile world and even the wider world of the Christian church, all of which led inevitably to the withdrawal of the Matthean community from these larger and dominant societies. The overall impression of the social setting of Matthew's church is that of an entirely alienated group with no home or support system outside its own borders. Each of these claims will be evidenced in turn.

1. The Matthean community and the Jewish world

1.1 The sectarian nature of the Matthean community

The relationship between the Matthean community and the wider Jewish world is an extremely complicated subject which cannot be given the full attention it deserves in this section. None the less, a general assessment of the issues is all that is required for the purpose at hand. As is becoming increasingly clear in the latest studies of this subject, the evidence of the gospel suggests that the Matthean community can be viewed as a Jewish sect opposed to formative Judaism in the period following the first Jewish war. Both the terms 'sect' and 'formative Judaism' require some explanation.

There are formidable problems with defining the word 'sect' and no one definition will please everyone. Yet all scholars would agree that in general terms we are dealing with a minority group which shares the basic outlook of the wider society or parent body but deviates quite consciously from that body over particulars, usually in a context of mutual hostility.[2] The best example of a Jewish sect from the time of Matthew is the group from Qumran. There is no doubt that the Qumran community shared the basic outlook of the wider Jewish world – the belief in one God, the importance of the covenant with that God, the observance of the Torah and so on – yet it consciously stood outside 'normative' or majority Judaism in the following ways. It traced its origins to a dissident member of the parent body, the Teacher of Righteousness, and rejected the official place of Jewish worship, the temple. The group at Qumran distanced itself, both physically and metaphorically, from the wider Jewish world and derided the leaders who controlled the parent

---

[2] See the discussions of Overman, *Matthew's Gospel*, pp. 8–9 and Stanton, *Gospel for a New People*, pp. 89–90 and the literature they cite.

body. Its sectarian nature is emphasised by the fact that it possessed its own rules and regulations and devised its peculiar interpretation of the Torah. It set strict boundaries around itself by the adoption of its own code of practice and also by the adoption of dualistic language which describes the respective natures of the insider and the outsider. As G. N. Stanton has noted, many of these sectarian motifs are paralleled in the gospel of Matthew,[3] and we shall deal with these shortly.

Regarding the term 'formative Judaism', this is used in the manner suggested by J. A. Overman which is itself based upon the earlier work of J. Neusner.[4] By 'formative Judaism', I mean the reorganisation and consolidation of Judaism in the period following the first Jewish war which was led by a coalition of the pre-70 Pharisees and those belonging to the scribal profession, but in which other groups participated as well. This was a lengthy process which did not take place, as the later stylised and idealised rabbinic accounts claim, immediately upon the founding of the rabbinic academy at Yavneh.[5] With the destruction of the temple, formative Judaism was firmly centred on the synagogue and the observance of the Torah. The pharisaic interpretation of the law was considered definitive, as too were the traditions of the elders which detail pharisaic practices not specifically enjoined in the Torah. At the time of the gospel of Matthew, this process of reconstruction, consolidation and legitimation was in its early phases and marked the middle stage between the fluidity of pre-70 Judaism and the more rigid Judaism of the later rabbinic period. This form of Judaism, although itself not constant and static in the period in question, therefore stands as the parent body with which the Matthean community was in dispute. By defining 'formative Judaism' in these terms, there is no implication that the reforming Pharisees and scribes represented all Jewish interests in all places. It is most probable that in addition to the Matthean community other Jewish groups, in Antioch and elsewhere, also came into conflict with this fledgling coalition of

---

[3] Stanton, 'Matthew and Judaism', p. 283 and his more recent and detailed discussion in *Gospel for a New People*, pp. 85–107.

[4] See Overman, *Matthew's Gospel*, pp. 35–71 for detailed discussion and literature cited there. A concise summary of Neusner's position, which has been stated many times, can be found in his 'The Formation of Rabbinic Judaism', pp. 3–42.

[5] Thus the view of W. D. Davies that Matthew's sermon on the mount was a direct response to Yavneh (*Sermon*, p. 315) is somewhat anachronistic. Despite this anachronism, Davies' discussion is still a valuable contribution to the subject.

forces before it eventually asserted complete dominance over its competitors.

There is no doubt that the gospel of Matthew shares much in common with the movement which we call formative Judaism. Both the gospel and the community for whom it was written are thoroughly Jewish in character and outlook. This point need not be argued in detail here. It is sufficient to state now that both groups shared the central doctrines of Judaism, the belief in one God and the central place of the Torah in the covenant relationship with this God (see further below). Moreover they had common practices such as alms-giving, prayer and fasting (6:1–18), and similar offices (prophets, wise men and scribes; 23:34).[6] These points of contact in terms of shared tradition and world view must be weighed against the differences between the two groups, differences which betray the sectarian or deviant nature of the Matthean community. An examination of the gospel reveals that the Matthean community unequivocally rejected the road which post-70 Judaism was taking and decided to take a different road in opposition to it. This is reflected in the vigorous polemic against the scribes and Pharisees who were beginning to emerge as the dominant party in formative Judaism.

Although in his gospel narrative the evangelist tends to blur the differences between the distinct groups which comprise the Jewish leadership, and presents them as one homogenous force which is totally united in its opposition to Jesus,[7] it is clear that the real villains of the gospel are the scribes and Pharisees. As J. A. Overman well says, 'The Jewish leadership is summed up and converges in the fixed Matthean formula "the scribes and the Pharisees".'[8] Matthew's polemic against the scribes and Pharisees is found throughout the gospel, but is most thoroughly expressed in chapter 23. While much of Matthew's polemic in this chapter stems from his sources, he has considerably sharpened and intensified it. The scribes and Pharisees are described as hypocrites (23:13, 15, 23, 25, 27, 29; cf. 6:2, 5, 16; 15:7; 22:18; 23:3), as blind men (23:16, 17,

---

[6] For further detail, see Saldarini, 'Matthew and Jewish–Christian Conflict', pp. 48–9. Cf. also Stanton, *Gospel for a New People*, p. 99.

[7] For comprehensive discussion of the evangelist's merging of the religious leadership into a unified whole, see van Tilborg, *Jewish Leaders*, pp. 1–6 and literature cited there. On the question of the role the Jewish leaders play in the Matthean story, J. D. Kingsbury's literary-critical analysis is most instructive. See his 'Developing Conflict between Jesus and the Jewish Leaders', pp. 57–73 and *Matthew as Story*, pp. 115–27.

[8] Overman, *Matthew's Gospel*, p.142. A similar point is made by Przybylski, 'Matthean Anti-Judaism', p. 190 and Meeks, 'Breaking Away', p. 109.

19, 24, 26; cf. 15:14;), children of Gehenna (23:15) and a brood of vipers (23:33; cf. 3:7; 12:34). They fail to practise what they preach (23:3), they place burdens on others (23:4), they love to be admired (23:5–7), they place their own tradition before the will of God (23:15–26) and are guilty of murder (23:29–36; cf. 22:6). As a result of their leadership roles, they lead the people astray (15:14), prevent them from entering the kingdom of heaven (23:13) and so make them twice as much children of Gehenna as they are (23:15). Both the scribes (9:4) and the Pharisees (12:34; 22:18) are singled out as being evil (πονηρός/πονηρία) which means in the context of Matthew's dualism that they belong on the side of Satan.[9] Since they themselves are evil, they are the appropriate leaders of 'this evil generation' (12:38–42; 16:1–4) and in no small way are responsible for it.

Some scholars have interpreted this stereotypical portrayal of the Jewish leaders as an indication of the distance between the Matthean community and the world of Judaism. One good example of this view is S. van Tilborg who points to the harsh polemic as proof that Matthew and his church had little, if any, contact with the local Jewish community. According to van Tilborg,

> Mt lived in a world in which Judaism was no longer a serious competitor. If one wishes to call the Jews who have refused to be converted hypocrites, evil people, murderers and imposters, there must be a fairly great and satisfactory distance on a historical level. This idea held by Mt can only be explained as being held by someone who, if he happened to come face to face with them, was still so absorbed in his own ideas that he had lost sight of reality.[10]

These words are one of the clearest descriptions of Matthew as an 'armchair theologian'. The evangelist is depicted as so absorbed in his own theological thoughts that he lives in his own world and is completely divorced from the real world. This singular portrayal of Matthew is rather difficult to accept. Only slightly more credible is the position of D. R. A. Hare who argues that the polemic reflects a past dispute not a current conflict between Matthew and his Jewish opponents.[11] The problem with this view is that it cannot account

---

[9]   So too van Tilborg, *Jewish Leaders*, p. 45.
[10] van Tilborg, *Jewish Leaders*, p. 171.
[11] Hare, *Jewish Persecution*, p. 96.

for the vigorous nature of the polemic. If the threat from the scribes and Pharisees is no longer an issue, why does Matthew pay so much attention to it?

It is now well recognised that polemical and stereotypical language such as we find in Matthew does not reflect the distance between the two parties. On the contrary, it reflects both physical and ideological proximity between the disputing groups, since its very purpose is to distance one party from the other. A general sociological rule of thumb is that the closer the relationship between dissenting groups, the more intense the conflict and the sharper the resultant polemic.[12] Consequently, the evangelist's polemical attack on the scribes and Pharisees indicates on the one hand the closeness of his community to the parent body, and on the other his attempt to put some distance between them. The minority group for whom Matthew is the spokesperson is thereby expressing its self-understanding as an entirely independent and distinct body over against that parent body.[13] Moreover, such polemic also confirms and legitimates the rigid drawing of the boundaries, the sectarian outlook, which Matthew's dualistic language is also intended to establish.[14] The parent body belongs on the side of Satan and is justifiably denounced, while the Matthean community belongs on the side of God. We shall say more about this point in the next chapter.

The sectarian or deviant nature of the Matthean community, which is evidenced in the evangelist's polemic, is confirmed by the fact that the evangelist's community had parted company with the official place of Jewish worship, in this case the synagogue, and perceived itself to be a rival and superior institution.[15] As is well known, Matthew uses different terms to define the assemblies of each group.[16] His Jewish opponents belong to the synagogue, an

---

[12] See Coser, *Social Conflict*, pp. 67–72. The relevance of Coser's work for understanding Matthew's polemic is accepted by Overman, *Matthew's Gospel*, pp. 146–7; Stanton, *Gospel for a New People*, pp. 98–9 and Przybylski, 'Matthean Anti-Judaism', p. 198.

[13] See Stanton, *Gospel for a New People*, pp. 96–7; Overman, *Matthew's Gospel*, pp. 142–3 and Przybylski, 'Matthean Anti-Judaism', p. 199.

[14] On the use of polemic to legitimate the sectarian viewpoint, see Stanton, *Gospel for a New People*, p. 105.

[15] Contra Hummel, *Auseinandersetzung*, pp. 28–33 who argues that although Matthew's community did not participate in the synagogue service, it still belonged to the synagogue association.

[16] For much of the following discussion I am indebted to Stanton, *Gospel for a New People*, pp. 97, 126–31 and Przybylski, 'Matthean Anti-Judaism', pp. 193–5. See

institution which is never depicted positively in Matthew but is always represented as an alien place. The synagogue is the place where hypocrisy in almsgiving (6:2) and prayer (6:5) is manifest and where the best seats are claimed by those who least deserve them (23:6). In accord with this negative view of the synagogue, Matthew refers to the faithful Jairus simply as a ruler rather than as a ruler of the synagogue as Mark describes him (Matt. 9:18//Mark 5:22). Matthew's intention to dissociate his community from this Jewish institution is further witnessed by his use of 'their synagogue(s)', an expression which he found only once in his sources (4:23//Mark 1:39) and which he inserts redactionally four times (9:35; 10:17; 12:9; 13:54), and 'your synagogues' when the Matthean Jesus directly addresses his Jewish opponents (23:34). By contrast with those who belong to the synagogue, the Matthean community is defined by a totally different term, 'the ekklesia' (ἡ ἐκκλησία).[17] That the ekklesia was founded by Jesus himself (16:18–19) both explains and legitimates its existence as a rival assembly to the synagogue, and he remains with it in the period between the resurrection and the parousia (18:20; 28:20). This church of Jesus (cf. 'my church' in 16:18) serves as the alternative to 'their synagogues', and this suggests that not only had the Matthean community separated from the synagogue, but it now consciously defined itself as a rival counterpart to it.[18]

The rivalry of the two institutions is indicated by a number of factors. One of these is that like the synagogue the Matthean community also contained scribes. Two texts in particular are important in this regard. In 23:34 the Matthean Jesus prophesies

also Hare, *Jewish Persecution*, pp. 104–5; Overman, *Matthew's Gospel*, pp. 60–1 and White, 'Crisis Management and Boundary Maintenance' pp. 215–16 n. 17.

[17] Contra Saldarini, 'Matthew and Jewish–Christian Conflict', pp. 41–2 who claims that Matthew has no special name for his group. Saldarini is rightly criticised on this point by Gundry, 'Social History of the Matthean Community', p. 64. However, Gundry goes too far in identifying the ekklesia with the whole Christian church (pp. 63–4), as too does Meier, 'Antioch', p. 67. We shall see later in this chapter that for Matthew the Christian movement was hardly a unity. This means he would be unlikely to use the term for his community as a covering term for the whole movement.

[18] Also of significance is Matthew's addition to the Marcan parable of the wicked tenants in 21:43, where Jesus tells the Jewish leaders, 'the kingdom of God will be taken away from you and given to a nation (ἔθνος) producing the fruits of it'. Israel is the nation which has lost the kingdom of God and the 'new nation' which inherits it is the Matthean community, the ekklesia. The evangelist thereby carefully distinguishes between his own group and the larger Jewish world which belongs to the synagogue. See Stanton, 'Matthew and Judaism', pp. 268–9 and Saldarini, 'Matthew and Jewish–Christian Conflict', pp. 42–3 n. 14.

that scribes will be among the group of martyrs who will die as they preach the message of Jesus, and in 13:52 he speaks positively of the scribes 'trained for the kingdom of heaven'. Both references certainly apply to the scribes in the Matthean community, one of whom was probably Matthew himself.[19] That Matthew's church contained scribes is confirmed by 7:29 where the evangelist compares the authority of Jesus with the authority of 'their scribes'. This terminology reflects a distinction between two rival groups of scribes, those who belong to the Matthean community and those who belong to 'their synagogues'.[20] The departure of the Matthean Christians had therefore caused a split in the scribal office of the synagogue and these two groups were now in opposition to one another. Matthew's intention to distance his group of scribes from those of the synagogue is given expression in his treatment of the title 'rabbi'. In the gospel only the false disciple Judas calls Jesus by this title (26:25, 49) and in 23:7b–8 the Matthean Jesus proclaims that the scribes and Pharisees love being called 'rabbi' and then instructs his disciples that none of them is to be called by this title. If, as seems likely, the Pharisees and their scribal associates were appropriating this title for themselves at this time, then the evangelist is making a clear distinction between the members of his own church and those who now lead the synagogue.[21] As was the case with Matthew's use of ekklesia, his break-away group refuses to adopt the terminology of the parent body and in doing so marks itself as an independent entity.

As a self-defined sect within the larger world of Judaism, the Matthean community developed its own practices concerning self-regulation. As with many deviant groups, there is more emphasis placed on group action than on a distinct hierarchy within the community.[22] In 23:8–12 the evangelist stresses the egalitarian

---

[19] For a detailed recent discussion, see Orton, *Understanding Scribe*, pp. 166–74.

[20] See Overman, *Matthew's Gospel*, pp. 115–17; Przybylski, 'Matthean Anti-Judaism', pp. 190–1. D. Orton makes the important point that the scribes of Matthew's community and those of the synagogue belong to the same Jewish office. He rightly argues that one should avoid calling the former 'Christian scribes' and the latter 'Jewish scribes' since such terminology ignores their fundamental similarity. See *Understanding Scribe*, pp. 139–40 and pp. 231–2 n. 10.

[21] See Overman, *Matthew's Gospel*, pp. 46–8 for full discussion. Cf. also Stanton, *Gospel for a New People*, p. 97.

[22] See Stanton, *Gospel for a New People*, p. 104. Cf. also Saldarini, 'Matthew and Jewish–Christian Conflict', p. 52 and White, 'Grid and Group in Matthew's Community', pp. 75–6.

nature of his community where no one is to be master of another, while 18:15–17 attributes to the ekklesia as a whole the power to expel unrepentant offenders from its midst.[23] Yet despite these texts it is clear that a certain hierarchy did exist within the Matthean community, although it might have been rather fluid at the time of the gospel's composition. The scribes of Matthew's group unquestionably assumed leadership roles of some sort,[24] and 5:22 seems to refer to a particular council within the church which dealt with matters of discipline.[25] In any event, the evangelist specifies that the authority of the church is such that its decisions are binding in the heavenly sphere (18:18) and again this claim is legitimated by tracing it back to Jesus himself (16:19).[26]

As is the case with many sectarian writings, the gospel of Matthew spells out clearly what is expected of those who comprise the ekklesia. The sermon on the mount in chapters 5–7 has with good reason been interpreted as the code or constitution of the Matthean community which orders and regulates the life of the ekklesia.[27] It spells out how community members should act

[23] There is some dispute over whether the advice to shun and exclude the unrepentant church member is directed to the wronged individual alone or to the whole church. If the former is adopted, then this text does not deal with exclusion from the church, but advises mere avoidance of the sinner by the wronged party within the context of the church. In favour of this position is the singular σοί in v.17 and this is the preferred reading of Bonnard, *Matthieu*, p. 275; France, *Matthew*, p. 249 and Thompson, *Matthew's Advice*, p. 185. Against this view is the fact that the dispute no longer concerned two individuals but was now between the sinner and the church as a whole, and that the next verse refers to the authority of the whole church. Moreover, it is inherently unlikely that Matthew's sectarian viewpoint would tolerate such uneasiness within the context of his church when cohesion and solidarity is all important. For the view that this text enjoins expulsion from the ekklesia, see Forkman, *Limits of the Religious Community*, pp. 124–32; cf. also Overman, *Matthew's Gospel*, pp. 103–4; Meier, 'Antioch', pp. 68–9; Davies and Allison, *Matthew*, II, p. 785; Gundry, *Matthew*, p. 368 and Beare, *Matthew*, p. 380.

[24] So correctly Overman, *Matthew's Gospel*, p. 117.

[25] So Overman, *Matthew's Gospel*, pp. 108–9 contra Guelich, *Sermon*, pp. 186–7; Luz, *Matthäus*, I, p. 252 and Davies and Allison, *Matthew*, I, p. 514 who argue that συνέδριον must refer either to the Jerusalem Sanhedrin or to a local Jewish court. Yet if Matthew's community had separated from the synagogue, it is almost impossible that its members would have sought resolution of disputes from those who controlled the parent body. Overman argues further that texts such as 5:25, 39b–40; 6:12 evidence the evangelist's view that church members should avoid the civil legal system at all costs, demonstrating again the sectarian outlook of the community. See *Matthew's Gospel*, pp. 106–8.

[26] Overman, *Matthew's Gospel*, pp. 104–6 argues that by couching the church's authority in the language of binding and loosing, Matthew is claiming the very authority for his community which the Pharisees were claiming at the time.

[27] See especially White, 'Grid and Group in Matthew's Community', *passim*;

toward God, toward one another and toward those outside the community. Since much of this code runs contrary to the way of life adopted by Matthew's Jewish opponents (i.e. 5:20; 6:1–18), the sermon both determines the boundaries between the ekklesia and the parent body and legitimates its own outlook over against the majority group. Tied up with this theme are the distinctive religious practices of the Matthean community which again stand in opposition to the practices of its opponents. As we might expect, these too are traced back to Jesus himself and are thereby given legitimacy. Jesus had given his ekklesia its own form of prayer (6:9–13) which, unlike the prayers of the 'hypocrites', is to be said in private and not in the open for all to hear (6:5–6). More importantly, Jesus had provided his church with a particular interpretation of the Torah. For Matthew, Jesus came to fulfil the law and not to abolish it (5:17). As we noted in chapter 5, the law was to remain functional until the passing of heaven and earth at the end of the age (5:18), but until that time it was to be followed according to the particular exegesis of Jesus (5:21–48) whose guiding principle was love of God and neighbour (22:34–40; cf. 7:12). Matthew strongly makes the point that this messianic interpretation contrasts sharply with the exegesis of his pharisaic opponents who followed the tradition of the elders.

This theme is given full attention in the so-called conflict stories, especially those which deal with the law, the tradition of the elders and the interpretation of scripture (12:1–8, 9–14; 15:1–20; 19:3–9; 22:34–40, 41–6). While the first four of these conflict stories were found in Mark (Mark 3:23–8; 3:1–6; 7:1–23; 10:2–12), Matthew has introduced both the Pharisees and the element of conflict into the last two (cf. also 12:39–42). His redaction at these points tells us about his social setting of conflict and the identity of his opponents. Moreover, where Mark sets the conflict within the context of keeping the law – the Pharisees abide by the law while Jesus does not – Matthew carefully edits his source and makes clear that the issue is not whether the Torah is valid but how it is to be correctly interpreted.[28] There is little doubt that we see here a current halakhic dispute between the pharisaic understanding of the law

Overman, *Matthew's Gospel*, pp. 94–101. Cf. the words of Meeks, 'Breaking Away', p. 111: 'The Sermon on the Mount reads like the ethic of a Jewish sect.'

[28] Full discussion of the conflict stories and Matthew's reinterpretation of the Marcan tradition cannot be undertaken here. More detailed studies of Matthew's redaction and his purpose of defending his own interpretation of the law against pharisaic opponents can be found in Hummel, *Auseinandersetzung*, pp. 26–56;

and the scriptures and the alternative exegesis of Matthew's community which it traced back to Jesus himself. Each of the opposing institutions therefore has its own authoritative tradition in terms of law observance. It seems fairly clear in view of its prominence in the gospel that the issue of the Torah and its correct interpretation was one of the contributing factors to the eventual separation of the Matthean community from the Jewish parent body.

The immediate circumstances leading to the split are not easy to determine. There is no evidence at all that those in the Matthean community were officially excluded from the synagogue service.[29] It is more probable that the former departed from the latter after a prolonged period of dispute. This conflict with the Pharisees might have begun prior to the Jewish war, since it is possible that some Pharisees would have been members of the Antiochene synagogue(s), but it is highly likely that it was greatly exacerbated in the years just prior to the composition of the gospel, the period following the Jewish war. Such a rapid escalation of the conflict can be explained in the light of the substantial migration from Palestine to neighbouring areas in the aftermath of the disastrous war against Rome. After the war the economic conditions of Palestine were extremely difficult and many Jews emigrated to Syria in general and to the capital Antioch in particular in the hope of a better life. It is quite probable that certain Pharisees and their supporters were involved in this migration and that they became

Overman, *Matthew's Gospel*, pp. 78–86; Hultgren, *Jesus and His Adversaries*, pp. 184–90 and Segal, 'Matthew's Jewish Voice', pp. 6–8.

[29] It is sometimes argued that the implementation of the *Birkath ha-Minim*, the 'blessing of the heretics' which comprised the twelfth of the eighteen benedictions (*Shemoneh Esreh*) in the synagogue service, was the direct cause of the break. For an earlier statement of this view, see Kilpatrick, *Origins*, pp. 109–11. The recent study by Segal also argues for the influence of the *Birkath ha-Minim* on the separation of Matthew's community from the synagogue, although he concedes that it might not have been the sole reason for the break. See his 'Matthew's Jewish Voice', pp. 33–4. This explanation, however, has been justly criticised. On the one hand, there are concrete problems in determining precisely when the *Birkath ha-Minim* was inserted into the series of benedictions and how it was implemented from region to region. On the other hand, it must be emphasised that the *Birkath ha-Minim* constitutes a sufficient but hardly a necessary cause for the separation of Matthew's church from the Jewish synagogue. Jewish Christians had engaged in conflict with non-Christian Jews from the earliest days of the Christian church, and doubtless many of the former group had left or had been forced to leave the synagogue because of this. The introduction of the twelfth benediction, whenever this was, thus probably formalised and standardised a process of painful separation which had a long prior history. For full discussion of this question, see Overman, *Matthew's Gospel*, pp. 50–6; Stanton, *Gospel for a New People*, pp. 142–5 and Hagner, '*Sitz im Leben*', pp. 251–4.

influential in the Jewish communities at Antioch.[30] These new arrivals and the Matthean Christians inevitably would have clashed over the messianic status of Jesus and the proper interpretation of the Torah, and this situation of worsening relations presumably led to the split.

1.2 Relations between the ekklesia and the Jewish world

The above discussion has so far proposed the view that the Matthean community had broken away from the synagogue and was now a well-defined sect which was in conflict with the parent body, pharisaic-led formative Judaism. But this does not provide the whole picture in terms of Matthew's relationship with the Jewish world. We must consider this situation of separation and resultant hostility in more concrete terms. Although the Matthean community had separated from the local synagogue, it is clear that not all links were severed with those who belonged to that institution. In all probability they could not be severed absolutely, since separation from the synagogue service did not necessarily entail geographical separation from the Jewish world. Many members of Matthew's church must have belonged to the 'Jewish quarter' of Antioch and remained there after the break.[31] Under these circumstances they would doubtless have come into contact, either through business or in the street or market-place, with the scribes and Pharisees themselves as well as those Jews over whom they exercised some influence. The fact that Matthew refers to the practices of the Pharisees in the streets in 6:2, 5 (cf. also 6:16) and in the market-place (23:7) strongly supports this statement. It ought to be borne in mind as well that in ancient Graeco-Roman cities living conditions were generally so cramped that people spent much of their waking time in public places rather than in their houses.[32] The members of the Matthean community could therefore hardly

---

[30] See Davies, *Sermon*, pp. 295–6. In order to explain Matthew's contact with pharisaism, some scholars place Matthew in Palestine where formative Judaism was most prominent. So, most recently, Overman, *Matthew's Gospel*, pp. 158–9. But given the clear lines of communication between Palestine and Syria which always existed and the fact of the post-war migration, the Antiochene hypothesis is still a viable one.

[31] According to Hare, *Jewish Persecution*, pp. 147–8 n. 4, the Jewish Christians in Matthew's church had left the Jewish quarter and now lived with their gentile friends. This is rather unlikely in view of Matthew's view of the wider gentile world which we shall discuss shortly.

[32] See Stark, 'Antioch as the Social Situation for Matthew's Gospel', pp. 192–3.

have avoided their opponents. In view of this, the original conflicts within the synagogue which led to the break would have been renewed afresh in an unofficial public context.

We would err, however, in thinking that this conflict was confined merely to 'academic' matters. This might have been the case while the Matthean Christians were still part of the synagogue and were treated as 'insiders', but it almost certainly would have changed after the split when they became 'outsiders'. There is good evidence in the gospel that at least some members of the Matthean community were the victims of local Jewish persecution. That such persecution was taking place is best evidenced in Matthew 5:10–12[33] which reads,

> Blessed are those who are persecuted for righteousness' sake, for theirs is the kingdom of heaven. Blessed are you when men revile you and persecute you and utter all kinds of evil against you falsely on my account. Rejoice and be glad, for your reward is great in heaven, for so men persecuted the prophets who were before you.

As most scholars recognise, verse 10 is a Matthean creation designed to introduce the two later verses which stem from Q (// Luke 6:22–3). This Matthean creation allows us to suppose not only that his community included 'those who are persecuted', but that the following verses reflect their situation. The Lucan parallel to these verses is only slightly different from its Matthean counterpart and probably stands closer to the original text of Q. In any event Matthew has clearly inserted the word 'persecute' (διώκω) in verses 11–12 which agrees with the presence of the word in verse 10 (cf. 5:44). Matthew's adoption of this material provides a glimpse of his community's concrete social setting.

The first thing which needs to be said is that he has taken over the Q motif that the ones responsible for the persecution are Jews;

---

[33] According to Hare's detailed study of the persecution theme in Matthew, all references to persecution in the gospel, including this text, apply to the missionaries of the evangelist's church. See *Jewish Persecution*, p. 125. Since he assumes that the evangelist's group no longer lived in the Jewish quarter (see note 31 above), Hare excludes the possibility that Matthew 5:10–12 could have referred to the local persecution of rank and file members. In view of this, he reads these verses through the eyes of 23:29–39 and 10:16–33, the two texts which do refer to the mistreatment of missionaries. But the very fact that this pericope appears in the sermon on the mount, which is addressed to all members of Matthew's community, means that it has a general application rather than a limited term of reference.

the ones who persecuted the prophets (the Jews) are also to blame for the present suffering. Matthew refers to two specific types of mistreatment, reviling and speaking evil. With regard to the first, ὀνειδίζω means insulting and abusive language or behaviour aimed at the object of abuse, and we are justified in presuming that some community members had been the recipients of such treatment. The second type of mistreatment refers to slander of a general nature. This slander might have included personal and direct insults and perhaps rumour-mongering as well. One possible instance of the latter might be reflected in Matthew 28:11–15 which states that certain Jews of the evangelist's time were accounting for the empty tomb of Jesus by blaming the disciples for the theft of the body. It is probable that this was not the only rumour which the Matthean church found itself trying to disprove.[34] Less easy to determine is what Matthew meant by the general notion of persecution. According to D. R. A. Hare, διώκω in 5:11 is best translated as 'violently oppose' which could include physical blows, the throwing of missiles and the use of dire threats.[35] Hare's translation is conditioned to some extent by his assumption that all references to persecution in Matthew apply to the missionaries of the Matthean community and not to the rank and file members (see note 33). But he is probably correct that the evangelist wishes to emphasise here the element of physical mistreatment which contrasts with the two forms of non-physical abuse also mentioned. If this is right, then we may conclude that in addition to insults and slander the Matthean community also had to contend with minor cases of physical assault (cf. 5:39).

The picture drawn by Matthew 5:10–12 is much as we would expect of a minority group which had broken away from the parent body, but which through design or accident maintained unofficial contact with the larger group. Insults, vindictive words, slander and even physical abuse are often the lot of those who choose to be different from the majority. This persecution of the Matthean community, however, should not be exaggerated. The fact that only a few passages allude to it is evidence enough that any persecution was sporadic and was perhaps initiated by only a few members of

[34]   Further potential rumours to which the evangelist responded might include the charge that Jesus was illegitimate which he addresses in 1:18–25 (so Saldarini, 'Matthew and Jewish–Christian Conflict', p. 38 n. 1), and the rumour that Jesus was in league with Satan to which he responds in 9:34; 10:25; 12:24, 27. On the second charge, see Stanton, *Gospel for a New People*, pp. 173–8.

[35]   Hare, *Jewish Persecution*, p. 119.

the opposing group. None the less, and this is the important point, any situation of persecution and hostility can escalate very quickly and it is reasonable to assume that the Matthean church as a whole lived with some trepidation on account of this ever-present possibility. This unease would have served to reinforce and perhaps even exaggerate the sense of alienation which occurred after the official break.

1.3 Matthean missionaries and the Jewish world

Matthew's major statements concerning Jewish persecution do not apply to the rank and file members of his community; they refer instead to the persecution of the group's missionaries. According to Hare's comprehensive study of this subject, such persecution by Jews of Matthean missionaries belongs only to the past. He arrives at this conclusion on account of his acceptance of the view that in Matthew the Jewish mission is over and the gospel is directed now only to the gentiles.[36] Yet, as argued in chapter 7, this hypothesis is quite implausible and it is far more likely that the evangelist enjoined the mission to the Jews up to the time of the parousia. In the light of this, the persecution of missionaries to which Matthew alludes encompasses both the past and the future.

The past persecution of the missionaries of Matthew's church is clearly related in the allegory of the wedding feast in Matthew 22:1–10 (cf. Luke 14:15–24). In verse 6 the evangelist relates that some of the messengers who delivered the invitation to the feast were mistreated and killed by those to whom they were sent. In response to this act, the king who holds the feast sends his troops to destroy the city of the murderers (verse 7). The latter event is an obvious reference to the destruction of Jerusalem by the Romans. Since this punishment is an immediate response to the murder of the envoys, there is no doubt that Matthew has in mind here Christian missionaries and not the Old Testament prophets. This text thus reveals the evangelist's view that certain missionaries had met their deaths at the hands of the Jews. The gravity of this crime for Matthew can be seen in his conviction that the destruction of Jerusalem and the temple was God's punishment for it. The expected persecution of Matthean missionaries in the future is highlighted in the mission discourse of chapter 10. It will be recalled

[36] Hare, *Jewish Persecution*, pp. 104–5, 146–62.

from the discussion in chapter 7 that this material probably enjoins a final mission to the Jews in Palestine before the arrival of the Son of Man, and there is no doubt that the evangelist expected these messengers to be persecuted by the Jews. The redactional verse 17 relates that they will be dragged before councils and flogged in their synagogues, while verse 23 contains the advice that they should flee from town to town to avoid such persecution. A number of later texts suggest that this mission in the last, desperate stage of the present era might also lead to death (10:29, 39).

A further relevant passage in this regard is 23:29–36 which appears towards the end of the polemical discourse against the scribes and Pharisees. Most of this material derives from Q (cf. Luke 11:47–51), but Matthew has extensively redacted it and appended verses 32–3 in the process. In verses 29–32 the evangelist makes the point that even though the scribes and Pharisees build and adorn the tombs and monuments of the prophets, and profess that they themselves would not have persecuted them, they are in reality no better than the past generations which did mistreat them. This point is explained in verse 34. In the Lucan version of this verse Jesus cites the Wisdom of God who says she will send prophets and apostles, some of whom will be killed and persecuted; with the possible exception of the reference to the apostles, it is generally accepted that Luke's text reflects the Q tradition.[37] Matthew substantially edits this verse. First, he omits the reference to the Wisdom of God and substitutes in its place the personal pronoun 'I', thus making Jesus the speaker. Moreover, he expands the list of those whom Jesus sends to include wise men and scribes in addition to prophets. Matthew also extends the list of crimes committed against these emissaries by the scribes and Pharisees. Some will be killed and crucified, while others will be scourged in the synagogue and persecuted from town to town.

This is a notoriously difficult passage to interpret, since it is not clear whether the evangelist is referring to past events, future events or even current events. The reference to crucifixion constitutes the chief difficulty. There is no evidence at all that Jews ever crucified Christians and this makes it difficult to perceive this passage, as Hare does, in terms of a past event from the perspective of the evangelist. Hare is well aware of this and opts to assign the

---

[37] See Schulz, *Q*, pp. 336–7; Gnilka, *Matthäusevangelium*, II, p. 298 and Gundry, *Matthew*, pp. 469–70.

crucifixion reference to the hand of a later glossator.[38] While such an explanation is not impossible, it does set a dangerous precedent whereby all uncomfortable sections of the gospel can be omitted from the discussion. A far better explanation of this material is to take it as a future reference which stands in agreement with the mission discourse of chapter 10. In support of this interpretation is the fact that all four crimes of 23:34 are mentioned in this particular chapter. The references to scourging and pursuit from town to town are found in 10:17, 23, while the statement about killing (ἀποκτείνω) finds a parallel in those who kill the body (τῶν ἀποκτεννόντων τὸ σῶμα) in 10:28. The crucifixion theme is likewise attested in the tradition relating to cross-bearing (10:38). In the light of these correspondences, 23:34 is best viewed as a comment on the mission discourse. The missionary activity described in both texts refers to the future and final mission to the Jews, an enterprise which Matthew believed would result in some missionaries following in the footsteps of Jesus and meeting their deaths by crucifixion.

The polemic reaches its climax in verses 35–6 where Matthew blurs the distinction between the past murderers of the prophets and their current descendants, the scribes and Pharisees, which he had established in verses 29–32. His current opponents are now charged with the crimes of their fathers. In verse 35 he adds 'whom you murdered' to the text of Q and so incriminates directly the scribes and Pharisees in the murder of Jeremiah, son of Barachiah.[39] All the righteous blood from the murder of Abel to that of Jeremiah will come upon these Matthean opponents. It is quite clear that Matthew here has left the arena of reasoned debate and entered the realm of abusive polemic. We may infer from this that Matthew's relations with the leaders of the parent body had sunk to such a point that abuse and polemic rather than sensible argumentation were adopted as the best weapons in the dispute. He therefore accuses the scribes and Pharisees of all violence done to the messengers of God in the past. While such an accusation is manifestly absurd and very unfortunate, we should not judge the evangelist too harshly for making it. Underlying these sorts of statements was a genuine fear for the forthcoming or present mission to the Jews of Palestine, a fear which was based upon past

---

[38] Hare, *Jewish Persecution*, pp. 89–91.

[39] So most scholars; Hare, *Jewish Persecution*, pp. 93–4; Shulz, *Q*, p. 338; Gnilka, *Matthäusevangelium*, II, p. 298 and Gundry, *Matthew*, p. 471.

and current hostilities. It would not have been lost on Matthew that the scribes and Pharisees were in the process of securing a stronghold in Palestine and this would have given the evangelist reason enough to expect the worst.

1.4 Summary

We may now summarise our discussion of the relations between the Matthean community and the wider Jewish world. Matthew's community is best seen as a self-conscious sect within a very fluid post-war formative Judaism. It had recently split from the synagogue after a period of bitter dispute and was in the process of defining and legitimating its sectarian nature vis-à-vis the parent body. This process of definition and legitimation was taking place in the context of harsh polemical relations with the scribes and Pharisees who were the leaders of the greater Jewish body. Although no longer within the synagogue, the members of Matthew's church maintained unofficial contact with their Jewish opponents and were probably subjected to minor bouts of persecution as a result. This persecution and the genuine fear of its escalation would have served only to increase the growing sense of alienation within the community. Such a fear is reflected in Matthew's pessimistic predictions concerning the future mission to the Jews of Palestine.

2. The Matthean community and the gentile world[40]

2.1 The gentiles in Matthew's narrative

The question of Matthew's relationship with the gentile world is also a very important one in terms of identifying the social setting of the Matthean community. For many scholars the issue is rather clear cut. Matthew's 'anti-Jewish' stance is completely counterbalanced by a wholly positive attitude to the gentiles, and there is no doubt that the gentiles receive some good press in his gospel as the following texts make clear. In the opening chapters, a number of gentile women are mentioned in Jesus' genealogy and the gentile magi travel to Bethlehem to find the infant Jesus and worship him. With regard to Jesus' ministry, Matthew composes two of his

---

[40] A far more detailed analysis of this subject can be found in Sim, 'Matthew and the Gentiles'.

formula quotations at 4:15–16 and 12:18–19 which state that Jesus is the light to the gentiles and that in his name the gentiles will hope. At Capernaum Jesus heals the servant of a centurion whose great faith in Jesus surpasses that of anyone in Israel (8:5–13). Jesus travels to the gentile regions of Gadara (8:28–34), and Tyre and Sidon (15:21–39), and performs miracles there. In the latter region, he heals a Canaanite woman and, as he did with the centurion, commends her great faith (15:22–8). The concluding part of the gospel also contains pro-gentile sentiments. Upon the death of Jesus, the centurion and the other guards at the foot of the cross confess him as the son of God (but see below), and at the very end of the gospel the command of the risen Jesus to his disciples to make disciples of all nations clearly includes the gentiles as well as the Jews.

This very brief survey of the relevant texts clearly paints a favourable picture of the gentiles. It is perhaps not surprising that a good many influential Matthean specialists have argued that the evangelist was in fact himself a gentile who, with the failure of the Jewish mission, now focused attention solely on the gentile world which had responded favourably to the Christian message. While both these conclusions exceed the evidence, it might reasonably be argued that the Jewish Matthew did look rather favourably upon the wider gentile world. We might assume that Matthew, having cut all ties with the institutionalised Jewish world and experiencing great hardship in the process, would now look to the gentile peoples, those who were responding appropriately to the gospel, as considerably more friendly and open to contact. As reasonable as this scenario appears on the surface, there is good evidence in the gospel that this was not the reality of the situation. The first thing which needs to be said is that, contrary to the view of many scholars, not all gentiles in the gospel narrative are depicted favourably. A glance at a number of passages confirms this point.

After performing the successful exorcism in Gadara, Jesus is asked by the gentile inhabitants to leave the area; since this amounts to a rejection of Jesus and the gospel, the Gadarenes are hardly portrayed in a positive light. More importantly, in the passion narrative it is the gentile Pilate who, along with the Jewish leaders and despite his handwashing, bears no small responsibility for the crucifixion of Jesus.[41] Further, the Roman soldiers in charge

---

[41] See the recent discussion of Cargal, 'His Blood be Upon Us and Upon our Children', pp. 107–8.

of Jesus' execution are hardly depicted in a favourable light (27:27–37). They place a crown of thorns on Jesus' head and dress him in a mock royal robe. They jeer at him, spit on him, beat him and, after crucifying him, cast lots for his garments. Since Matthew explicitly identifies these soldiers with the ones who declare that Jesus is the Son of God in 27:54 (cf. 27:36 and 27:54), it is not so certain that their later statement is intended to be taken in a positive sense. The fact that they make their confession solely out of fear in the face of the terrifying apocalyptic events which Matthew inserts into the Marcan account (27:51b–3), is a pointer in this direction. I have argued in detail elsewhere that the common understanding of these soldiers and their 'confession' in the context of the Matthean narrative is mistaken, and that rather than depicting these torturers and murderers as models of gentile faith, Matthew uses this episode to prefigure the judgement where the terrified wicked will learn Jesus' true identity as they stand before his throne of glory and realise the nature of their eternal fate (cf. Matthew 25:31–46).[42] On this understanding of the pericope, the soldiers are not examples of good and faithful gentiles; rather, as the torturers and murderers of the messiah, they are gentiles of the worst type.

We see then that Matthew's narrative is not wholly favourable to gentiles. The Gadarenes, Pontius Pilate and the Roman executioners of Jesus serve as examples of wicked gentiles who are contrasted with the good gentiles such as the centurion of Capernaum. This introduces an important point which is all too often forgotten. Precisely the same contrast between good and evil figures appears in Matthew's portrayal of his Jewish characters. Just as there are wicked Jews in Matthew's narrative, the scribes and Pharisees for example, so too are there good Jews who stand in contrast to the wicked. Examples of this type are the parents of Jesus, John the Baptist and the disciples of Jesus, not to mention Jesus himself! Therefore the proposition that Matthew intends to stereotype all Jewish figures as wicked and all gentile characters as positive does not hold up to scrutiny on either count.[43] It is based upon a very selective reading of the evidence and ignores the point that each group has a mixture of good and bad. The gentile world in Matthew's gospel is thus not

[42] Sim, 'Confession of the Soldiers', pp. 401–24.
[43] So too Levine, *Salvation History*, pp. 274–5 and Davies and Allison, *Matthew*, I, pp. 23–4.

as open and friendly as is commonly thought. Just as Matthew specifies that Jesus was rejected and murdered by the Jews, so too does he specify that the gentiles were not innocent of either crime. Having made this important point, we may now move on to an even more significant category of evidence concerning the evangelist's attitude toward the gentile world.

2.2 Anti-gentile statements in Matthew

A number of Matthean pericopae unambiguously betray an anti-gentile perspective. In many scholarly discussions these particular texts either are explained away as Matthew's conservative retention of traditional material or are conveniently forgotten altogether. Neither approach is fair to the evangelist. Since these texts appear in his gospel and were not omitted by him, they must be given due consideration. When they are taken into account, they shed considerable light on the social setting of the evangelist and his church. Four passages, two of which derive from Q (5:46–7//Luke 6:32–3; 6:31–2//Luke 12:29–30), and two of which are unique to Matthew (6:7–8; 18:15–17), belong together and will be considered first.

Matthew 5:46–7 appears in the section of the sermon on the mount which deals with love of enemies and is the least critical of the gentiles. It reads, 'For if you love those who love you, what reward have you? Do not even the tax-collectors do the same? And if you salute only your brethren, what more are you doing than others? Do not even the gentiles (οἱ ἐθνικοί) do the same?' The Lucan version says much the same thing, except that for 'tax-collectors and 'gentiles' Luke twice uses 'sinners' (ἁμαρτωλοί). Since ἁμαρτωλοί is a favourite Lucan word, it is generally agreed that at these points the Lucan version is secondary, and that Matthew has followed Q in using 'tax-collectors' and 'gentiles'.[44] Implementing our policy of taking seriously the text of the gospel as it stands, it matters little whether Matthew has copied from Q here or inserted it into his source. The important point is that these verses contain an unfavourable reference to gentiles, albeit a comparatively mild one. This tradition specifies that the readers of the gospel must do much more than the two groups in question, tax-collectors and gentiles. While neither group is criticised or attacked

---

[44] So Schulz, *Q*, p. 129; Gnilka, *Matthäusevangelium*, I, p. 189; Davies and Allison, *Matthew*, I, p. 559 and Luz, *Matthäus*, I, p. 312, contra Gundry, *Matthew*, p. 99.

openly, they are so implicitly in view of the inherent contrast.[45] The second Q passage is Matthew 6:31–2 which is presented in similar wording in Luke 12:29–30. The Matthean version reads, 'Therefore, do not be anxious saying, "What shall we eat?" or "What shall we drink?" or "What shall we wear?". For the gentiles (τὰ ἔθνη) seek all these things, and your heavenly father knows you need them all.' In this case Luke also writes 'gentiles', so it is clear that the word stood in Q. It appears then that once again Matthew has taken from his tradition without change a text which views the gentiles in an unfavourable light; they are misguided at best and ignorant at worst because they concern themselves with mundane matters. As with 5:46–7, Matthew urges his readers not to model themselves on gentile practice.

The third relevant text, again featuring in the sermon on the mount, is Matthew 6:7–8 which acts as an introduction to the Lord's Prayer, and reads as follows, 'And in praying, do not heap up empty phrases as the gentiles (οἱ ἐθνικοί) do; for they think that they will be heard for their many words. Do not be like them, for your heavenly father knows what you need before you ask him.' This is a stronger criticism of the gentiles than is found in either of the two Q passages examined above. The origin of this material is uncertain, but it most probably stems from a special source.[46] None the less, the significant point is that we find the gentile world criticised, this time for its religious practice. Gentile prayers are denounced by the evangelist for their length and empty content. The readers are again instructed not to emulate this aspect of gentile life. It is significant that this anti-gentile material follows a tradition which criticises hypocritical (on Matthew's terms) Jewish prayer (6:5–6). This arrangement is quite deliberate and shows that Matthew wished to compare the Christian Lord's Prayer with hypocritical Jewish prayer and with wordy gentile prayer and, of course, affirm its superiority over both.

The final text for consideration, 18:15–17, appears in the chapter treating church regulations and is the most important of all. This pericope specifies the procedure to be adopted when one member has a grievance with another member. At first the wronged

---

[45] This point is acknowledged by Gnilka, *Matthäusevangelium*, I, p. 194; Davies and Allison, *Matthew*, I, p. 559; Luz, *Matthäus*, I, p. 312 and Guelich, *Sermon*, pp. 232–3.

[46] A special source is postulated by Davies and Allison, *Matthew*, I, p. 587 and Luz, *Matthäus*, I, p. 330, while Matthean composition is affirmed by Guelich, *Sermon*, p. 319 and Gundry, *Matthew*, p. 104.

individual is to discuss the issue with the offender alone. If this fails, he or she is to try again but this time in the presence of two or three witnesses (cf. Deut. 19:15). Failing even this, the matter is to be brought to the attention of the ekklesia and if the wrongdoer does not listen to the church, he or she is to be treated as a tax-collector and a gentile. Since the point at issue is that the sinner is to be expelled from the community (see note 23) and therefore shunned and ignored, we may infer from this that the Matthean community largely avoided contact with the gentile world. Despite attempts to lessen the pejorative tone of this pericope, there is no other way to understand it.[47]

These four texts are very significant. The first three fall within the Matthean community's code of practice, the sermon on the mount, which serves to establish the boundaries around the group. Just as this code urges the readers not to emulate the practice of their Jewish opponents, so too does it advise that the irreligious practices of the gentile world are to be avoided. The Matthean ekklesia is therefore consciously distinct from both the larger Jewish world and the wider gentile society. The final text from chapter 18 specifies just how tightly drawn the boundaries are in terms of the gentile world. One should exclude and avoid an unrepentant community member in the same manner as one would a gentile.

Apart from these four texts which explicitly criticise the gentiles, there are other indications in the gospel of Matthew of the relationship between the evangelist's church and the gentile world. In both the mission discourse and the apocalyptic discourse, there are references to malevolent gentile treatment of Christians. Matthew 24:9b specifies that at the time of the eschatological woes, the Matthean church will be hated by all nations (diff. Mark 'by all'). Since this verse appears in the section of Matthew's timetable which had already been fulfilled, we may infer that this perception of hatred was the present experience of the evangelist at the time he wrote. The first half of this verse (24:9a) speaks of Christian martyrdom and, while the evangelist probably had in mind some murder of Christians by Jews, it is almost certain in view of what follows immediately after that he is referring to gentile acts of murder as well. We shall return to this point shortly. Matthew also expects gentile persecution of the missionaries to Israel. After relating the expected persecution of the missionaries by the Jews in

---

[47] So correctly Stanton, 'Matthew and Judaism', p. 277.

10:17, Matthew then turns to gentile persecution. Matt 10:18 refers to the missionaries being dragged before governors and kings to bear testimony before them and the gentiles. This verse bespeaks not only persecution at an official level by gentile officials,[48] but also that they act with the assent of the whole gentile world. Since Matthew has added καὶ τοῖς ἔθνεσιν in this verse (cf. Mark 13:9), he indicates the affinity between these administrators and the gentile world they represent. This is reinforced in verse 22 in which Matthew, following Mark 13:13, states that the missionaries will be hated by all on account of their allegiance to Jesus. It is presumably these gentile officials who, at the instigation of the Jews, will be responsible for the crucifixion of certain missionaries in the final mission to Israel (10:38; 23:34). This gentile persecution of the missionaries in Palestine ties in with our exegesis of 24:28 which was argued in chapter 4. In the very final days before the end, the Romans will align themselves with the antichrist and increase the suffering of 'those in Judea', the missionary elements of the Matthean community.

The mission discourse and the apocalyptic discourse, therefore, together indicate that Matthew's view of the gentile world was not as positive as some scholars think. His community had suffered at the hands of the gentiles and was expecting to suffer even more as the eschatological timetable progressed according to divine plan. At the time the gospel was composed, this community perceived itself to be universally hated by the gentile nations. These two discourses thus reinforce the attitude inherent in the texts which were examined earlier. The gentile world is not just a godless place; it is a very dangerous place and for this reason contact with gentiles should be kept to a minimum.

2.3 An explanation of Matthew's anti-gentile attitude

Can we probe more deeply and attempt to explain Matthew's position on the question of the gentile world? Certainly a partial answer is provided by the evangelist's Jewish heritage. He betrays a suspicion of and contempt for the irreligious 'pagan' world which were current in some Jewish circles. But surely there is more to it than this. The answer, I would suggest, lies in Matthew's references to gentile persecution of his community. In this respect, Matthew

---

[48] For comprehensive discussion of the question whether this material refers to gentile persecution, see Hare, *Jewish Persecution*, pp. 106–8.

24:9 is of the greatest significance. Here the evangelist speaks of a past persecution of his community which was so serious that some of his fellow church members met with death while those who lived through it perceived that they were universally hated by all the nations. Can we identify with more precision this gentile persecution of the Matthean community? It might be argued that the evangelist had in mind the Neronian persecution, but this can be ruled out on the grounds of both date and location. Nero's persecution occurred in the early sixties, some fifteen or so years before the composition of the gospel. More importantly, it was basically confined to Rome and did not, so far as we know, affect the Christians of Syria where Matthew was written. A far better explanation which is consistent with both the date and location of the gospel is that Matthew is referring to gentile persecution of his community both during and following the Jewish war.

This subject is best introduced by recounting the gentile persecution of the Jews which occurred in this period. These events are well known and can be summarised here quickly.[49] At the time of the first Jewish uprising against Rome, the Jews of the eastern regions of the Roman empire, including the Jews of Syria, were persecuted and massacred by their gentile neighbours. The purported location of Matthew and his church, Antioch on the Orontes, was initially spared this ordeal, but after a Jewish apostate spread rumours that the Jews were planning to burn the city, they were then persecuted mercilessly and many were killed. This gentile violence against the Jews of Antioch was renewed at the end of the Jewish war when they were again accused by the same apostate of lighting certain fires which destroyed parts of the city. Although their innocence was confirmed by an enquiry of the Roman governor, relations between the Jews and the gentiles in Antioch remained extremely strained. This is amply demonstrated by the fact that when the triumphant Titus passed through Antioch a little later, he was twice approached by the gentile population to expel the Jews from the city, a request which he refused. A further request to strip the Jews of their privileges was also rejected by Titus. Although we have no direct information about the relations between the two groups in the period following these events, it can be safely assumed that they remained uneasy at best and hostile at worst. Many of the gentiles of Antioch would still have resented their Jewish citizens and

---

[49] See the discussion of Meeks and Wilken, *Jews and Christians in Antioch*, pp. 4–5 and the relevant ancient sources cited there.

wished their departure from the city, while the Jews no doubt lived in great fear that any spark could ignite the anti-Jewish feeling which the Jewish war had caused and lead to further outbreaks of violence against them.

It may be safely assumed that the Matthean church did not escape this violence. If, as argued above, Matthew's community had only very recently parted company with institutionalised Judaism, then there is a good chance that the evangelist and many members of his church were still attached to the synagogue when the persecutions took place. But even if they had left the synagogue by this time, and this possibility must not be excluded, it is still likely that they suffered at the hands of the gentile persecutors. Since we are dealing with mob violence, it is unlikely that a bloodthirsty mob, intent on harming all Jews, would have known or cared about the finer details of the theological dispute between traditional synagogue Jews and their Jewish Christian opponents. We also need to remember that the members of Matthew's community, despite their departure from the synagogue, still considered themselves as Jews and followed a traditional Jewish lifestyle. Thus, no matter when we date the departure of the Matthean community from the larger Jewish world, the probability is that these Jewish Christians suffered the same fate as other Jews in the terrifying pogroms during and after the Jewish war against Rome, and it is to these events that Matthew 24:9a refers. The rift between the evangelist's church and the parent body which had occurred in the meantime would not have affected either group's attitude toward the gentile world. Though in conflict with one another, each of them would have viewed their gentile neighbours with extreme bitterness and fear.

In some respects the Matthean community might have been even more fearful of the gentile world than were the 'mainstream' Jews. After the split with the parent body, Matthew and his readers could place no real faith in the gentile (Roman) authorities, despite the protective actions of the Roman governor in stopping the earlier violence against the Jews. The reason for this is that the members of the Matthean community were not merely Jews; they were Christians as well. While their Jewish status made them prone to gentile mob violence, their Christian status made their position precarious vis-à-vis the Roman empire. It was, as Matthew well knew, the Roman governor who put Jesus to death on the cross, no matter how much Jewish participation he suspected in this matter. Moreover, the official persecution of the Christians by Nero was proof enough that the Roman authorities were not above persecutions of their own. We also need to remember that the mission discourse indicates that the missionaries of this church expected to be mistreated by gentile officials.

When we look at matters in this way, it is clear that Matthew and his church had good reason to be fearful of the gentile world. Not only could they be attacked by gentile mobs for being Jews, but they could be persecuted by the gentile authorities for being Christians as well. In the light of its extremely precarious and vulnerable position, it is quite understandable that it was critical of the surrounding gentile society and adopted a policy of avoiding and shunning it. Also comprehensible is that this minority Jewish group perceived itself to be hated by all the nations (24:9b). In recent years it had come into conflict with both the gentile world and the larger Jewish world.

These points are all but forgotten in scholarly discussions of the effects of the Jewish war on the Matthean community. All too often the emphasis is placed on Jewish persecution of the church when formative Judaism sought to establish solidarity and exclude those groups which were perceived to threaten that unity. J. P. Meier's discussion of the Matthean community at Antioch is a good example of this tendency. While he acknowledges that the Matthean community expected some official gentile persecution, he does not refer at all to the gentile mob violence which the Jews of Antioch suffered and how this might have affected the Jews in Matthew's group.[50] Only by ignoring this can Meier claim that since the (whole) church's mission to the Jews had been a failure and the mission to the gentiles a relative success, '... even conservative Jewish Christians at Antioch and elsewhere would find it more and more difficult to put obstacles in the way of a full-scale circumcision-free mission to the Gentiles. Increasingly, the Gentiles appeared to be the church's main if not only future, especially after the Jewish War.'[51] But this scenario completely overlooks the historical fact of gentile persecution of Jews at this time and the great probability that the Matthean community was caught up in these events. For Meier's view to be credible, we must imagine that

---

[50] Meier, 'Antioch', pp. 48–9.
[51] Meier, 'Antioch', pp. 47–8. Other scholars who have argued that in the aftermath of the Jewish war the Matthean community turned to the gentile world include Brown, 'Gentile Mission', pp. 215–18 and LaVerdiere and Thompson 'New Testament Communities in Transition', pp. 571–82.

the conservative Jewish Christians in Antioch miraculously escaped the persecutions and that the gentile world held no fears for them. This is a difficult proposition to believe. It is far more likely, as Matthew 18:17 and other texts show, that the Jewish war, far from bringing the Matthean community and the gentile world closer together, actually drove a firm wedge between them.

2.4 The gentiles in the Matthean community

Having made the above points, however, it must be emphasised that Matthew is not against all people of non-Jewish background. He clearly enjoins the gentile mission which had been commanded by the risen Lord (cf. 28:19), and he acknowledges that certain gentiles can be viewed with approval. On these grounds alone, it is inherently probable that some gentiles were part of the Matthean community. But what makes these gentiles acceptable is the fact that they have to all intents and purposes left the gentile world and become (Matthean) Christians; by association with Matthew's community these people in a real sense cease to be gentiles. In short, they are now insiders rather than outsiders. Matthew's anti-gentile sentiments, therefore, are directed at those who remain in the realm of the gentiles, just as his anti-Jewish statements are directed at those who reside in the world of formative Judaism.[52] It is these gentiles, true gentiles from Matthew's perspective, who are to be treated with suspicion and avoided. As to the number and status of the gentiles in the Matthean community, the evidence is not absolutely clear. A number of inferences, however, can be made on the basis of the existing evidence. It is almost certain that Jews comprised the greater part of the Matthean community and that gentile membership was comparatively small.[53] The fact that this community perceived itself as a sect within formative Judaism and was involved in thoroughly Jewish issues is evidence enough of this. Moreover, the probability that the Matthean community had only recently parted company with the synagogue also points in this direction.

[52] This point is rightly made by Levine, *Salvation History*, p. 35. A similar view is proposed by Meier, 'Antioch', p. 69 n. 157. Neither scholar, however, really addresses the issue that the remainder of the gentile world is to be avoided at all costs, the very point of 18:17. They seem more concerned to prove that Matthew is not totally anti-gentile since he accepts gentiles into his community.

[53] So most recent studies; Overman, *Matthew's Gospel*, p. 157; Przybylski, 'Matthean Anti-Judaism', p. 192; Hagner, '*Sitz im Leben*', p. 255 and Saldarini, 'Matthew and Jewish–Christian Conflict', pp. 59–60.

On the much debated questions whether the male gentiles were circumcised and whether all of them were expected to follow the whole Torah, the evidence implies that they were on both counts.[54] Matthew's clear statements that the whole law, which includes circumcision for males as the mark of entry to the covenant community, remains valid up to the time of the parousia (5:17–19) must be given full force. We can hardly suppose that the gentiles in Matthew's church were excluded from this command to keep the Torah in its entirety.[55] It is sometimes argued that since the command to evangelise the world in 28:19 mentions baptism and not circumcision as the mark of entry to the Matthean community, the latter rite was not practised on gentile converts.[56] But this argument completely overlooks the focus of the Matthean mission which was oriented primarily toward the Jews rather than the gentiles (Matt. 10; 23:34–6),[57] in which case the command to circumcise would be rather superfluous. Under these circumstances Matthew understandably preferred to focus on the rite which inducted one into his deviant Jewish group. We must take into account as well the great probability that in so far as the great commission does advert to a gentile mission that circumcision as a mark of entry was understood by both author and reader alike. Had Matthew's community abandoned this most Jewish of practices we should expect some defence of this stance in the material which treats the conflict with formative Judaism. It is also important to remember that when the evangelist refers to pharisaic proselytism in 23:15 he does not mention circumcision for the obvious reason that it was taken for granted. Matthew 28:19 should therefore be read in the same way.

2.5 Summary

We are now in a position to draw some conclusions about the relationship between the Matthean community and the gentile world. It is very probable that Matthew's church had been caught

---

[54] So correctly Overman, *Matthew's Gospel*, p. 157; Saldarini, 'Matthew and Jewish–Christian Conflict', p. 49 and White, 'Crisis Management and Boundary Maintenance', pp. 241–2 n. 100.

[55] This position, however, is adopted by Davies and Allison, *Matthew*, I, pp. 492–3.

[56] So Davies and Allison, *Matthew*, I, p. 493; Meier, 'Antioch', p. 62; Hagner, '*Sitz im Leben*', p. 258 and Segal, 'Matthew's Jewish Voice', p. 22.

[57] For full discussion of this point, see Sim, 'Matthew and the Gentiles', pp. 39–44 and literature cited there.

up in the pogroms against the Jews which the Jewish war had triggered. The effect of this persecution was that this community perceived itself to be universally hated by all the nations (24:9). For this reason, the Matthean group was fearful of the gentile world and adopted a policy of avoiding and shunning it. When we add together the respective relationships which Matthew's community enjoyed with the wider Jewish and gentile worlds, then the picture becomes a very sorry one. Matthew's ekklesia appears completely alienated from both worlds and related to each of them with feelings of bitterness, hostility and fear.

3. The Matthean community and the wider Christian church

The relationship between the Matthean community and the wider Christian church must also be considered if we are to understand fully the social setting of Matthew's gospel. It might be thought that the evangelist's group, whatever problems it had with the Jewish and gentile spheres, would not have had any difficulties with the wider Christian church; for all its Jewishness, it was after all a Christian institution which could easily have turned to its fellow Christian churches for support. As reasonable as this scenario sounds, however, a fresh examination of Matthew's gospel within its historical context demonstrates the inherent implausibility of this suggestion. There is every reason to think that the Matthean community was alienated from the broader Christian movement, and that this in turn only exacerbated its sense of isolation and despair. In what follows we need to bear in mind that Matthew's church was a law-observant Jewish sectarian group which did not enjoy good relations with the gentile world.

It is widely recognised that Matthew perceived the Christian church as a whole to be a *corpus mixtum*. This is clearly stated in the parable of the wedding feast where the mission of the messengers ('all whom they found') gathers both good and bad to the festivities (22:10). It is along these lines that one should view the parables of the tares and the net and their respective redactional interpretations (Matt. 13:24–30, 36–43, 47–50). In the material dealing with the tares, Matthew emphasises that the Son of Man has sown good seed in a field (the world), while the devil has sown weeds amongst the seed. The two must grow together until the judgement when the angels of the Son of Man will uproot the evildoers out of his kingdom and cast them into the fire. While some scholars have argued that Matthew intended 'the world' to be taken literally, so that the contrast is between Christians and the remainder of humanity,[58] this is not likely. Against the literal interpretation is the fact that the angels of the Son of Man gather the sinners out of his kingdom (verse 41). This reference to the kingdom of the Son of Man (cf. 16:28; 20:21) seems more appropriate to the church than to the whole world. It is important to note that Matthew has the whole Christian church in mind here and not merely his own community. This is evident from the universal nature of the word he chooses, 'the world'; had he intended to refer only to his own community, we might expect him to have used ekklesia. It is also suggested by the fact that the passage advises letting the weeds grow amongst the wheat until the judgement. Since Matthew's church practised exclusion of its own wicked members (18:17), he cannot be speaking only of his own church.[59] He is plainly referring to the Christian movement in general where his own community did not possess the authority or the means to expel troublemakers. For Matthew, therefore, the Christian church as a whole comprises both good and bad members.[60] Matthew incorporates this distinction between Christians into his developed dualistic scheme. The righteous have their origin in Jesus, while the wicked work in the service of Satan.

Matthew provides us with a description of the ones in the Christian church whom he considers to be the weeds. They are described in 13:41 as those who cause sin and as doers of lawlessness (τοὺς ποιοῦντας τὴν ἀνομίαν). Although Matthew does not expand upon this in the present context, he had earlier in his narrative referred to a specific group of such lawless figures. In 7:15–23 the false prophets who signal the nearness of the end are depicted as charismatics and workers of lawlessness (οἱ ἐργαζόμενοι τὴν ἀνομίαν) who are rejected by Jesus at the eschatological judgement (cf. 13:41–2). These people are nominally Christians but appear not to be members of the Matthean

---

[58] See, for example, Gundry, *Matthew*, p. 275 and Schweizer, *Matthew*, p. 311. Davies and Allison, *Matthew*, II, pp. 408–9 adopt a similar position, but define the contrast in terms of believing Christians and unbelieving Israel (p. 430).

[59] So correctly Davies and Allison, *Matthew*, II, p. 409, although they draw the wrong conclusion from it (see note 58 above).

[60] Those supporting the view that Matthew is speaking of good and bad within the Christian church include Bornkamm, 'End-Expectation', p. 44; Barth, 'Matthew's Understanding of the Law', pp. 59–60; Gnilka, *Matthäusevangelium*, II, p. 502; Marguerat, *Le Jugement*, p. 440; Beare, *Matthew*, p. 312; France, *Matthew*, p. 275 and Zumstein, *La Condition*, p. 382.

community. Two points speak in favour of their 'outsider' status. First, Matthew never speaks of expelling these troublemakers (cf. 18:17) which suggests that the leaders of his own church had little or no authority over them. The best he can do is direct his readers to have nothing at all to do with them. Secondly, Matthew implies that these figures have come into the Matthean community from outside. He informs his readers that they should beware of these false prophets 'who come to you in sheep's clothing' (7:15). This suggests that these people are Christian outsiders who come into the Matthean community and practise what the evangelist considers to be false prophecy and lawlessness.

What does Matthew mean by lawlessness? Many scholars have argued that the law-observant Matthew relates the term to the keeping of the Torah and that he was in conflict with certain antinomians who were active in his community.[61] For other scholars, however, ἀνομία has little or nothing to do with disobeying the commands of the Torah. Rather, as the other New Testament occurrences of the word show (cf. Rom 4:7; 6:19; 2 Cor. 6:14; 2 Thess. 2:3, 7–8; Tit. 2:14; 1 John 3:4), it applies more generally to wickedness or sinfulness which runs contrary to the will of God.[62] Of these two views the first and more narrow one is by far the more plausible. It was argued earlier that the Jewish sectarian outlook of Matthew places heavy emphasis upon the proper interpretation of the law and that Jesus' interpretation of it forms one of the boundaries which marks off the evangelist's *ekklesia* from the remainder of Judaism. Given the importance of the law (νόμος) for Matthew, one can hardly believe that he intended ἀνομία in any other way than as the opposite of Torah-fulfilment according to the definitive exegesis of Jesus.[63] Certainly we should not adopt the broader definition of the term merely on

---

[61] See Barth, 'Matthew's Understanding of the Law', pp. 73–5, 159–64 and Hummel, *Auseinandersetzung*, pp. 64–6. This position is generally followed by Zumstein, *La Condition*, pp. 171–200 (but see further note 63 below). Cf. the blunt comment of Segal, 'Matthew's Jewish Voice', p. 21, 'Matthew uses the word ἀνομία, lawlessness, to mean rejection of the law.'

[62] See Davies, *Sermon*, pp. 202–6; Davies and Allison, *Matthew*, I, pp. 718–19; Guelich, *Sermon*, pp. 402, 410; Stanton, 'Origin and Purpose', pp. 1909–10; France, *Matthew*, pp. 109–10 and Davison, 'Antinomian Polemic in Matthew', pp. 617–35.

[63] This point is not properly appreciated by those who fail to interpret ἀνομία in a legalistic sense. W. D. Davies, for instance, argues that while ἀνομία does not refer to the breaking of the Jewish law, it could apply to the breaking of the law which is God's will revealed in the words of Jesus in the sermon (*Sermon*, p. 205). Davies is followed by Zumstein, *La Condition*, pp. 172–3 and Marguerat, *Le*

the basis of its use in the remainder of the New Testament. It hardly needs saying that we must interpret words and themes on the basis of the gospel alone and not read them through the eyes of other early Christian writers. Matthew's special emphasis on the law distinguishes him in many ways from the remainder of the New Testament and we should expect his meaning of ἀνομία to do likewise. Just as Matthew perceives insiders to be marked by their observance of the law according to Jesus' interpretation of it, so too does ἀνομία characterise those outside the ekklesia who fail to live by this standard. Lawlessness can therefore denote those Jews who do not properly interpret the law. Thus in 23:23 the Matthean Jesus accuses the scribes and Pharisees of not keeping the law properly and this then leads to the charge of lawlessness (23:28). On the other hand, ἀνομία can be used to describe those who do not keep the law at all. This is its meaning in 7:23. There is no suggestion that these Christian false prophets improperly observe the law; rather, they seem not to follow the law in any respect.

In support of this is Matthew 5:17–19, which appears earlier in the sermon on the mount and which speaks of the validity of the law in the present age. The first verse begins with the solemn pronouncement of the Matthean Jesus that he has not come to abolish the law and the prophets. This must be seen as a response to the claim that he had indeed come to abolish them.[64] Since the scribes and Pharisees appear in the immediate context (5:20), it is tempting to see them behind this charge.[65] However, because this issue deals with the nature of Jesus' mission, it is more likely that Matthew is voicing a Christian claim here. While Matthew's Jewish opponents seemingly directly and openly attacked Jesus as a deceiver, they would hardly have passed comment on the significance of his ministry in the manner implied in 5:17. If the evangelist is opposing a Christian point of view in this verse, then the ones promoting it can only be those Christians from outside

---

Jugement, p. 200. But how is the law any less Jewish or any less legalistic after the Matthean Jesus has given it his definitive and distinctive interpretation?

[64] Contra Strecker, *Weg*, p. 137 n. 4 who argues that Matthew was not responding to a claim that Jesus had dispensed with the law but was merely addressing a theoretical possibility. This view, however, portrays the evangelist as an 'arm-chair theologian' quietly musing over potential theological matters and not really concerned with the concrete issues of his day.

[65] Thus Overman, *Matthew's Gospel*, pp. 88–9; Stanton, *Gospel for a New People*, p. 49; Davies and Allison, *Matthew*, I, pp. 483, 501 n. 54 and Beare, *Matthew*, pp. 138–9.

the evangelist's community whom Matthew later in the sermon calls 'workers of lawlessness'.[66] They fail to do the will of God (7:21) which includes, amongst other things, obeying the Torah as Jesus had interpreted it.

If lawlessness means failure to obey the law properly or failure to keep it at all, then what are we to make of the division within the general Christian church in 13:36–43? While most scholars view the inter-church division in this text in very general moral terms – the church is composed of both good and bad members – Matthew's conscious use of ἀνομία in this redactional text gives it a specific term of reference: *it is a division based primarily upon observance of the law*. Matthew spells out concretely in this text that all lawless Christians derive ultimately from Satan, while his own law-obser-vant version of Christianity derives from Jesus himself (cf. 16:18). On this interpretation the odd reference in the parable proper to the sleeping men who allow the devil to sow weeds amongst the wheat (13:25) must be applied to the leaders of the earliest church whom Matthew believed were completely oblivious to the Satan-induced nature of the law-free mission.

Matthew's division of Christianity into law-observant Christianity (including his ekklesia) and its law-free counterpart is further evidenced in the material which precedes and follows the tradition dealing with the antinomians. If we take 7:13–27 as a unit, then the following interpretation presents itself. In the redactional pericope of the two ways (7:13–14), the wide gate and the easy way which lead to destruction and through which many will enter can easily be applied to law-free Christianity. In numerical terms the law-free version of Christianity was by Matthew's time considerably larger than the law-observant form, and there is no doubt that the way of life which rejects the Torah is far easier than the way which obeys it. After he has spelt out the dangers of following the lawless false prophets in 7:15–23, the evangelist picks up the theme of the two ways in the parable of the two houses (7:24–7). The Lucan version of this Q material (6:47–9) contrasts two builders who construct houses but only one of whom provides proper foundations for the house by building on a rock. In Matthew the comparison is brought out more fully. Those who hear and do the words of Jesus will be like the wise man who built his house upon a rock, while those who do not heed them will be like the foolish man who built

[66]   So correctly Barth, 'Matthew's Understanding of the Law', pp. 67, 73.

his house upon the sand; as we might expect the wise will weather the storm and the foolish will not. For Matthew more so than for Luke the contrast is between those who build upon the rock and those who do not. This reference to the rock clearly relates to the ekklesia built upon Peter (the rock) in 16:18,[67] while the alternative way which leads to destruction (cf. 7:13) is doubtless the antinomian position which has just been attacked. In this manner the two major varieties of Christianity are compared and contrasted, as they are later in the gospel in 13:36–43.

These texts thus spell out very plainly Matthew's view of the wider Christian community. He strongly opposes the very principle of law-free Christianity and sets his own community (and perhaps other similar groups) against it. It is clear that just as Matthew constructed boundaries around his community in relation to the gentile world and the remainder of the Jewish world, so too does he construct boundaries around it with regard to the wider Christian world. Law-free Christians are considered outsiders in the same way as Matthew's Jewish opponents and gentiles are deemed to be outsiders and they are likewise to be avoided at all costs. It might be objected that the Christian Matthew could hardly have considered matters in this way. But on what grounds should we believe that the law-keeping Matthew felt any affinity with law-free Christianity? If we can accept that the Jewish Matthew could oppose the world of formative Judaism, then why could not the Christian Matthew have attacked certain sections of the wider Christian church? More to the point, if he could condemn the scribes and Pharisees for not following the law properly, then it is almost to be expected that he would have little sympathy with those who rejected entirely the validity of the law. This is a point which is too often overlooked.

Even more, however, can be said on this subject. Matthew's opposition to law-free Christianity was not merely a matter of principle; a further examination of this subject renders it very probable that at the time of the gospel's composition Matthew's law-observant brand of Christianity had much to fear from its law-free counterpart. At this point in the discussion, it must be readily conceded that we possess little in the way of concrete data for

---

[67] Contra Davies and Allison, *Matthew*, I, p. 721 who see no reference at all to the rock in 16:18. On the other hand, a number of other scholars do note a connection, though they make little attempt to analyse its significance. See, for example, Guelich, *Sermon*, p. 404 and Gundry, *Matthew*, p. 134.

reconstructing the relationship between the different streams which comprised the Christian church in the time of Matthew. But we can put forward quite reasonable and historically probable hypotheses on the basis of the evidence we do possess. For instance, it is reasonable enough to suppose that a law-observant Christian Jewish group in or around the year 80 would have felt seriously threatened by the law-free stream of early Christianity. The following points make this supposition a reasonable one.

To begin with and as noted above, the predominantly gentile, law-free wing of the church was numerically superior to the predominantly Jewish and law-observant stream. We can fully appreciate Matthew understanding his community to be an island of law-keeping righteousness in a sea of gentile lawlessness, especially when we recall the evangelist's attitude toward gentiles as a whole. More important, however, is the fact that the status and protection which law-observant Christians enjoyed while the Jerusalem church was in the ascendant disappeared in the wake of the Jewish war. Prior to the events of 66–70, the law-abiding Jerusalem church, which was headed until 62 by James the brother of Jesus, attempted to exercise some control over the diaspora churches and the gentile mission, and Galatians 2:11–14 is one example of its success. It is true to say that while the Jerusalem church existed the law-observant party within the church always posed a threat to law-free Christianity. All this changed, however, in the aftermath of the Jewish war which witnessed not just the destruction of Jerusalem but the effective disappearance of the Jerusalem church. In this sense the Jewish war against the Romans must have been just as much a disaster for law-observant Christian Jews as it was for non-Christian Jews. In one fell swoop the group which protected the interests of law-keeping Christianity was gone and communities such as Matthew's must have felt particularly vulnerable as a result. One almost certain consequence of these events was that the mission without the law progressed unimpeded. While this mission presumably concentrated on finding new gentile converts, it would doubtless have encountered certain pockets of law-observant Christianity. In these situations the previous trend would have been completely reversed and law-abiding Christians would have found themselves under threat from the law-free party. This resurgence of the law-free mission after 70 and its threat to those Christians who upheld the law is seemingly reflected in Matthew's conflict with those antinomian missionaries to whom he refers in the sermon on the mount. That this mission was meeting with some success is perhaps indicated by 24:11–12. In this redactional section of the apocalyptic discourse, Matthew affirms that towards the very end of the age, the present time from his perspective, the (lawless) false prophets will lead many astray and lawlessness will increase as a result.

Whether these missionaries belonged to a resurgent Paulinism or to another stream of law-free Christianity is difficult to say. It has been argued that Matthew intended to discredit Paul and his gospel in a number of texts (5:18; 13:25) and that he promoted Peter as the apostle *par excellence* to counter the influence of Paul.[68] But as W. D. Davies has shown, none of the evidence for this view is particularly convincing.[69] These missionaries might have been Paulinists, but since law-free Christianity was not exclusively Pauline it is quite possible that they belonged to another strand.[70] It does not really matter in the present context. The important point is that Matthew disapproved fiercely of law-free Christianity in any form, and perceived it to be a considerable threat to his own community. The above reconstruction of the probable relationship between law-free Christianity and its law-keeping alternative shows that Matthew's point of view is both historically credible and entirely understandable.

If the above reconstruction of Matthew's community and the broader Christian movement is correct, then we find that the alienation of the former was complete. Not only was it alienated from the Jewish and gentile worlds, but this law-observant church which had recently lost its power base in Jerusalem was completely alienated from the wider Christian world which preached a law-free gospel and was composed mainly of gentiles. There is good evidence in the gospel that some missionaries from this stream of

---

[68] See Brandon, *Fall of Jerusalem*, pp. 232–6 and, more recently, Segal, 'Matthew's Jewish Voice', pp. 21–2. H. D. Betz has argued that the sermon on the mount is a pre-Matthean unity composed by a Jewish Christian group which was directly opposing Paul. See his *Essays on the Sermon on the Mount*, pp. 20–2. For a critique of this hypothesis, see Stanton, *Gospel for a New People*, pp. 309–18.

[69] Davies, *Sermon*, pp. 334–40. See too Barth, 'Matthew's Understanding of the Law', pp. 159–64 who does not see the antinomians as representatives of Paul, but as hellenistic libertines.

[70] On the problems of using biased, polemical texts to identify the opponents under attack, see Barclay, 'Mirror-Reading a Polemical Letter', pp. 73–93. Although Barclay focuses on Paul's letter to the Galatians, his comments are applicable to Matthew as well. We can be sure that Matthew is opposing what he considers to be law-free Christians, but we can say almost nothing more about them.

Christianity had arrived in Matthew's community and so posed a real threat to it.

4. Alienation from the world at large

The Matthean community's conflicts with the wider Jewish and Christian worlds, as well as its negative view of the gentile world, meant ultimately that it had no support system other than itself. Its members were thus forced by necessity to withdraw from the world at large and take refuge in the ekklesia alone. This in turn led inevitably to an intense feeling of isolation and alienation, and the whole world outside the community became a place to be feared and avoided. There are a number of pointers which reveal the intensity of the alienation experienced by the community in terms of its relation to the larger world. One of these is Matthew 18:7a which states, 'Woe to the world for temptations to sin.' This unparalleled tradition stands in the middle of a Q section which deals with temptations and the one who brings them (Matt. 18:6–8//Luke 17:1–2) and its origin is uncertain. Since the object or recipient of the woe form in Matthew is always depicted negatively – indeed that is the very purpose of this form of speech – then we must interpret the reference to the world here in negative terms. The world at large receives a woe because it contributes to or is responsible for an upsurge in temptations to sin.[71] This clearly points to the Matthean community's alienation from the wider world.[72] Another indication of this viewpoint is provided by 5:13–16. Here the evangelist first describes his community in sectarian terms as the salt of the earth and the light of the world which shines before men.[73] In the second description, the community is depicted as a shining beacon of righteousness by contrast with those who live outside it in the larger world.

That Matthew considered that his community members should place no reliance on institutions or individuals outside the ekklesia

[71] See Thompson, *Matthew's Advice*, pp. 109–10; Stanton, 'Matthew and Judaism', p. 277. This interpretation necessitates taking ἀπό in a causal sense. On this point, see Thompson, *Matthew's Advice*, p. 109 n. 38 and literature cited there. Some scholars take the reference to the world in Matthew 18:7 in a positive sense and argue that Matthew here is expressing sympathy for the world. For example, Schweizer, *Matthew*, p. 364 renders this sentence as 'How terrible for the world (on account of the coming temptations)', but this ignores the force of the woe form.

[72] So correctly Stanton, 'Matthew and Judaism', p. 277.

[73] So too Stanton, 'Matthew and Judaism', pp. 277–8.

is evident from his omission of the Marcan account of the strange exorcist (Mark 9:38–40). This Marcan passage describes the disciples telling Jesus how they rebuked an exorcist who was casting out demons in Jesus' name. Jesus instructs them that they should not have done this on the grounds that 'he that is not against us is for us'. Matthew omits this pericope in view of his belief that those outside the community cannot share its goals and aspirations. His own attitude is reflected in the Q logion in 12:30 (//Luke 11:23) which makes the opposite point to the Marcan saying, 'He who is not with me is against me, and he who does not gather with me scatters.' By his adoption of the Q tradition and his omission of the Marcan passage, Matthew clearly promotes the view that only those within the ekklesia stand with Jesus, while all those outside necessarily stand against him.[74] We may infer from all these texts that the alienated Matthean community could view all the different components of the outside world as a single entity. Its outlook was that ultimately the world is divided into two groups, the ekklesia and the remainder of the world.

5. Conclusions

The results of this chapter provide a very bleak picture of the social setting of the Matthean community once it is placed in its proper historical and geographical context. That context is the region of Syria in the years following the Jewish war. This period saw the rise of pharisaic-led formative Judaism which contributed to a large degree to the break between Matthew's church and the larger Jewish world. The relations between the two groups were dominated by bitterness and hostility as the Matthean ekklesia attempted to legitimate its sectarian existence and the parent body subjected it to some degree of persecution in response. The Jewish war had also witnessed an extensive persecution of the Jews by the gentiles, and it is clear that Matthew's community was caught up in these terrible events. This means that while this group was in conflict with the Jewish parent body, it had a very uneasy relationship with its gentile neighbours. The gospel advocates a policy of avoiding the gentile world which indicates the depth of fear occasioned by the recent pogroms. The events of 66–70 contributed to the social setting of the Matthean ekklesia in one further and

---

[74] Cf. Overman, *Matthew's Gospel*, pp. 110–11.

important way. With the destruction of Jerusalem came the destruction of the Jerusalem church and the loss of law-observant Christianity's power base. Those communities which still observed the law had lost both power and prestige and were now easy prey to those of the law-free wing who took the opportunity to turn the tables on the earlier situation when they themselves were under threat. There is good evidence in the gospel that such law-free missionaries had entered the evangelist's community and had even enjoyed some moderate success.

The social setting of this Antiochene Christian Jewish group is thus one of extreme crisis occasioned by the effects of the Jewish war. As a law-observant Christian community, it now had little in common with the world of formative Judaism, even less in common with the remainder of the Christian world and nothing at all in common with the wider gentile society. The Jewish war had to all intents and purposes decimated all its external support systems. It could not now turn to the greater Christian church for help in its conflict with the synagogue, nor could it expect any assistance from any Jewish sources in its conflict with the law-free party within Christianity. Similarly, it could expect to find no allies in either the Jewish or the Christian world in its tense relationship with its gentile neighbours. The Matthean community was essentially cut off and deeply alienated from all external institutions, be they Jewish, Christian or those of the gentile authorities, and consequently approached them all with a mixture of fear, bitterness and hostility. We can well understand why Matthew composed 24:9–12, which deals with universal hatred of the elect and the problems of lawlessness, to provide his readers with the clue that they were living in the final period of the era. Moreover, the outlook of the evangelist was particularly bleak. Having been persecuted by the gentiles and presently experiencing persecution at the hands of the Jewish parent group, Matthew expected such ill-treatment from both parties in the future. Under these circumstances the only place of refuge was within the community itself and this can be seen in the process of drawing rigid boundaries around the group and withdrawal from the wider world.

It is clear that the complex social setting of the Matthean community as reconstructed here is more than sufficient to explain its embracement of apocalypticism and its recourse to apocalyptic eschatology. This community conforms to the general pattern of groups which adopt and promote this religious perspective. It was a small minority or sectarian group experiencing considerable hardship at the hands of outsider groups and was as a result completely alienated from the wider world. In the next chapter, we shall consider how Matthew's particular scheme serves to respond to the crises facing his community.

9

THE FUNCTION OF APOCALYPTIC ESCHATOLOGY IN THE GOSPEL OF MATTHEW

As noted in chapter 2, the function of apocalyptic eschatology in a given document is directly related to the social setting which underlies it, and is used to respond to it. The gospel of Matthew is no exception to this rule. Thus the purpose of the gospel material reflecting this particular perspective is to confront and combat the situation(s) of crisis which the evangelist's community faced. Like other representatives of apocalypticism, Matthew uses apocalyptic eschatology in order to construct a 'symbolic universe' which conflicts with those of the wider societies from which his community is alienated. While he doubtless rejects out of hand the gentile world view, Matthew also dismisses the respective world views of the Jewish parent body and the law-free and dominant wing of Christianity, and replaces them with one which reinforces and legitimates the beliefs and hopes of his own group. Just as the apocalyptic authors used great figures of the past to present and lend authority to their own views of reality, so too does Matthew. By adopting the gospel genre from Mark, Matthew uses no less a figure than Jesus the messiah, son of God and Son of Man to convey and authorise this new symbolic universe. In doing so, Matthew gives his alternative vision of reality an authority and legitimacy which it might not have carried had he not expressed it on the lips of Jesus. The author of Revelation does precisely the same thing, although he appeals to the words of the present, risen Jesus rather than to his teaching prior to his death and resurrection. Since Matthew's apocalyptic eschatology is closely associated with contemporary Jewish (and Christian) apocalyptic-eschatological schemes, it is almost to be expected that his scheme would serve the same general functions as theirs. This is precisely the case. The five general functions of this distinctive religious perspective which were identified in chapter 2 all play a part in Matthew's particular scheme. We shall examine each of these in turn.

1. Identification and legitimation

An important function of the evangelist's apocalyptic eschatology is that it both identifies and legitimates the sectarian nature of the Matthean community. Like other proponents of apocalypticism, Matthew adopts a markedly dualistic perspective which divides humanity into the good and the wicked along the lines of his perception of the world. To this end he accepts the concept of the two ways and constantly juxtaposes and contrasts the two groups using a variety of antithetical terms which describes the nature of each and immediately draws boundaries around them. Needless to say, according to Matthew's perception of the world his community assumes the mantle of the righteous or the good, while the ones opposed to it are identified as the wicked. This is not, however, simply a moral division within humanity. As argued in chapter 3, the evangelist incorporates this human division into a cosmic struggle between the supernatural forces of good and evil. In this scheme all humans pledge allegiance either to the side of Jesus (and God) or to the side of Satan, the evil one (ὁ πονηρός), and there is no middle ground in this conflict. Matthew's acceptance of this world view clearly betrays his developed sense of alienation from the larger world which was established in the previous chapter. As with the Qumran community and the author of Revelation, who propose similar perceptions of the cosmic order, this extreme sense of alienation leads Matthew to the view that his community is playing an important part in a much larger drama. The hostile nature of the wider society can only be explained by postulating an underlying demonic influence.

The evangelist does not merely present this aspect of his symbolic universe as an abstract notion; he relates it in concrete terms to the particular social setting of his community. He takes pains to identify his righteous community, the ekklesia, with the side of the heavenly forces. It was founded by Jesus himself (13:37–8a; 16:18) and it continues the battle against Satan which Jesus himself had initiated (10:7; 16:18; 24:15–28). Moreover, its peculiar beliefs and practices, which can all be traced back to Jesus and which serve further to draw the boundaries around the group, are in turn legitimated. The identification of the ekklesia as the group which remains true to God and Jesus and performs their will thus legitimates its minority status as well as its own sectarian practices and beliefs.

On the other hand, Matthew identifies all those outside the

community as being in league with Satan. He emphasises that the two major threats to his community, law-free Christianity and formative Judaism, both work for the forces of evil against the will of God. He specifies that the former owes its origin to the devil and he solidifies the relationship by describing its proponents as sons of the evil one (13:38b-9a). In both 13:49 and 22:10 he again refers to this group of Christians as evil (πονηρός) and he similarly identifies the lawless false prophets who have infiltrated his community and pose a direct threat to it (7:17–18). Likewise, the leaders of formative Judaism, the scribes and Pharisees, are themselves described as evil (πονηρός/πονηρία; 9:4; 12:34–5; 22:18) and so placed in the camp of the evil one. Hence, in one fell swoop, the respective viewpoints of the two major opposition groups are completely discredited. Their identification as allies of Satan serves in turn to illegitimate their respective beliefs and practices. There are no direct statements in Matthew concerning the evil nature of the gentile world and its association with Satan, except perhaps for 24:28 which might refer to the coalition of the antichrist and the Romans at the end of the age, but this was doubtless an assumption by Jewish author and reader alike. Matthew reinforces his dualistic perspective by adopting the myth of the final eschatological conflict between good and evil. Here, as also in Revelation and the War scroll from Qumran, the final events in history witness the polarisation of the two sides into their respective camps. Jesus will return as the military Son of Man leading the heavenly armies in order to come to the aid of the embattled righteous.

The marked dualistic aspect of Matthew's apocalyptic eschatology therefore serves a number of important functions for Matthew's beleaguered minority community. It identifies the true natures of the ekklesia and the remainder of the world by relating the stance of each in the cosmic conflict, and it serves to reinforce the validity of the former and the illegitimacy of the latter. The readers of the gospel can feel secure in the knowledge that they remain true to the will of God in a world which has generally deserted him. Their alienation from the world is thus interpreted in a positive rather than a negative light.

2. Explanation of current circumstances

In addition to identifying and legitimating the existence of the ekklesia, Matthew's apocalyptic-eschatological scheme enables his readers to accept more readily the present dire circumstances which threaten them. His particular world view possesses great explanatory power in this regard. At one level the critical situation of the group becomes easier to justify when it is depicted in terms of the cosmic conflict. Since the Matthean community is in conflict not merely with human groups but with powerful demonic forces, its plight becomes more comprehensible if not more bearable. An even more important element in this respect, however, is the concept of historical determinism. The current situation has not happened merely by historical chance in the aftermath of the Jewish war, nor is it a sign that God has deserted his elect and left them to the mercy of Satan and his allies. On the contrary, the present plight of the ekklesia is an essential part of God's predetermined historical and eschatological plan. Once again Matthew does not relate this notion in an abstract way; he applies it to the concrete situation of his readers throughout the gospel, but particularly in his revision of the Marcan apocalyptic discourse. The rejection of the gospel by the majority of Jews and the resultant conflict it brings, the murder of certain community members in the gentile persecutions of the Jews, the arrival of lawless false prophets in the Matthean ekklesia and the general upsurge in lawlessness toward the end of the age, were all prophesied by Jesus himself and thus had to occur in the manner predicted. The righteous enclave of the ekklesia must bear its share of suffering, both now and in the future, as the eschatological woes work their way to their determined conclusion. This explanation of current events (and any future suffering) serves in turn to offer comfort to members in their time of distress. The current situation is occurring within God's divine plan and with his consent; despite appearances that God has deserted the ekklesia, the harsh reality of its situation of crisis is not contrary to the divine will but is in perfect accord with it.

3. Encouragement and hope for the future[1]

As noted in chapter 2, there is more to the concept of determinism than just offering a valid explanation of current events and the comfort which such knowledge affords. Perhaps of more importance is its purpose in offering hope for the future. The corollary of

---

[1]   That Matthew's apocalyptic eschatology serves to encourage his readers and give them hope for the future is noted by Hagner, 'Apocalyptic Motifs', p. 75; Stanton, 'Matthew and Judaism', p. 280 and Cope, 'Role of Apocalyptic', p. 118.

the belief that the past was determined and fulfilled prophecy to the letter and that the present is similarly unfolding as predicted is that the future too will come to pass according to the prophecies of an authoritative figure. Like the historical review of the apocalyptic genre, Matthew uses the fulfilment of past prophecies, both of the Old Testament prophets and of Jesus himself, to give conviction to his own future expectations. These expectations are presented in turn as predictions by the Matthean Jesus. Of utmost importance in this regard is the promise that Jesus will return as judgemental Son of Man. As noted in Part II, Matthew emphasises time and again not only that Jesus will return at the end of the age, but that he will return for the sole purpose of judgement. His return will see the vindication of the righteous who have followed him faithfully and the punishment of the wicked who have opposed him. Predictions of this sort serve in no small way to raise the spirits of those who are now oppressed and alienated. For their continuing allegiance to the one who brings the judgement and for their steadfastness in a threatening world, they will receive rewards beyond measure. They will be given treasures in heaven and eternal life in the new creation where evil no longer threatens them, and they will be transformed into angels (22:30; cf. 13:43, 17:2 and 28:3). In view of their assured future state, they are able to receive eschatological blessings now (5:3–12).

The notion of the imminence of these end events clearly plays an important role in providing concrete hope for the future. Not only can Matthew's readers live in certainty that the present circumstances will be reversed and that they will receive wonderful eschatological rewards, they can likewise be assured that this will take place in the imminent future. Although he occasionally states that the parousia will come soon (16:28; 24:34), the evangelist spells this out for his readers by constructing his own timetable of the end and placing his own time toward the end of it (24:4–14; cf. 10:23). Like all apocalyptic-eschatological writers with the exception of the authors of Daniel and Revelation, Matthew is careful not to nominate a precise day for the parousia (24:36). While such a practice of naming a day would be fruitful in the short term since it would raise group expectations, it might prove to be a disastrous policy in the long term if the end did not arrive on the specified day. Since the aim of the imminent end expectation is to raise the hopes of his readers and not to dishearten them, Matthew strongly affirms the nearness of the end but just as strongly denies that the precise day is known. In view of this, the evangelist exhorts his readers to watch continually. They must remain in a state of preparedness for the return of the Son of Man (24:37–25:13) and put their trust in the prophecies that it will occur in the imminent future.

In conjunction with this hope for the future are those exhortations to remain steadfast in the short but desperate time which remains. Matthew reminds his readers that with the climax of the end-time woes only those in the ekklesia who endure to the end will be saved (10:22b; 24:13) and he encourages such steadfastness by affirming that the days of tribulation have been shortened on their account (24:22). These texts perform a consolatory function by spelling out that the necessary suffering of the last times will be shortlived and well worth the hardship it brings. Those who remain steadfast will be relieved of their suffering by the arrival of the Son of Man in the imminent future. It is not surprising that the mission discourse contains further hortatory material, since Matthew envisaged great hardship and persecution to be the lot of those who embark upon this final mission to the Jews of Palestine. These figures will encounter both human opponents and the supernatural forces of the antichrist (cf. 16:18; 24:15). Matthew affirms that the missionaries will be aided by the holy spirit in times of trouble (10:19–20) and exhorts them to fearless confession (10:26–33). They should not fear their enemies (verses 26, 28), since they are of enormous importance to God (verse 31), and those amongst them who lose their lives will be awarded eternal life (verse 39).

4. Vengeance and consolation

Like most apocalyptic-eschatological schemes, Matthew's version does not merely treat the eschatological fate of the righteous; he also deals with the ultimate fate of the wicked. The evangelist depicts the fate of this group in the harshest of terms. One important function of this motif is to satisfy the desire for vengeance on the part of himself and his readers.[2] Just as they are given hope in the light of their vindicated status after the judgement, so too can they be satisfied and consoled that those who contribute to their present suffering will be punished without mercy in the imminent future. They will be excluded from the eschatolo-

---

[2] This element is noted, if somewhat understated, by Cope, 'Role of Apocalyptic', p. 118.

gical kingdom and consigned to the gloom and flames of Gehenna where they will burn forever. The vengeful nature of this theme can be clearly seen from Matthew's constant descriptions of the horror of the plight of the wicked; they will weep in misery and gnash their teeth in rage. By presenting this material, the evangelist oversteps a mark which is crossed by few other apocalyptic-eschatological schemes. His constant use of this unpleasant theme signals the depth of his community's pain and suffering and its understandable desire to punish those responsible. Once more the evangelist does not present this theme of the fate of the wicked in general terms; he applies it to the actual situation of his readers by specifying that all groups of opponents will meet the same fiery fate.

Matthew devotes considerable space to the end-time fate of his Jewish opponents, particularly the scribes and Pharisees. These figures can now receive eschatological woes in view of the terrible punishments they will face (ch. 23). They will be called to judgement on account of their blasphemy against the holy spirit, a crime for which there is no forgiveness (12:31–7), and they will be condemned in the judgement by the queen of the south and the Ninevites (12:41–2). Their fiery fate is indicated by the fact that they are 'sons of Gehenna' (23:15) who will not escape the judgement of Gehenna (23:33). The judgemental proclamation of John the Baptist (3:7–12) is also addressed to Matthew's Jewish enemies and speaks of their final destination in terms of the fiery furnace. The Baptist asks the Pharisees and Sadducees who warned them of the coming wrath (verse 7) and then goes on to explain the nature of this imminent catastrophe. The axe is laid to the root of the trees and every tree which does not produce good fruit is cut down and thrown into the fire (verse 9). The judge has a winnowing fork in hand to clear his threshing floor, and he will burn the chaff with unquenchable fire (verses 11–12). All these texts make the point that the Jewish leaders with whom Matthew's group is in dispute will ultimately receive their just punishments. As sons of Gehenna, they will spend eternity there amongst the unquenchable flames.

Although Matthew focuses primarily on the fate of the Jewish leaders with whom he is in dispute, he does condemn to eternal punishment a wider group of Jews. We need to remember that for Matthew the new age will see the judgement of the whole twelve tribes of Israel (19:28). The Galilean towns which rejected Jesus will suffer on the day of judgement (11:20–4), as will those which fail to heed the message of the missionaries (10:15). Such punishment of an unspecified number of Jews also appears to be the point of the Q material which he inserted into the centurion of Capernaum pericope. After Jesus tells the centurion that he has not found such faith in Israel (verse 10), he then relates in verses 11–12 that many will come from the east and west and sit in the kingdom, while the sons of the kingdom will be cast to the outer darkness where they will weep and gnash their teeth. Many exegetes interpret 'the many' as faithful gentiles like the centurion who will share in the kingdom, whereas the 'sons of the kingdom' is taken as the Jewish nation as a whole which will be rejected at the eschaton.[3] But even though this material is found immediately after Jesus' praise of a gentile, neither part of this interpretation is as soundly based as is usually claimed. The first part does not square with Matthew's anti-gentile sentiments which he clearly expresses elsewhere, and the second part ignores the primarily Jewish constituency of Matthew's community as well as its continuing mission to the Jews. In other words, neither wholesale praise of the gentile world nor complete condemnation of the Jewish world seems to fit the evangelist's point of view.

A more probable reading of the text in the light of Matthew's sectarian outlook is that he wishes to make the point that gentiles are included among the righteous, while many or most Jews are excluded. For Matthew, mere Jewishness was no longer sufficient for salvation (cf. 3:9). The determining factor now was membership in the ekklesia and this was open to both Jew and gentile provided they obeyed its rules and observance of the Torah. Matthew 8:11–12 thus appears to expand the number of Jews who will meet with punishment far beyond his direct scribal and pharisaic opponents. His sectarian and dualistic viewpoint leads him ultimately to condemn all those of Jewish descent, be they direct opponents or not, who stand outside his ekklesia or who do not respond to its missionary message. Since there is no middle ground on Matthew's terms, all Jews outside the ekklesia will receive the same terrible punishment at the judgement.

Just as Matthew speaks of the horrible fate of his Jewish opponents, so too does he promote a similar fate for his Christian enemies. He states in 7:15–23 that the law-free missionaries who have come into his community will be denied and excluded from

---

[3] So Marguerat, *Le Jugement*, pp. 243–57; Zumstein, *La Condition*, pp. 362–71; Schweizer, *Matthew*, p. 213 and Gundry, *Matthew*, pp. 144–5.

the kingdom by Jesus the Son of Man (verses 22–3) and that their ultimate fate will be punishment by fire (verse 19; cf. 3:10). Moreover, just as the evangelist seemingly condemns all Jews outside his ekklesia and not merely direct opponents, so too does he see fit to consign to eschatological punishment all Christians of the law-free wing. This is the point of the interpretation of the parable of the tares in 13:36–43. Here Matthew expresses his view that this type of Christianity which refuses to follow the Torah in the manner specified by Jesus has its origin in Satan and that all its representatives, immediate opponents or otherwise, will be punished by eternal fire. The shorter parable of the net and its interpretation in 13:47–50 make much the same point, though lacking the detail of the earlier tradition. The parable of the wedding garment in 22:11–13 has a similar purpose. The wicked in the church, those outside Matthew's community, will be excluded from the kingdom and cast into the outer darkness.

It has not been lost on commentators that Matthew depicts the fate of the wicked in the (general) Christian church in the same terms as he describes the fate of wicked Jews.[4] In the redactional 7:19 the Matthean Jesus repeats the words of the Baptist in 3:10 (from Q) that those trees which do not bear good fruit will be thrown into the fire. Since the former is addressed to Christian opponents while the latter applies to Jewish enemies, these pericopae link together absolutely the fate of these two groups of Matthean opponents. The same can be said of the similarity in wording between 8:12 and 22:13. Each of these refers to expulsion to the outer darkness and the weeping and gnashing of teeth, but one adverts to Jews (8:12) and the other to Christians (22:13).[5] The editorial Matthew 13:36–43, which relates to law-free Christians, has ties with the 'anti-Jewish' traditions of both 3:7–12 and 8:11–12. On the one hand, it is linked to the former in the sense that it employs harvest symbolism to represent the final judgement, although the metaphors are not precisely the same. While the Baptist material contrasts wheat and chaff, the Matthean Jesus refers to good seed and weeds. None the less, both texts agree that the unacceptable part of the harvest will be burned. The words of

[4]   See Marguerat, *Le Jugement*, pp. 400–1.
[5]   This link is stronger than is normally supposed. I have argued elsewhere that the man without the wedding garment in 22:11–13 is a composite figure, referring both to the wicked in the church (cf. 22:10) and to the Jewish leaders of the broader context. See Sim, 'Man without the Wedding Garment', pp. 165–78.

the Matthean Jesus speak explicitly of the fiery furnace (verse 42), and the same imagery is implied if not stated in the Baptist tradition. On the other hand, Matthew 13:36–43 recalls 8:12 by referring to the weeping and gnashing of teeth as the response of the wicked to their punishment. The parable of the net is also closely related to these two 'anti-Jewish' texts. Although it lacks the harvest metaphor, it does refer to the furnace of fire (cf. 3:12) and to the weeping and gnashing of teeth (cf. 8:12).

It is clear from the above that Matthew deliberately describes the eschatological fate of his two major groups of opponents in similar terms. What applies to one applies just as much to the other. We may infer from this that Matthew's sectarian perspective does not distinguish between them in any meaningful sense. Though formative Judaism and law-free Christianity might be worlds apart in terms of belief and practice, each of them stands on the side of Satan and each poses a substantial threat to Matthew and his community. For this reason both groups are earmarked for the same terrible punishment at the hands of the Son of Man. The evangelist's emphasis on this point has a number of purposes, but one of these is to comfort his community that these opponents who are responsible for its current misery will meet with just retribution at the final judgement.

Unlike the predictions of the final fate of the Jews and Christians outside the ekklesia, there is no Matthean pericope which is specifically related to the fate of those in the wider gentile world. There are two possible explanations for this lack of detailed material, neither of which excludes the other. The first is that it was probably understood by author and reader alike that the 'pagan' world would be severely judged and punished at the eschaton and no definitive statement was necessary. Secondly, and as noted in the previous chapter, at the time of the gospel's composition the Matthean community was in direct dispute primarily with other groups of Jews and Christians and not with the gentile world. The gentiles had persecuted Matthew's group in the past and were expected to persecute it in the future, but since his community had minimal contact with the gentile world when the gospel was written the threat it posed at that time was not as immediate as that posed by the scribes and Pharisees and the law-free stream of Christianity. This might explain why less attention is given to the judgement of the gentile world. But Matthew by no means ignores the eschatological fate of the gentiles. He addresses this subject in his colourful description of the final judgement in 25:31–46. This tradition emphasises the completely universal nature of the judgement of the Son of Man by specifying that all the nations will stand before his throne of glory awaiting the final separation (verse 32). The gentiles along with everyone else obviously take part in this event. According to verse 41 the fate of all the wicked, gentiles included, is that they will be cast into the eternal fire which has been prepared for the devil and his angels. Thus in this last pericope of the final discourse in the gospel, Matthew carefully works out the eschatological climax to his concept of dualism. All those humans who are aligned with Satan in the cosmic conflict, be they Jew, Christian or gentile, will be identified concretely with him and sent to the same place of punishment. It is here that all the different groups which the evangelist perceives as enemies are blended into a single entity.

The tradition of the final separation is important in another respect as well. Of specific interest are the criteria which it proposes for the universal judgement, since these directly relate to the overall function of the passage. Matthew states that salvation or punishment is inextricably tied up with the treatment of 'the least of my (the Son of Man's) brothers' (verse 40; cf. verse 45). That the treatment of these individuals is tantamount to treatment of the Son of Man himself shows the close relationship between them. It is common to take this description in a universal sense, according to which the least of my brethren refers to the poor and needy of the whole world. On this view, the Matthean Jesus identifies with all the deprived persons of the world and will judge people, including those in the church, on the basis of their treatment of them. The evangelist is therefore spelling out what is required of true Christians and issuing a warning on the penalty for not performing this duty.[6] This interpretation of the phrase, though widespread, must be deemed rather improbable in the light of Matthew's sectarian outlook. It presumes that the Matthean community is 'world-open' when in fact it was closing itself off from the outside world. As noted in the previous chapter, for Matthew the wider world is a place to be feared and avoided, and it is difficult to accept that he would have given much thought to the needy outside his community. Moreover, it is inherently unlikely that Matthew's concept of dualism would have tolerated the explicit identification of Jesus

---

[6]   So Marguerat, *Le Jugement*, pp. 508–11; Zumstein, *La Condition*, pp. 339–40; Gnilka, *Matthäusevangelium*, II, p. 375; Bornkamm, 'End-Expectation', pp. 23–4; Schweizer, *Matthew*, pp. 477–80 and Beare, *Matthew*, p. 495.

with anyone outside his group. A further and perhaps over-whelming problem for this view is that the use of 'brother' points to a community setting rather than a general or universal context (cf. 5:22–4, 47; 7:3–5; 12:49–50; 18:15, 21, 35; 23:8; 28:10).

For this reason, many other exegetes argue that 'the least of my brothers' must be given a Christian application. While some of these argue that Matthew has in mind all Christians,[7] this too is unlikely in the light of his view that many, perhaps most, Christians will be found wanting on the day of judgement. We are left then with only two alternatives for the meaning of this phrase in the context of the gospel. Either it refers to the Matthean ekklesia as a whole, or it applies to a particular group within that community. The first of these alternatives certainly fits the sectarian viewpoint of Matthew; the world will be judged on the basis of its treatment of the righteous community. But against this interpretation is the fact that the list of requirements which need to be met – food and drink, a warm welcome, clothing and visits when sick or in prison – seems not to be applicable to a domiciled group. Rather, such requirements are more appropriate to a missionary context (cf. 10:8–9, 40–2). In the light of this, some exegetes identify 'the least of my brethren' to whom these kindnesses must be extended as the missionaries of the Matthean community.[8] Those who have pro-vided these comforts will receive eternal life (cf. 10:42), while the fire of Gehenna awaits those who have not.

What is the purpose of this pericope? As noted above, it was not intended to exhort Matthew's readers to help the needy of the wider world. Nor was it intended to exhort those outside the community to treat the Matthean ekklesia (or its missionaries) well, since the gospel was written exclusively for insiders and not for distribution outside the borders of the community. The function of this pericope is rather determined by the manner in which it would have been read by the leading characters in the narrative, the missionaries themselves. From all accounts the law-observant mission of the Matthean community had not been a great success. By comparison with the law-free mission, it had probably experienced only partial success amongst the gentiles, while its mission to

---

[7] See Friedrich, *Gott im Bruder?*, pp. 238–9, 248–9, 253–4 and Gray, *Least of My Brothers*, pp. 357–8, though Gray does admit the possibility that the term might refer to a restricted group of Christians.

[8] For full defence of this interpretation, see Lambrecht, 'Parousia Discourse', pp. 335–9 and literature cited there. Cf. also Cope, 'Sheep and Goats', pp. 39–41 and Stanton, 'Matthew and Judaism', pp. 279–80.

the Jews was marked by a high failure rate. As we know from chapter 10 of the gospel, the forthcoming (or current) mission to the Jews of Palestine was expected to be more of a disaster than a success. The missionaries would meet with rejection, persecution and death at the hands of both Jews and gentiles. Once we approach 25:31–46 in this light, then it becomes clear that the real focus of the passage falls less on those few (if any) who treat the messengers well and are rewarded with salvation, and more on the majority who mistreat them and receive eternal punishment for their trouble. Consequently, the purpose of this pericope is not to encourage the missionaries in the expectation that they can expect kindness in their enterprise. On the contrary, its function is to meet the missionaries' need for vengeance and consolation. They can be satisfied and consoled that the many who have rejected and mistreated them in the past and who will do so in the future will receive their just punishment at the hands of the Son of Man.[9]

It is no coincidence that Matthew selects the material in 25:31–46 to conclude the final major discourse of the Matthean Jesus. Not only does he use this pericope to spell out the universal nature of the final judgement, but he singles out how the missionary component of his community stands in relation to it. This is perhaps to be expected in the light of the emphasis the evangelist places on the last mission to Israel and his pessimistic predictions of the mistreatment the messengers will receive. Unlike chapter 10, which is concerned primarily with words of comfort and exhortation, the tradition of the great separation functions primarily to satisfy the missionaries' desire for vengeance on their particular opponents. This in turn performs a consolatory function which is necessary for the successful completion of the task. They can undertake their mission firm in the knowledge that those who oppose them are earmarked for the eternal fires of Gehenna.

In this section we have noted one of the evangelist's important uses of apocalyptic eschatology, particularly the abundant material relating to the horrific punishments awaiting the wicked. Matthew emphasises this particular element and uses it to satisfy his apocalyptic community's psychological need for vengeance on those who are responsible for their suffering. All those outside the

---

[9]   A similar exegesis is given by Stanton, *Gospel for a New People*, pp. 221–30, who interprets this pericope in terms of its apocalyptic-eschatological function. Like many commentators, however, Stanton stops short of identifying its function in terms of the need to satisfy a desire for vengeance.

ekklesia who contribute to their current dire circumstances – Jew, Christian and gentile – will be considered as a unity and consigned to the everlasting torment of Gehenna. The importance of this theme is even more marked in view of the particular ethic of the Matthean community. Owing to the high ethical demands of Jesus' interpretation of the Torah, the ekklesia was prohibited from taking its own revenge upon its enemies, even if it were in a position to do so. Jesus had commanded that his followers love their enemies and even pray for them (5:44) and that they should not retaliate when they were wronged (5:38–42). They were expected to be as perfect as their heavenly father (5:48) and live according to the golden rule (7:12) and the double love commandment (22:34–40). These demands must have posed some problems for Matthew's community and raised doubts in their minds about the justice of God. How can God be just when he allows the righteous to suffer and the wicked to prosper and does not allow the former to take revenge on the latter? It is obvious from our discussion that Matthew responds to this problem in the same manner as other apocalyptic-eschatological thinkers. He provides an eschatological solution. Since the opponents of the ekklesia will be punished without mercy at the judgement, the members of the community can rest assured that God is just. While Matthew does not appeal to Deuteronomy 32:35, 'Vengeance is mine, I will repay', as do Paul in Romans 12:19 and the author of Hebrews (10:30), he is firmly in agreement with this sentiment (cf. 16:27). The righteous can take heart that God (or Jesus Son of Man) will balance the ledger at the eschaton and exact vengeance on their behalf.

5. Group solidarity and social control

A further important use Matthew makes of his apocalyptic-eschatological scheme concerns the related themes of group solidarity and social control. As noted in chapter 2, communities which are alienated from and threatened by outside forces cannot tolerate dissension within their own ranks; group solidarity is all-important and must be maintained at all costs. In order to make this point, the evangelist abandons hard-line determinism and enjoins the concept of free will with regard to individual behaviour. The readers are free to choose how they act, and can decide for themselves whether to heed Matthew's advice or to ignore it. As a means of promoting group solidarity, Matthew enjoins his readers to get along with one another and to protect one another. He states that community members should not be judgemental toward one another (7:1–5), they should be humble like children (18:1–4) and that forgiveness should be an essential part of community life (18:21–2). In addition, the evangelist exercises a genuine pastoral concern for the weaker members of his community, the so-called little ones. They are not to be despised for their weakness by stronger group members, since it is God's will that they will be saved (18:10–14). And he stresses that whoever is responsible for putting temptation in their way will themselves be severely punished (18:6–7); though it is not stated in so many words, an eschatological punishment is almost certainly in view.

As a means of ensuring group solidarity and social harmony within his community, Matthew, like other apocalyptic-eschatological authors, attempts to impose a good measure of control over its members. The eschatological material reviewed in the previous section plays an important part in this respect. Spelling out the terrible eschatological fate of those outside the ekklesia, while satisfying the need for vengeance (see above), also puts considerable pressure on those waverers in the community who might be tempted to leave it and join either the ranks of formative Judaism or the law-free wing of Christianity.[10] The implicit threat that leaving the community entails horrible penalties thus serves to make less steadfast members reconsider their position and remain within it, thereby preserving the harmony of the community. A further and more important strategy which Matthew adopts is the explicit threat that those within his group who do not act as they should will themselves meet the same punishment as the opponents outside the ekklesia. Much of the gospel's judgemental material is devoted to this theme and it clearly reflects the intensely alienated situation of the Matthean community and its need for total solidarity. Similar emphasis on this theme is found in Revelation and the Qumran literature which both betray an alienated, sectarian perspective. Matthew's threats apply both to inter-personal relations within the community and to deviant behaviour which breaches the recognised code of the ekklesia. Each type of wicked behaviour, however, has the same eschatological implications.

In terms of inter-personal relations, we first meet the evangelist's

---

[10] To this extent Marguerat's view (*Le Jugement*, pp. 398–405) that the fate of Israel serves as a warning to Matthew's readers is correct, though his overall argument is quite different from that which is presented here.

view on this subject in the sermon on the mount, the community's code of conduct. In 5:22, the Matthean Jesus directly addresses the situation of his community and specifies the sanctions for angry behaviour toward a fellow group member; whoever is angry with a brother shall be liable to judgement, whoever insults his brother shall go before the community council and whoever says 'fool' will be destined for the Gehenna of fire. It might seem that in this instance the punishment far outweighs the crime, but such a severe sanction illustrates the importance Matthew places on social cohesion. Since anger and bitterness between community members can have a detrimental effect on the whole group, social harmony must be preserved at all costs, even by threat of eschatological damnation. A similar notion appears in the parable of the unforgiving servant which concludes the 'ecclesiological discourse' (18:23–35). After spelling out the necessity of forgiveness within the community (18:21–2), Matthew moves on to the eschatological implications of not forgiving one's brother. This parable describes how a servant was forgiven a huge debt by his master, but then refused to forgive the debts of those who owed him. When his master heard of this, he admonished the wicked servant (δοῦλε πονηρέ) and delivered him to the jailors. The point of this parable is provided in the admonition of verse 35: 'So also my heavenly father will do to every one of you, if you do not forgive your brother from your heart.' Since this application is a clear reference to the eschaton, this tradition serves as a warning that those who do not truly forgive in the context of the Matthean community will themselves not be forgiven at the time of the judgement and will be punished accordingly. Just as anger and insulting words are to be eliminated from the ekklesia, so is the attitude of forgiveness forcefully enjoined.

Similar exhortations to proper behaviour within Matthew's group are also given in the eschatological discourse. In the parable of the good and wicked servants (24:45–51), those leaders of the community who abuse their positions of authority because they mistakenly believe that the return of Jesus is delayed will be justly punished when he returns. This text testifies to Matthew's strong conviction that leadership must be responsible and any divergence from this standard will be greeted with severe sanctions. Since this pericope states that any wicked leader will be put with the hypocrites, we are meant to infer that they will be consigned to the same place of punishment as the scribes and

Pharisees, the fire of Gehenna where they will weep and gnash their teeth. This is an important point for it means that Matthew makes no distinction between the ultimate fate of the wicked inside the ekklesia and the fate of those outside it. The parable of the talents in Matthew 25:14–30 also seems to issue a warning to community leaders. In this text a man goes on a journey and entrusts his property to his servants. The man in the narrative is no doubt Jesus and the servants are presumably the leaders of the church who are given care of his ekklesia. The point of the parable is that those given a measure of responsibility should exercise it properly and not abuse or ignore it. The faithful servants will be rewarded, while the one who reneged on his responsibilities will be cast into the outer darkness with the concomitant weeping and gnashing of teeth. Once again Matthew not only makes the overall point that actions within the community incur eschatological punishments, but he stresses as well that these sanctions will be the same as those which non-community members will receive (cf. 8:12; 22:13).

Matthew also refers to eschatological punishments for breaking the code of the community. This point is most forcefully stated in the sermon on the mount and the discourse concerning church order in chapter 18. In 5:27–8 the evangelist warns against a lustful look which is tantamount to the commission of physical adultery. He then advises that it is better to sacrifice sinful limbs and organs than to be thrown whole into Gehenna (5:29–30). Precisely the same point is made in 18:8–9 where Matthew repeats this advice. These texts thus impose a very clear imperative on community members to observe the rules of the community. Any unrepentant breach of the ekklesia's code of conduct will be met with the most severe of punishments at the time of reckoning. In both texts the evangelist spells out the moral requirements of life within his community and warns by threat of eschatological punishment that dissident behaviour will not be tolerated.

Matthew probably hoped that explicit threats of this sort would suffice to control and regulate the behaviour of his community members. But mechanisms were in place to counter those members upon whom these measures did not have the desired effect. As noted in chapter 8, the Matthean community exercised the right of expulsion from its ranks (18:15–17). After such expulsion, the individual in question immediately ceased to be an insider and became an outsider who, like all those outside the community, faced the prospect of eschatological punishment. In this way the very threat of excommunication is itself a useful tool for social control. Moreover, on those occasions when the threat was not successful and expulsion was actually practised, this measure would have served to maintain social stability by ridding the ekklesia of dissident and potentially destructive elements.

It ought to be mentioned as well that Matthew resorts to eschatological threats within the sphere of missionary activity. Just as there can be no break in the ranks within those domiciled in the community, so too is it imperative for missionaries to band together when confronted by hostility and rejection. Matthew's exhortations to fearless confession which were noted above are tempered with the threat of eschatological sanction for improper performance of duty. This is first mentioned in 10:28 where the missionaries are advised not to fear those who can kill only the body; rather, they should fear God who can destroy both body and soul in Gehenna. The implicit threat of 10:28 is worked out more fully in verses 32–3 where the Matthean Jesus states that in the judgement he will acknowledge those missionaries who acknowledge him and deny those who deny him. Failure to remain steadfast therefore has an eschatological penalty. Although there is no doubt that Matthew genuinely attempts to comfort those missionaries embarking on the final and dangerous mission to Palestine, he keeps his priorities firmly in focus. Consolation must be balanced by threats when group solidarity is all-important.

It is plain from the above that Matthew, in similar vein to other representatives of apocalypticism, believed that group solidarity and social harmony must be maintained at all costs and by any means available. In order to ensure that such conditions prevailed in his community, Matthew attempts to impose social control over its members by encouraging a common standard of behaviour and discouraging any deviation from it. His major weapon in this enterprise is his apocalyptic-eschatological material which presents the judgement as a two-edged sword. Those members who faithfully follow the code of conduct can expect eternal life as a reward, while those who break the code and put the community at risk will be horribly punished alongside the wicked outside the ekklesia. As noted in the Introduction, almost all scholars who examine this hortatory element of Matthew's gospel conclude that the evangelist was basically interested in paraenesis for its own sake. They argue that Matthew simply wished to urge his readers to strive for the standard of the higher righteousness which Jesus himself had set.[11] But this explanation does not account for the evangelist's adoption of such extreme measures to convey this point. The suggestion of G. N. Stanton that Matthew's paraenesis serves to promote group solidarity[12] is a step in the right direction, but it still does not go far enough. For Matthew, group solidarity is achieved by the imposition of social control. He attempts to impose such control by offering both the 'carrot' of eternal life as an angel for conformity and the 'stick' of eternal burning for dissident behaviour.

This brings us to a very important question. Are we to believe that the evangelist deliberately uses 'scare tactics' to impose his own will on those within his community? No matter how unsavoury such a proposition might be, honesty compels us to answer this question in the affirmative. The gospel is replete with threats, both actual and implicit, addressed to those within his community and it can hardly be denied that Matthew plays on the natural fears of his readers to cajole them to his own point of view.[13] But having acknowledged this less than attractive side to the evangelist, we should not ourselves judge him too harshly, nor should we cast aside too quickly the common depiction of him as a 'caring pastor' for his troubled community.[14] On the interpretation of Matthew presented above, he is very much concerned with his community and exercises a genuine pastoral care over its members. His chosen methods for doing so might not appeal to everyone, but he

[11] See the discussion of Bornkamm, Trilling, Strecker, Marguerat and Cope in the Introduction. D. Hagner attempts to take this point a step further by arguing that the evangelist exhorts his readers to moral conduct in order to avoid the moral passivity which the prior notion of determinism could engender. See 'Apocalyptic Motifs', pp. 75–6. While there is doubtless an element of truth in Hagner's assertion, it still does not provide a complete explanation of Matthew's intentions.

[12] Stanton, 'Matthew and Judaism', p. 282. His discussion of this point is rather brief, however.

[13] This seems to be acknowledged by R. Mohrlang, *Matthew and Paul*, p. 49: 'In general, it is the threat of judgement and loss of the kingdom which is the dominant motivating force for ethics throughout the Gospel.' Trilling, *Wahre Israel*, p. 126 also comments on the evangelist's use of threat in the service of paraenesis, and Cope, 'Role of Apocalyptic', pp. 118–19 seems to adopt this position as well. On the other hand, France, *Matthew*, p. 269 denies that Matthew 'advocates a discipleship based on fear'. Marguerat, who constantly refers to the threat (menace) of judgement, stands in agreement with France. He suggests that Matthew's emphasis on the fate of the condemned is not meant to terrify his readers, though he adds that this might have been the motivation of other apocalyptic authors! (*Le Jugement*, p. 174).

[14] The pastoral function of the gospel has been emphasised by Thompson, *Matthew's Advice*, pp. 258–64 and, more recently, France, *Matthew*, pp. 251–6.

obviously saw them as necessary if his sectarian group was to survive its current crisis of conflict with and alienation from the wider world. In such a situation, dissension and disharmony are simply self-destructive and must be prevented at any cost. Consequently, and for the good of his community as a whole, Matthew sought to avoid these problems by adopting a solution which seemed best to him and which was a tried and true method of other apocalyptic-eschatological groups, the threat of eschatological sanction for non-acceptable behaviour.

6. Conclusions

This chapter has attempted to isolate the primary functions which Matthew's scheme of apocalyptic eschatology or his symbolic universe plays in his gospel. These functions are found in many apocalyptic-eschatological texts but are directly related by Matthew to the crises which his community faced in the aftermath of the Jewish war. Matthew uses the dualistic component of this religious perspective to legitimate both the existence and sectarian nature of his community and to invalidate the symbolic universes of the wider societies. The ekklesia stands on the side of God and Jesus in the cosmic struggle while those who oppose it, be they Jew, Christian or gentile, are aligned with Satan. Moreover, the evangelist uses apocalyptic eschatology to explain the current circumstances of his sectarian group. Since all events have been predetermined in advance, the present plight of the ekklesia can be readily explained as in full accord with the will of God and not as contrary to it; God has deemed that the righteous enclave must suffer at the hands of Satan and his allies as history draws to its conclusion. This emphasis on the determination of history also provides hope for the future. The members of the ekklesia can take heart that the predictions of the imminent return of the Son of Man in judgement will certainly come to pass just as earlier predictions had been fulfilled. The judgement of the Son of Man will see the vindication of the righteous and the terrible punishment in the fire of Gehenna of the wicked who are responsible for their suffering. These two sides of the judgement offer hope and consolation on the one hand and satisfy the need for vengeance on the other. Each motif is stark testimony to the absolutely critical situation of the Matthean community and reflects its acute sense of despair. But Matthew also issues a stern warning to his readers. Since the survival of the community is absolutely dependent upon group solidarity, Matthew attempts to impose this by use of the threat of judgement. Those within the ekklesia who cause disruption by any means will be punished in the same manner as the opponents of the group. Like the scribes and Pharisees of formative Judaism and the false prophets of law-free Christianity, the dissidents within the Matthean community will be placed in the fire and darkness of Gehenna where they will weep and gnash their teeth. Matthew thus constructs his apocalyptic-eschatological scheme which he places on the lips of Jesus to meet the needs of a community which was faced by a particularly critical social setting. All at once his symbolic universe offers this sectarian group justification, explanation, hope, consolation, exhortation, vengeance and warning.

SUMMARY OF PART III

In this section we have tried to explain why Matthew adopted and promoted his particular apocalyptic-eschatological scheme. It was argued that the answer lies in the social setting of the community for whom he wrote. This sectarian Jewish group was experiencing an extremely critical situation in the aftermath of the Jewish war. It had departed from the Jewish parent body and was now in open conflict with it, and it felt extremely threatened by law-free Christianity which had now assumed an ascendant role after the destruction of the Jerusalem church. Relations between the gentile world and the Matthean community were also not amicable in view of past hostilities and expected future conflict. All these factors led to the withdrawal of the Matthean ekklesia from the wider world and the necessity to seek support only from within its own borders. It became, in short, an apocalyptic community. As the spokesperson for this group, the evangelist responded to this desperate situation in a tried and true manner which had well served both Jewish and Christian groups facing similar situations of crisis. He abandoned the symbolic universes of the opposing parties and constructed one of his own which validated his group's hopes and aspirations. This symbolic universe identified the members of the community as the suffering righteous who would soon be vindicated and their opponents as the Satan-influenced wicked who would soon experience unspeakable suffering as punishment for their crimes. By doing so, the evangelist satisfied his readers' need for hope and consolation on the one hand, and for vengeance on the other. His scheme of apocalyptic eschatology was also designed to maintain group solidarity in the face of these extreme outside pressures. This was absolutely necessary if the group was to survive the current crisis.

CONCLUSIONS

This study of Matthew's gospel has attempted to reconstruct and to understand its important apocalyptic-eschatological component. It was stated in the Introduction that since no full-scale study of this theme had yet been undertaken, the present work was an attempt to fill this gap. The first Part of the study was devoted to the general concepts of apocalyptic eschatology and apocalypticism in the time of Matthew. It was argued that these phenomena are necessarily related, the one denoting a distinctive religious perspective and the other its underlying social movement, and that neither is confined to the apocalyptic literature. While it was conceded that this religious perspective or vision of reality was an unsystematic phenomenon and that one can hardly speak of *an* apocalyptic theology, it was argued that eight characteristics recur with great frequency in the apocalyptic-eschatological schemes of the evangelist's day. An apocalyptic-eschatological perspective or world view, therefore, consists of a substantial cluster of these motifs.

Two of these characteristics, dualism and determinism, are not in themselves eschatological, but they provide the context in which the eschatological themes function. The former relates in almost every case to a fundamental division between the righteous and the wicked in the human world. In some apocalyptic groups this dualistic perception of the human world is associated with a similar division in the cosmic realm where a struggle for supremacy rages between God and Satan and their respective angelic allies. The deterministic component of apocalyptic eschatology concerns the broad sweep of history. The course of history has been fixed in advance by God and cannot be changed. On an individual level, the apocalyptic writers tend to focus less on hard determinism and emphasise that humans have free will and are thus responsible for their actions. The six remaining characteristics of apocalyptic eschatology are all eschatological in nature and take as their point of departure the dualistic notion of the two ages; the present age will be succeeded by a new era. The final period of the present age will witness many terrible events which will intensify the suffering of the righteous, including in many schemes a final conflict between the righteous and the wicked. This situation will then be reversed by the arrival of a saviour figure, either God or his agent, whose appearance signals the turning of the ages. The arrival of this figure leads in turn to the final and universal judgement. The righteous will be vindicated and receive eternal salvation, while the wicked, both human and angelic, will be punished forever in the fire and gloom of Gehenna. Almost all apocalyptic-eschatological schemes affirm that this series of events will occur in the imminent future, although this particular belief could be expressed in a number of ways.

It was argued that this perception of reality has a concrete social setting. Apocalypticism is embraced by sectarian or minority groups which experience a situation of crisis and a resultant sense of alienation from the wider society, and the use of apocalyptic eschatology is a direct response to these dire circumstances. This religious perspective presents a new and authoritative symbolic universe which is at odds with the world view of the outside world, but one which reinforces and validates the experience of the group which adopts it. By spelling out that according to God's predetermined plan the suffering righteous will be vindicated and the wicked oppressors horribly punished in the imminent future, it serves a number of basic functions. These include legitimation of the group in question, hope for the future, the desire for vengeance and the necessity for group solidarity until the eschaton.

Part II of this study was concerned with a full reconstruction of Matthew's particular apocalyptic-eschatological scheme. It was argued that the evangelist readily adopted and promoted the eight major characteristics of this perspective which were analysed in Part I. He adopts a developed type of cosmic dualism similar to those which are found in the Qumran literature and the book of Revelation. According to Matthew's scheme, the cosmos is divided into two opposing supernatural groups which are engaged in a battle for supremacy. The human world is similarly divided into two camps and each person must decide whether he or she pledges allegiance to the side of heaven or to the side of Satan. Matthew also promotes the notion of historical determinism on the one hand, and the concept of individual free choice on the other.

His end-time scenario conforms to that of the Jewish apocalyptic-eschatological schemes, although it is presented in strictly Christian terms. The end of the present age will be characterised by a period of upheaval which would increase the suffering of the righteous. According to Matthew's timetable of the end, the series of events comprising the eschatological woes was well advanced and the turning of the ages was imminent. The final event in history would be a major assault against the righteous by the demonic forces of Satan led by the antichrist. This attack would be met and defeated by the saviour figure, Jesus Son of Man, who would arrive on the clouds of heaven accompanied by his angelic army. The Son of Man would ascend his throne of glory and preside over the final judgement. Matthew's distinctive presentation of the Son of Man is a perfect synthesis of his Christian and Jewish Son of Man sources, both of which are reinterpretations of the one like a son of man in Daniel 7:13–14. The judgement which the Son of Man brings is the climax of the evangelist's eschatological scheme. The righteous will be vindicated and live forever as angels, while the wicked will suffer forever in the fire of Gehenna where they will weep and gnash their teeth. Matthew's description of the horrific fate of the wicked stands much more in line with Jewish apocalyptic-eschatological schemes than with their Christian counterparts. Of all the early Christian literature, only the Apocalypse emphasises that the lot of the wicked will be everlasting torture by fire. Hence, the judgement in Matthew is not, as many scholars have claimed, a colourless event which lacks concrete details. Since the dual themes of reward and punishment are the climax of Matthew's apocalyptic-eschatological scenario to which everything else points, it is clear that Matthew's scheme is particularly vindictive and vengeful. On the basis of the evangelist's fervent promotion of apocalyptic eschatology, we are entitled to consider his community as an apocalyptic group.

The third Part of this study attempted to account for the evangelist's adoption and promotion of his particular vision of reality. To this end, it was argued that the explanation lies in the social setting of the Matthean community which found itself facing a number of crises in the aftermath of the Jewish war. It had separated from the Jewish parent body and was in open conflict with it. Moreover, it had experienced persecution at the hands of its gentile neighbours and expected more to come. Finally, the Jewish war had witnessed the destruction of the Jerusalem church and the power base of law-observant Christianity. This situation in turn led to a resurgence of law-free Christianity and there is good evidence in the gospel that Matthew believed this form of Christianity posed a considerable threat to his community. These three factors contributed to the Matthean ekklesia's alienation from the outside world. With the disintegration of all its former external support systems, Matthew's community had no choice but to become a self-supporting unit or face extinction on account of the pressures it faced. It attempted to accomplish this by embracing apocalypticism in so far as it adopted an apocalyptic-eschatological perspective or symbolic universe to which the evangelist gives expression.

Matthew's apocalyptic eschatology is therefore a direct response to the situations of crisis which his community faced. By adopting a markedly dualistic vision of the cosmos, it identifies the sectarian Matthean community as the embattled righteous who stand firmly on the side of the heavenly world in the cosmic conflict. The remainder of the world, by contrast, is identified as being in league with Satan. This identification of each group serves to legitimate the Matthean community and to discredit all those who stand outside it and against it. Matthew's particular scheme also offers an explanation for the current dire circumstances of his group. The righteous community must suffer as the predetermined eschatological woes draw to their conclusion. But its members can take heart that the present situation will be reversed in the imminent future. Jesus the Son of Man will soon arrive to vindicate the righteous and to punish the wicked. The members of the ekklesia can thereby be consoled that their suffering and endurance will be more than adequately compensated and that their demands for vengeance will be met. All outsider groups which threaten the Matthean community are earmarked for the fire of Gehenna. But in order to promote group solidarity, which is essential for any minority group in threatening circumstances, Matthew makes clear that the judgement is a two-edged sword. Membership in the ekklesia is not sufficient for one to be numbered among the righteous at the judgement. One needs to be a true member of the group by following its code of practice and refraining from dissident behaviour. The evangelist therefore threatens his readers that

improper behaviour within the group will see the offender punished in the same horrific manner as the outsiders.

Matthew lends authority to his apocalyptic-eschatological
scheme by placing it on the lips of an authoritative figure, namely
Jesus the Son of Man who will return at the eschaton and preside
over the judgement. He uses as his vehicle of expression the gospel
genre which he inherited from Mark and which provided the scope
to present other themes which were of concern to him. The fact that
Matthew presents his apocalyptic eschatology in a gospel and not
in an apocalypse reinforces the point that this world view is not
confined to the apocalyptic genre (nor is it always found there).
This point had been conceded in the case of the Qumran community, but the fact that Matthew's scheme is as detailed as any other
makes it all the more necessary to revise the misleading terminology
in this area of study. Finally, it hardly needs saying that Matthew's
apocalyptic eschatology is not the most appealing aspect of the
gospel. His division of the human world into two distinct camps,
his vengeful view of the fate of the wicked complete with graphic
descriptions of their suffering, and his use of threats to influence his
readers to adopt his own point of view are not likely to find favour
with many readers of the gospel today. It is understandable that
many Matthean studies have either avoided altogether or at least
played down these particular elements of the gospel. Yet Matthew's
apocalyptic eschatology looms so large in the gospel that it cannot
be dispensed with so easily. We must accept that it is an integral
part of the gospel and attempt to explain its presence there. The
sociological explanation offered here is an attempt to do this. By
reconstructing the social setting of the evangelist and his readers,
and by examining the functions which this religious perspective
plays in the gospel, we can understand why apocalyptic eschatology, including its unattractive elements, is such a prominent
theme in the gospel of Matthew. It is clear from this study that
Matthew's adoption and promotion of this theme was tied inextricably to his historical and social circumstances. Had the Jewish war
not eventuated and had the Matthean community not had to face
the problems it did, it is probable that Matthew would have written
a gospel 'more acceptable' to modern readers. But the Jewish war
did happen and it did impact severely on Matthew's community in
a number of ways. The evangelist obviously believed that drastic
circumstances require drastic measures and he responded to these
crises in a manner which was readily available to him and which

was used approvingly in his cultural and historical setting. While we might not today share Matthew's world view or approve of his methods in responding to his community's needs, we do him a great disservice if we do not try to understand him as a child of his time. When we acknowledge this, we find that Matthew did compose his gospel as a caring pastor for his troubled community. He constructed a symbolic universe which was designed to see his readers through the current crises and the troubling times which lay ahead.

SELECT BIBLIOGRAPHY

Albright, W. F. and C. S. Mann. *Matthew*, AB 26, Garden City, Double-day, 1971.

Allen, W. C. *A Critical and Exegetical Commentary on the Gospel according to S. Matthew*, ICC, Edinburgh, T.& T. Clark, 1907.

Allison, D. C. *The End of the Ages Has Come: An Early Interpretation of the Passion and Resurrection of Jesus*, Edinburgh, T. & T. Clark, 1987.

Allison, D. C. *The New Moses: A Matthean Typology*, Edinburgh, T. & T. Clark, 1993.

Aune, D. E. *Prophecy in Early Christianity and the Ancient Mediterranean World*, Grand Rapids, Eerdmans, 1983.

Barclay, J. M .G. 'Mirror-Reading a Polemical Letter: Galatians as a Test Case', *JSNT* 31 (1987), 73–93.

Barrett, C. K. *The Gospel according to St. John*, 2nd edn, London, SPCK, 1978.

Barth, G. 'Matthew's Understanding of the Law', in G. Bornkamm, G. Barth and H. J. Held, *Tradition and Interpretation in Matthew*, London, SCM, 1963, pp. 58–164.

Bartnicki, R. 'Das Trostwort an die Jünger in Mt 10.23', *TZ* 43 (1987), 311–19.

Bauckham, R. J. *Jude, 2 Peter*, WBC 50, Waco, Tx., Word Books, 1983.

Bauckham, R. J. 'The Book of Revelation as a Christian War Scroll', *Neotestamentica* 22 (1988), 17–40.

Beare, F. W. *The Gospel according to Matthew*, Oxford, Basil Blackwell, 1981.

Betz, H. D. *Essays on the Sermon on the Mount*, Philadelphia, Fortress Press, 1985.

Black, M. *The Book of Enoch or 1 Enoch*, SVTP 7, Leiden, Brill, 1985.

Blenkinsopp, J. 'Interpretation and the Tendency to Sectarianism: An Aspect of Second Temple History', in E. P. Sanders, A. I. Baumgarten and A. Mendelson (eds.), *Jewish and Christian Self-Definition* vol. II, London, SCM, 1981, pp. 1–26.

Bonnard, P. *L'évangile selon saint Matthieu*, Neuchâtel, Delachaux & Niestlé, 1963.

Bornkamm, G. 'End-Expectation and Church in Matthew', in G. Born-kamm, G. Barth and H. J. Held, *Tradition and Interpretation in Matthew*, London, SCM, 1963, pp. 15–51.

Boyd, W. J. P. 'Gehenna – According to J. Jeremias', in E. A. Livingstone (ed.), *Studia Biblica 1978 II: Papers on the Gospels*, JSNTSS 2, Sheffield, Sheffield Academic Press, 1980, pp. 9–12.

Brandenburger, E. *Das Recht des Weltenrichters: Untersuchung zu Matthäus 25,31–46*, SBS 99, Stuttgart, Katholisches Bibelwerk, 1980.

Brandon, S. G. F. *The Fall of Jerusalem and the Christian Church*, London, SPCK, 1951.

Broer, I. 'Das Gericht des Menschensohnes über die Völker', *BuL* 11 (1970), 273–95.

Brooks, S. H. *Matthew's Community: The Evidence of his Special Sayings Material*, JSNTSS 16, Sheffield, Sheffield Academic Press, 1987.

Brown, R. E. *The Gospel according to John*, 2 vols., AB 29, 29A, 2nd edn, Garden City, Doubleday, 1980.

Brown, S. 'The Mission to Israel in Matthew's Central Section (Mt 9 35–11 1)', *ZNW* 69 (1978), 73–90.

Brown, S. 'The Matthean Apocalypse', *JSNT* 4 (1979), 2–27.

Brown, S. 'The Matthean Community and the Gentile Mission', *NovT* 22 (1980), 193–221.

Büchsel, F. 'παλιγγενεσία', *TDNT*, I, pp. 686–9.

Burnett, F. W. *The Testament of Jesus-Sophia: A Redaction-Critical Study of the Eschatological Discourse in Matthew*, Lanham, University Press of America, 1981.

Burnett, F. W. 'παλιγγενεσία in Matt. 19:28: A Window on the Matthean Community?', *JSNT* 17 (1983), 60–72.

Callaway, P. R. *The History of the Qumran Community: An Investigation*, JSPSS 3, Sheffield, Sheffield Academic Press, 1988.

Campbell, K. M. 'The New Jerusalem in Matthew 5.14', *SJT* 31 (1978), 335–63.

Cargal, T. B. '"His Blood be Upon Us and Upon our Children": A Matthean Double Entendre?', *NTS* 37 (1991), 101–12.

Catchpole, D. R. 'The Poor on Earth and the Son of Man in Heaven: A Re-Appraisal of Matthew xxv. 31–46', *BJRL* 61 (1979), 355–97.

Charette, B. *The Theme of Recompense in Matthew's Gospel*, JSNTSS 79, Sheffield, Sheffield Academic Press, 1992.

Charles, R. H. (ed.). *The Apocrypha and Pseudepigrapha of the Old Testament*, 2 vols., Oxford, Clarendon, 1913.

Charlesworth, J. H. (ed.). *The Old Testament Pseudepigrapha*, 2 vols., London, Darton, Longman and Todd, 1983, 1985.

Collins, A. Yarbro. 'The Revelation of John: An Apocalyptic Response to a Social Crisis', *CMT* 8 (1981), 4–12.

Collins, A. Yarbro. 'Persecution and Vengeance in the Book of Revelation', in D. Hellholm (ed.), *Apocalypticism in the Mediterranean World and the Near East: Proceedings of the International Colloquium on Apocalypticism, Uppsala, August 12–17, 1979*, Tübingen, Mohr [Siebeck], 1983, pp. 729–50.

Collins, A. Yarbro. *Crisis and Catharsis: The Power of the Apocalypse*, Philadelphia, Westminster Press, 1984.

Collins, A. Yarbro. 'Insiders and Outsiders in the Book of Revelation and its Social Context', in J. Neusner and E. S. Frerichs (eds.), *'To see*

*Ourselves as Others See Us': Christians, Jews, 'Others' in Late Anti-
quity*, Chico, Scholars Press, 1985, pp. 187–218.

Collins, A. Yarbro. 'Vilification and Self-Definition in the Book of Revelation', *HTR* 79 (1986), 308–20.

Collins, J. J. *The Sibylline Oracles of Egyptian Judaism*, SBLDS 13,
Missoula, Scholars Press, 1974.

Collins, J. J. 'Apocalyptic Eschatology as the Transcendence of Death',
CBQ 36 (1974), 21–43.

Collins, J. J. *The Apocalyptic Vision of the Book of Daniel*, HSM 16,
Missoula, Scholars Press, 1977.

Collins, J. J. 'Introduction: Towards the Morphology of a Genre', *Semeia*
14 (1979), 1–19.

Collins, J. J. *The Apocalyptic Imagination: An Introduction to the Jewish
Matrix of Christianity*, New York, Crossroad, 1984.

Collins, J. J. 'Was the Dead Sea Sect an Apocalyptic Movement?', in L. H.
Schiffman (ed.), *Archaeology and History in the Dead Sea Scrolls*,
JSPSS 8, Sheffield, Sheffield Academic Press, 1990, pp. 25–51.

Collins, J. J. 'Genre, Ideology and Social Movements in Jewish Apocalypticism', in J. J. Collins and J. H. Charlesworth (eds.), *Mysteries and
Revelations: Apocalyptic Studies since the Uppsala Colloquium*, JSPSS
9, Sheffield, Sheffield Academic Press, 1991, pp. 11–32.

Conzelmann, H. *1 Corinthians*, Hermeneia, Philadelphia, Fortress Press,
1975.

Cope, O. L. 'Matthew xxv:31–46. "The Sheep and the Goats" Reinterpreted', *NovT* 11 (1969), 32–44.

Cope, O. L. ' "To the Close of the Age": The Role of Apocalyptic Thought
in the Gospel of Matthew', in J. Marcus and M. L. Soards (eds.),
*Apocalyptic and the New Testament: Essays in Honour of J. Louis
Martyn*, JSNTSS 24, Sheffield, Sheffield Academic Press, 1989,
pp. 113–24.

Coser, L. *The Functions of Social Conflict*, New York, Free Press, 1964.

Crosby, M. H. *House of Disciples: Church, Economics and Justice in
Matthew*, Maryknoll, Orbis, 1988.

Davids, P. H. *The Epistle of James: A Commentary on the Greek Text*,
NIGTC, Grand Rapids, Eerdmans, 1982.

Davidson, M. J. *Angels at Qumran: A Comparative Study of 1 Enoch
1–36,72–108 and Sectarian Writings from Qumran*, JSPSS 11, Sheffield,
Sheffield Academic Press, 1992.

Davies, P. R. *1QM, The War Scroll from Qumran*, Rome, Biblical Institute
Press, 1977.

Davies, P. R. 'Eschatology in the Book of Daniel', *JSOT* 17 (1980) 33–53.

Davies, P. R. 'Eschatology at Qumran', *JBL* 104 (1985), 39–55.

Davies, P. R. 'The Social World of Apocalyptic Writings', in R. E.
Clements (ed.), *The World of Ancient Israel: Sociological, Anthropological and Political Perspectives*, Cambridge, University Press, 1989,
pp. 251–71.

Davies, W. D. *The Setting of the Sermon on the Mount*, Cambridge,
University Press, 1964.

Davies, W. D. and D. C. Allison. *A Critical and Exegetical Commentary on the Gospel according to Saint Matthew*, 2 vols., ICC, Edinburgh, T. & T. Clark, 1988, 1991.

Davison, J. E. '*Anomia* and the Question of an Antinomian Polemic in Matthew', *JBL* 104 (1985), 617–35.

De Jonge, M. *The Testaments of the Twelve Patriarchs: A Commentary*, in association with H. W. Hollander, Leiden, Brill, 1985.

Denis, A.-M. *Introduction aux pseudépigraphes grecs d'ancien Testament*, SVTP 1, Leiden, Brill, 1970.

Dexinger, F. *Henochs Zehnwochenapokalypse und offene Probleme der Apokalyptikforschung*, Leiden, Brill, 1977.

Donaldson, T. L. *Jesus on the Mountain: A Study in Matthean Theology*, JSNTSS 8, Sheffield, Sheffield Academic Press, 1985.

Dunn, J. D. G. *Romans*, 2 vols., WBC 38a, 38b, Dallas, Word Books, 1988.

Dupont, J. *Les Trois Apocalypses Synoptiques*, LD 121, Paris, Cerf, 1985.

Elliott, J. H. *What is Social-Scientific Criticism?*, Guides to Biblical Scholarship, Minneapolis, Fortress Press, 1993.

Esler, P. F. *Community and Gospel in Luke–Acts: The Social and Political Motivations of Lucan Theology*, SNTSMS 57, Cambridge, University Press, 1987.

Fenton, J. C. *The Gospel of Saint Matthew*, PNTC, Harmondsworth, Penguin, 1963.

Feuillet, A. 'Le Sens du Mot Parousie dans l'évangile de Matthieu: Comparaison entre Matth. xxiv et Jac. v, i-xi', in W. D. Davies and D. Daube (eds.), *The Background of the New Testament and its Eschatology*, Cambridge, University Press, 1956, pp. 261–80.

Fiorenza, E. Schüssler. 'The Phenomenon of Early Christian Apocalyptic: Some Reflections on Method', in D. Hellholm (ed.), *Apocalypticism in the Mediterranean World and the Near East: Proceedings of the International Colloquium on Apocalypticism, Uppsala, August 12–17, 1979*, Tübingen, Mohr [Siebeck], 1983, pp. 295–316.

Fiorenza, E. Schüssler *The Book of Revelation: Justice and Judgment*, Philadelphia, Fortress Press, 1985.

Fischer, U. *Eschatologie und Jenseitserwartung im Hellenistischen Diasporajudentum*, BZNW 44, Berlin, de Gruyter, 1978.

Forkman, G. *The Limits of the Religious Community: Expulsion from the Religious Community within the Qumran Sect, within Rabbinic Judaism, and within Primitive Christianity*, CBNTS 5, Lund, Gleerup, 1972.

France, R. T. *Matthew: Evangelist and Teacher*, Exeter, Paternoster Press, 1989.

Frankmolle, H. *Jahwebund und Kirche Christi*, NTAbh 10, 2nd edn, Münster, Aschendorf, 1984.

Friedrich, J. *Gott im Bruder? Eine Methodenkritische Untersuchung von Redaktion, Überlieferung und Traditionen in Mt 25, 31–46*, CTM 7, Stuttgart, Calwer, 1977.

Gaston, L. *No Stone on Another: Studies in the Significance of the Fall of Jerusalem in the Synoptic Gospels*, NovTSup 23, Leiden, Brill, 1970.

Geddert, T. L. *Watchwords: Mark 13 in Markan Eschatology*, JSNTSS 26, Sheffield, Sheffield Academic Press, 1989.

Geist, H. *Menschensohn und Gemeinde: Eine redaktionskritische Untersuchung zur Menschensohnprädikation im Matthäusevangelium*, FB 57, Würzburg, Echter, 1986.

Gill, R. *Theology and Sociology: A Reader*, London, Geoffrey Chapman, 1987.

Glasson, T. F. 'The Ensign of the Son of Man (Matt. xxiv. 30)', *JTS* 15 (1964), 299–300.

Gnilka, J. *Das Matthäusevangelium*, 2 vols., HTKNT, Freiburg, Herder, 1986, 1988.

Goulder, M. D. *Midrash and Lection in Matthew*, London, SPCK, 1974.

Grabbe, L. L. 'The Social Setting of Early Jewish Apocalypticism', *JSP* 4 (1989), 27–47.

Grant, F. C. *The Gospels: Their Origin and Their Growth*, London, Faber and Faber, 1957.

Grässer, E. *Das Problem der Parusieverzögerung in den Synoptischen Evangelien und in der Apostelgeschichte*, BZNW 22, 3rd edn, Berlin, de Gruyter, 1977.

Gray, S. *The Least of My Brothers, Matthew 25:31–46: A History of Interpretation*, SBLDS 114, Atlanta, Scholars Press, 1989.

Guelich, R. A. *The Sermon on the Mount: A Foundation for Understanding*, Waco, Tx., Word Books, 1982.

Gundry, R. H. *Matthew: A Commentary on His Literary and Theological Art*, Grand Rapids, Eerdmans, 1982.

Gundry, R. H. 'A Responsive Evaluation of the Social History of the Matthean Community in Roman Syria', in D. L. Balch (ed.), *Social History of the Matthean Community: Cross-Disciplinary Approaches*, Minneapolis, Fortress Press, 1991, pp. 62–7.

Hagner, D. A. 'Apocalyptic Motifs in the Gospel of Matthew: Continuity and Discontinuity', *HBT* 7 (1985), 53–82.

Hagner, D. A. 'The *Sitz im Leben* of the Gospel of Matthew' in K. H. Richards (ed.), *SBL 1985 Seminar Papers*, Atlanta, Scholars Press, 1985, pp. 243–69.

Hahn, F. 'Die eschatologische Rede Matthäus 24 und 25', in L. Schenke (ed.), *Studien zum Matthäusevangelium: Festschrift für Wilhelm Pesch*, SBS, Stuttgart, Katholisches Bibelwerk, 1988, pp. 109–26.

Hanson, P. D. 'Apocalypticism', in K. Crim et al. (eds.), *IDBSupp*, Nashville, Abingdon, 1976, pp. 28–34.

Hanson, P. D. *The Dawn of Apocalyptic: The Historical and Sociological Roots of Jewish Apocalyptic Eschatology*, rev. edn, Philadelphia, Fortress Press, 1979.

Hanson, P. D. 'Apocalyptic Literature', in D. A. Knight and G. M. Tucker (eds.), *The Hebrew Bible and its Modern Interpreters*, Chico, Scholars Press, 1985, pp. 465–88.

Hare, D. R. A. *The Theme of Jewish Persecution of Christians in the Gospel according to St Matthew*, SNTSMS 6, Cambridge, University Press, 1967.

Hare, D. R. A. *The Son of Man Tradition*, Minneapolis, Fortress Press, 1990.

Hare, D. R. A. and D. J. Harrington. ' "Make Disciples of all the Gentiles" (Mt 28:19)', *CBQ* 37 (1975), 359–69.

Harrington, D. J. *The Gospel of Matthew*, Sacra Pagina 1, Collegeville, Michael Glazier, 1991.

Hartmann, L. L. and A. A. Dilella. *The Book of Daniel*, AB 23, Garden City, Doubleday, 1978.

Hellholm, D. 'The Problem of Apocalyptic Genre and the Apocalypse of John', in K. H. Richards (ed.), *SBL 1982 Seminar Papers*, Chico, Scholars Press, 1982, pp. 157–98.

Hemer, C. J. *The Letters to the Seven Churches in their Local Setting*, JSNTSS 11, Sheffield, Sheffield Academic Press, 1986.

Hengel, M. *Judaism and Hellenism: A Study of their Encounter in Palestine during the Early Hellenistic Period*, 2 vols., London, SCM, 1974.

Higgins, A. J. B. *Jesus and the Son of Man*, London, Lutterworth Press, 1964.

Higgins, A. J. B. *The Son of Man in the Teaching of Jesus*, SNTSMS 39, Cambridge, University Press, 1980.

Hill, D. *The Gospel of Matthew*, NCB, London, Marshall, Morgan and Scott, 1972.

Hill, D. 'False Prophets and Charismatics: Structure and Interpretation in Matthew 7,15–23', *Biblica* 57 (1976), 327–48.

Himmelfarb, M. *Tours of Hell: An Apocalyptic Form in Jewish and Christian Literature*, Philadelphia, Fortress Press, 1983.

Hoffmann, P. *Studien zur Theologie der Logienquelle*, NTAbh 8, Münster, Aschendorf, 1972.

Holmberg, B. *Sociology and the New Testament: An Appraisal*, Minneapolis, Fortress Press, 1990.

Hooker, M. *The Son of Man in Mark*, London, SPCK, 1967.

Hultgård, A. *L'eschatologie des Testaments des Douze Patriarches*, 2 vols., Uppsala, Almqvist & Wiksell, 1977, 1981.

Hultgren, A. J. *Jesus and his Adversaries*, Minneapolis, Augsburg, 1979.

Hummel, R. *Die Auseinandersetzung zwischen Kirche und Judentum im Matthäusevangelium*, BEvT 33, 2nd edn, Munich, Kaiser, 1966.

Isenberg, S. R. 'Millenarianism in Greco-Roman Palestine', *Religion* 4 (1974), 26–46.

Jeremias, J. 'γέεννα', *TDNT*, I, pp. 657–8.

Jeremias, J. 'πύλη', *TDNT*, VI, pp. 921–8.

Jeremias, J. *The Prayers of Jesus*, London, SCM, 1967.

Jeremias, J. *The Parables of Jesus*, 3rd edn, London, SCM, 1972.

Kee, H. C. *Christian Origins in Sociological Perspective*, London, SCM, 1980.

Kilpatrick, G. D. *The Origins of the Gospel according to St. Matthew*, Oxford, Clarendon, 1946.

Kingsbury, J. D. *The Parables of Jesus in Matthew 13*, London, SPCK, 1969.

Kingsbury, J. D. 'The Developing Conflict between Jesus and the Jewish Leaders in Matthew's Gospel: A Literary-Critical Study', *CBQ* 49 (1987), 57–73.

Kingsbury, J. D. *Matthew as Story*, 2nd edn, Philadelphia, Fortress Press, 1988.

Knibb, M. A. *The Ethiopic Book of Enoch*, 2 vols., Oxford, Clarendon, 1978.

Knibb, M. A. 'The Date of the Parables of Enoch: A Critical Review', *NTS* 25 (1979), 345–59.

Knibb, M. A. 'The Second Book of Esdras', in R. J. Coggins and M. A. Knibb, *The First and Second Books of Esdras*, Cambridge, University Press, 1979, pp. 76–305.

Knibb, M. A. 'Prophecy and the emergence of the Jewish apocalypses', in R. J. Coggins, A. Phillips and M. A. Knibb (eds.), *Israel's Prophetic Tradition: Essays in Honour of Peter Ackroyd*, Cambridge, University Press, 1982, pp. 155–80.

Koch, K. *The Rediscovery of Apocalyptic*, SBT 2/22, London, SCM, 1972.

Kümmel. W. G. *Introduction to the New Testament*, rev. edn, London, SCM, 1975.

Lambrecht, J. 'The Parousia Discourse: Composition and Content in Mt. xxiv-xxv', in M. Didier (ed.), *L'évangile selon Matthieu: Rédaction et Théologie*, BETL 29, Gembloux, Duculot, 1972, pp. 309–42.

Lambrecht, J. *Out of the Treasure: The Parables in the Gospel of Matthew*, LTPM 10, Louvain, Peeters Press, 1991.

Lang, F. 'πῦρ', *TDNT*, VI, pp. 928–48.

Langton, E. *Essentials of Demonology: A Study of Jewish and Christian Doctrine, Its Origin and Development*, London, Epworth, 1949.

Laverdiere, E. A. and W. G. Thompson, 'New Testament Communities in Transition: A Study of Matthew and Luke', *TS* 37 (1976), 567–97.

Levine, A.-J. *The Social and Ethnic Dimensions of Matthean Salvation History: 'Go nowhere among the Gentiles...'(Matt 10:5b)*, SBEC 14, Lewiston, Edwin Mellen, 1988.

Lindars, B. *Jesus Son of Man: A Fresh Examination of the Son of Man Sayings in the Gospels*, Grand Rapids, Eerdmans, 1984.

Lohmeyer, E. *Das Evangelium des Matthäus*, revised by W. Schmauch, MeyerK, 3rd edn, Göttingen, Vandenhoeck & Ruprecht, 1962.

Lührmann, D. *Die Redaktion der Logienquelle*, WMANT 33, Neukirchen-Vluyn, Neukirchener, 1969.

Luz, U. 'Die Erfüllung des Gesetzes bei Matthäus', *ZTK* 75 (1978), 398–435.

Luz, U. *Das Evangelium nach Matthäus*, 2 vols., EKKNT I/1–2, Zürich, Benziger, 1985, 1990.

McDermott, J. M. 'Mt. 10:23 in Context', *BZ* 28 (1984), 230–40.

McKnight, S. 'A Loyal Critic: Matthew's Polemic with Judaism in Theological Perspective', in C. A. Evans and D. A. Hagner (eds.), *Anti-Semitism and Early Christianity: Issues of Polemic and Faith*, Minneapolis, Fortress Press, 1993, pp. 55–79.

Malina, B. J. and J. H. Neyrey, *Calling Jesus Names: The Social Value of Labels in Matthew*, Sonoma, Cal., Polebridge Press, 1988.

Marguerat, D. *Le Jugement dans l'évangile de Matthieu*, Le Monde de la Bible, Geneva, Labor et Fides, 1981.

Marshall, I. H. *1 and 2 Thessalonians*, NCB, London, Marshall, Morgan and Scott, 1983.

Marxsen, W. *Mark the Evangelist: Studies on the Redaction History of the Gospel*, Nashville, Abingdon, 1969.

Meeks, W. A. *The First Urban Christians: The Social World of the Apostle Paul*, New Haven, Yale University Press, 1983.

Meeks, W. A. 'Social Functions of Apocalyptic Language in Pauline Christianity', in D. Hellholm (ed.), *Apocalypticism in the Mediterranean World and the Near East: Proceedings of the International Colloquium on Apocalypticism, Uppsala, August 12–17, 1979*, Tübingen, Mohr [Siebeck], 1983, pp. 687–705.

Meeks, W. A. 'Breaking Away: Three New Testament Pictures of Christianity's Separation from the Jewish Communities', in J. Neusner and E. S. Frerichs (eds.), *'To see Ourselves as Others see Us': Christians, Jews, 'Others' in Late Antiquity*, Chico, Scholars Press, 1985, pp. 93–115.

Meeks, W. A. and R. L. Wilken. *Jews and Christians in Antioch in the First Four Centuries of the Common Era*, SBLSBS 13, Missoula, Scholars Press, 1978.

Meier, J. P. 'Salvation History in Matthew: In Search of a Starting Point', *CBQ* 37 (1975), 203–15.

Meier, J. P. *Law and History in Matthew's Gospel: A Redactional Study of Mt. 5:17–48*, AnBib 71, Rome, Biblical Institute Press, 1976.

Meier, J. P. 'Nations or Gentiles in Matthew 28:19?', *CBQ* 39 (1977), 94–102.

Meier, J. P. 'Antioch', in R. E. Brown and J. P. Meier, *Antioch and Rome*, New York, Paulist Press, 1983, pp. 11–86.

Michaelis, W. 'ὁδός', *TDNT*, V, pp. 42–96.

Milik, J. T. *The Books of Enoch*, Oxford, Clarendon, 1976.

Milikowsky, C. 'Which Gehenna? Retribution and Eschatology in the Synoptic Gospels and in Early Jewish Texts', *NTS* 34 (1988), 238–49.

Mohrlang, R. *Matthew and Paul: A Comparison of Ethical Perspectives*, SNTSMS 48, Cambridge, University Press, 1984.

Moloney, F. *The Johannine Son of Man*, BSR 14, 2nd edn, Rome, Libreria Ateneo Salesiano, 1978.

Morgan, R. *Biblical Interpretation*, Oxford, University Press, 1988.

Murphy, F. J. *The Structure and Meaning of Second Baruch*, SBLDS 78, Atlanta, Scholars Press, 1985.

Myers, J. M. *I and II Esdras*, AB 42, Garden City, Doubleday, 1974.

Neusner, J. 'The Formation of Rabbinic Judaism: Yavneh from 70–100', in H. Temporini and W. Haase (eds.), *ANRW* II,19,2, Berlin, de Gruyter, 1979, pp. 3–42.

Nickelsburg, G. W. E. *Resurrection, Immortality and Eternal Life in Intertestamental Judaism*, HTS 26, Cambridge MA, Harvard University Press, 1972.

Nickelsburg, G. W. E. 'Eschatology in the Testament of Abraham: A Study of the Judgement Scene in the Two Recensions', in G. W. E. Nickelsburg (ed.), *Studies on the Testament of Abraham*, SBLSCS 6, Missoula, Scholars Press, 1976, pp. 23–64.

Nickelsburg, G. W. E. 'The Apocalyptic Message of 1 Enoch 92–105', *CBQ* 39 (1977), 309–28.

Nickelsburg, G. W. E. *Jewish Literature Between the Bible and the Mishnah*, Philadelphia, Fortress Press, 1981.

Nickelsburg, G. W. E. 'Social Aspects of Palestinian Jewish Apocalypses', in D. Hellholm (ed.), *Apocalypticism in the Mediterranean World and the Near East: Proceedings of the International Colloquium on Apocalypticism, Uppsala, August 12–17, 1979*, Tübingen, Mohr [Siebeck], 1983, pp. 641–54.

Nickelsburg, G. W. E. 'The Apocalyptic Construction of Reality in 1 Enoch', in J. J. Collins and J. H. Charlesworth (eds.), *Mysteries and Revelations: Apocalyptic Studies since the Uppsala Colloquium*, JSPSS 9, Sheffield, Sheffffield Academic Press, 1991, pp. 51–64.

Orton, D. E. *The Understanding Scribe: Matthew and the Apocalyptic Ideal*, JSNTSS 25, Sheffield, Sheffield Academic Press, 1989.

Osei-Bonsu, J. 'The Intermediate State in the New Testament', *SJT* 44 (1991), 169–94.

Overman, J. A. *Matthew's Gospel and Formative Judaism: The Social World of the Matthean Community*, Minneapolis, Fortress Press, 1990.

Painter, J. *The Quest for the Messiah: The History, Literature and Theology of the Johannine Community*, Edinburgh, T. & T. Clark, 1991.

Pesch, R. *Das Markusevangelium*, 2 vols., HTKNT, 2nd edn, Freiburg, Herder, 1980.

Pryke, J. 'Eschatology in the Dead Sea Scrolls', in M. Black (ed.), *The Scrolls and Christianity*, London, SPCK, 1969, pp. 45–57.

Przybylski, B. 'The Setting of Matthean Anti-Judaism', in P. Richardson and O. Granskou (eds.), *Anti-Judaism in Early Christianity*, I, Waterloo, Wilfred Laurier, 1988, pp. 181–200.

Rad, G. von. 'The City on the Hill', in G. von Rad, *The Problem of the Hexateuch and Other Essays*, London, Oliver and Boyd, 1966, pp. 232–42.

Reddish, M. G. *Apocalyptic Literature: A Reader*, Nashville, Abingdon, 1990.

Robinson, J. A. T. 'The "Parable" of the Sheep and the Goats', *NTS* 2 (1955–6), 225–37.

Rowland, C. C. *The Open Heaven: A Study of Apocalyptic in Judaism and Early Christianity*, London, SPCK, 1982.

Rowland, C. C. *Christian Origins: An Account of the Setting and Character of the most Important Messianic Sect of Judaism,* London, SPCK, 1985.

Russell, D. S. *The Method and Message of Jewish Apocalyptic*, London, SCM, 1964.

Sabourin, L. 'Apocalyptic Traits in Matthew's Gospel', *RSB* 3 (1983), 19–36.

Sabourin, L. *The Gospel according to St. Matthew*, 2 vols., Bombay, St Paul, 1982.

Saldarini, A. J. 'The Gospel of Matthew and Jewish–Christian Conflict', in D. L. Balch (ed.), *Social History of the Matthean Community: Cross-*

Disciplinary Approaches, Minneapolis, Fortress Press, 1991, pp. 38–61.

Sanders, E. P. 'The Genre of Palestinian Jewish Apocalypses', in D. Hellholm (ed.), *Apocalypticism in the Mediterranean World and the Near East: Proceedings of the International Colloquium on Apocalypticism, Uppsala, August 12–17, 1979*, Tübingen, Mohr [Siebeck], 1983, pp. 447–59.

Sayler, G. *Have the Promises Failed? A Literary Analysis of 2 Baruch*, SBLDS 72, Chico, Scholars Press, 1984.

Schenk, W. *Die Sprache des Matthäus: Die Text-Konstituenten in ihren makro- und mikrostrukturellen Relationen*, Göttingen, Vandenhoeck & Ruprecht, 1987.

Schiffman, L. H. 'Jewish Sectarianism in Second Temple Times', in R. Jospe and S. Wagner (eds.), *Great Schisms in Jewish History*, New York, KTAV, 1981, pp. 1–46.

Schiffman, L. H. *The Eschatological Community of the Dead Sea Scrolls: A Study of the Rule of the Congregation*, SBLMS 38, Atlanta, Scholars Press, 1989.

Schulz, S. *Die Stunde der Botschaft: Einführung in die Theologie der vier Evangelisten*, 2nd edn, Zürich, Zwingli, 1970.

Schulz, S. *Q. Die Spruchquelle der Evangelisten*, Zürich, Theologischer Verlag, 1972.

Schürer, E. *The History of the Jewish People in the Age of Jesus Christ (175 B.C.- A.D. 135)*, revised by G. Vermes, F. Millar, M. Black and M. Goodman, 3 vols. in 4 parts, Edinburgh, T. & T. Clark, 1973, 1979, 1986, 1987.

Schweizer, E. *Matthäus und seine Gemeinde*, SBS 71, Stuttgart, Katholishes Bibelwerk, 1971.

Schweizer, E. *The Good News according to Matthew*, London, SPCK, 1976.

Segal, A. F. 'Matthew's Jewish Voice', in D. L. Balch (ed.), *Social History of the Matthean Community: Cross-Disciplinary Approaches*, Minneapolis, Fortress Press, 1991, pp. 3–37.

Senior, D. P. *The Passion Narrative according to Matthew: A Redactional Study*, BETL 39, Louvain, University Press, 1975.

Sim, D. C. 'The Man Without the Wedding Garment (Matthew 22:11–13)', *HeyJ* 31 (1990), 165–78.

Sim, D. C. 'Matthew 22:13a and 1 Enoch 10:4a: A Case of Literary Dependence?', *JSNT* 47 (1992), 3–19.

Sim, D. C. 'The Meaning of παλιγγενεσία in Matthew 19:28', *JSNT* 50 (1993), 3–12.

Sim, D. C. 'The "Confession" of the Soldiers in Matthew 27:54', *HeyJ* 34 (1993), 501–24.

Sim, D. C. 'The Gospel of Matthew and the Gentiles', *JSNT* 57 (1995), 19–48.

Sim, D. C. 'Jewish and Christian Apocalypticism in the Ancient World: Problems and Prospects', in M. Dillon (ed.), *Religion in the Ancient World: New Themes and Approaches*, Amsterdam, Hakkert, 1995, pp. 491–504.

Sim, D. C. 'The Social Setting of Ancient Apocalypticism: A Question of Method', forthcoming in *JSP*.

Smalley, S. *1,2,3 John*, WBC 51, Waco, Tx., Word Books, 1984.
Smith, M. 'What is Implied by the Variety of Messianic Figures?', *JBL* 78 (1959), 66–72.
Stanley, J. E. 'The Apocalypse and Contemporary Sect Analysis', in K. H. Richards (ed.), *SBL 1986 Seminar Papers*, Atlanta, Scholars Press, 1986, pp. 412–21.
Stanton, G. N. 'The Origin and Purpose of Matthew's Gospel: Matthean Scholarship from 1945–80', in H. Temporini and W. Haase (eds.), *ANRW* II,25,3, Berlin, de Gruyter, 1985, pp. 1889–1951.
Stanton, G. N. 'The Gospel of Matthew and Judaism', *BJRL* 66 (1984), 264–84.
Stanton, G. N. *A Gospel for a New People: Studies in Matthew*, Edinburgh, T. & T. Clark, 1992.
Stark, R. 'Antioch as the Social Situation for Matthew's Gospel', in D. L. Balch (ed.), *Social History of the Matthean Community: Cross-Disciplinary Approaches*, Minneapolis, Fortress Press, 1991, pp. 189–210.
Stendahl, K. *The School of St. Matthew and its Use of the Old Testament*, ASNU 20, Uppsala, Almqvist & Wiksells, 1954.
Stone, M. E. 'Lists of Revealed Things in the Apocalyptic Literature', in F. M. Cross, W. E. Lemke and P. D. Miller Jr (eds.), *Magnalia Dei. The Mighty Acts of God: Essays on the Bible and Archaeology in Memory of G. Ernest Wright*, Garden City, Doubleday, 1976, pp. 414–52.
Stone, M. E. 'Coherence and Inconsistency in the Apocalypses: The Case of "the End" in 4 Ezra', *JBL* 102 (1983), 229–43.
Stone, M. E. 'Apocalyptic Literature', in M.E. Stone (ed.), *Jewish Writings of the Second Temple Period: Apocrypha, Pseudepigrapha, Qumran Sectarian Writings, Philo, Josephus*, CRINT 2/2, Philadelphia, Fortress Press, 1984, pp. 383–441.
Stone, M. E. 'The Question of the Messiah in 4 Ezra', in J. Neusner, W. S. Green and E. Frerichs (eds.), *Judaisms and Their Messiahs at the Turn of the Christian Era*, Cambridge, University Press, 1987, pp. 209–24.
Stone, M. E. *Features of the Eschatology of IV Ezra*, HSM 35, Atlanta, Scholars Press, 1989.
Stone, M. E. *Fourth Ezra*, Hermeneia, Minneapolis, Fortress Press, 1990.
Strecker, G. *Der Weg der Gerechtigkeit: Untersuchung zur Theologie des Matthäus*, FRLANT 82, 3rd edn, Göttingen, Vandenhoeck & Ruprecht, 1971.
Streeter, B. H. *The Four Gospels: A Study of Origins*, London, Macmillan, 1924.
Stuhlmacher, P. *Der Brief an der Römer*, NTD 6, Göttingen/Zürich, Vandenhoeck & Ruprecht, 1989.
Sturm, R. E. 'Defining the Word "Apocalyptic": A Problem in Biblical Criticism', in J. Marcus and M. L. Soards (eds.), *Apocalyptic and the New Testament: Essays in Honour of J. Louis Martyn*, JSNTSS 24, Sheffield, Sheffield Academic Press, 1989, pp. 17–48.
Suggs, M.J . 'The Christian Two Ways Tradition: Its Antiquity, Form, and Function', in D. E. Aune (ed.), *Studies in New Testament and Early Christian Literature: Essays in Honor of Allen P. Wikgren*, NovTSup 33, Leiden, Brill, 1972, pp. 60–74.

Suter, D. *Tradition and Composition in the Parables of Enoch*, SBLDS 47, Missoula, Scholars Press, 1979.

Theisohn, J. *Der auserwählte Richter: Untersuchungen zum traditions- geschichtlichem Ort der Menschensohngestalt der Bilderreden des Äthio- pischen Henoch*, SUNT 12, Göttingen, Vandenhoeck & Ruprecht, 1975.

Thompson, L. L. *The Book of Revelation: Apocalypse and Empire*, Oxford, University Press, 1990.

Thompson, W. G. *Matthew's Advice to a Divided Community: Mt. 17,22–18,35*, AnBib 44, Rome, Biblical Institute Press, 1970.

Thompson, W. G. 'An Historical Perspective in the Gospel of Matthew', *JBL* 93 (1974), 243–62.

Tilborg, S. van. *The Jewish Leaders in Matthew*, Leiden, Brill, 1972.

Tödt, H. E. *The Son of Man in the Synoptic Tradition*, London, SCM, 1965.

Trilling, W. *Das Wahre Israel: Studien zur Theologie des Matthäusevange- liums*, ETS 7, 3rd edn, Munich, Kösel, 1964.

Tuckett, C. M. *Reading the New Testament*, London, SPCK, 1987.

Vanderkam, J. C. *Textual and Historical Studies in the Book of Jubilees*, HSM 14, Missoula, Scholars Press, 1977.

Vanderkam, J. C. *Enoch and the Growth of an Apocalyptic Tradition*, CBQMS 16, Washington, Catholic Biblical Association of America, 1984.

Vanderkam, J. C. 'The Prophetic-Sapiential Origins of Apocalyptic Thought', in J. D. Martin and P. R. Davies (eds.), *A Word in Season: Essays in Honour of William McKane*, JSOTSS 42, Sheffield, Sheffield Academic Press, 1986, pp. 163–76.

Vermes, G. *The Dead Sea Scrolls in English*, 3rd edn, Sheffield, Sheffield Academic Press, 1987.

Vielhauer, P. 'Apocalypses and Related Subjects: Introduction', in E. Henneke and W. Schneemelcher (eds.), *New Testament Apoc- rypha*, 2 vols., Philadelphia, Westminster Press, 1965, II, pp. 581–607.

Walker, R. *Die Heilsgeschichte im Ersten Evangelium*, FRLANT 91, Göttingen, Vandenhoeck & Ruprecht, 1967.

Watson, F. *Paul, Judaism and the Gentiles: A Sociological Approach*, SNTSMS 56, Cambridge, University Press, 1986.

Weaver, D. J. *Matthew's Missionary Discourse: A Literary Critical Ana- lysis*, JSNTSS 38, Sheffield, Sheffield Academic Press, 1990.

Webber, R. C. 'Group Solidarity in the Revelation of John', in D. J. Lull (ed.), *SBL 1988 Seminar Papers*, Atlanta, Scholars Press, 1988, pp. 132–40.

White, L. J. 'Grid and Group in Matthew's Community: The Righteous- ness/Honor Code in the Sermon on the Mount', *Semeia* 35 (1986), 61–90.

White, L. M. 'Crisis Management and Boundary Maintenance: The Social Location of the Matthean Community', in D. L. Balch (ed.), *Social History of the Matthean Community: Cross-Disciplinary Approaches*, Minneapolis, Fortress Press, 1991, pp. 211–47.

Willett, T. W. *Eschatology in the Theodicies of 2 Baruch and 4 Ezra*, JSPSS 4, Sheffield, Sheffield Academic Press, 1989.

Wilson, R. R. 'From Prophecy to Apocalyptic: Reflections on the Shape of Israelite Religion', *Semeia* 21 (1982), 79–95.

Yadin, Y. *The Scroll of the War of the Sons of Light against the Sons of Darkness*, Oxford, University Press, 1962.

Ziesler, J. *Paul's Letter to the Romans*, TPINTC, London, SCM, 1989.

Zumstein, J. *La Condition du croyant dans l'évangile selon Matthieu*, OBO 16, Göttingen, Vandenhoeck & Ruprecht, 1977.

INDEX OF PASSAGES CITED

INDEX OF MODERN SCHOLARS

INDEX OF SUBJECTS